Engraved by C. J. Anderton at J. M. Butler's establishment

Henry Reed

LECTURES

ON

ENGLISH LITERATURE,

From Chaucer to Tennyson.

By HENRY REED.

FIFTH EDITION, REVISED AND CORRECTED.

PHILADELPHIA:
J. B. LIPPINCOTT & CO.
1860.

COLLINS, PRINTER.

TO

My Widowed Sister,

WHO, FOR THE SAKE OF THE LIVING, HAS NOBLY BORNE HER SORROW FOR THE DEAD,

This Memorial Volume

IS AFFECTIONATELY INSCRIBED.

W. B. R.

CONTENTS.

LECTURE III.

THE ENGLISH LANGUAGE.

LECTURE IV.

EARLY ENGLISH LITERATURE.

LECTURE V.

LITERATURE OF THE SIXTEENTH CENTURY.

LECTURE VI.

LITERATURE OF THE SEVENTEENTH CENTURY, WITH INCIDENTAL SUGGESTIONS ON SUNDAY READING.

LECTURE IX.

CONTEMPORARY LITERATURE.

LECTURE X.

TRAGIC AND ELEGIAC POETRY.

LECTURE XI.

LITERATURE OF WIT AND HUMOUR.

LECTURE XII.

THE LITERATURE OF LETTER-WRITING.

INTRODUCTORY NOTICE.

My duty in editing this volume is a very simple one:—to state, with frankness and precision, the circumstances of its publication, and, if need be, to disarm criticism by the absence of any thing like pretension on the part of him whose posthumous work is now given to the reading world of his own countrymen. Immediately on my brother's death in the autumn of last year, or as soon (and with me it was very soon) as all hope of possible rescue had faded away, my attention was turned to his manuscript lectures, delivered in different courses at the University of Pennsylvania. I knew that, as popular lectures, or rather essays at lectures, they had been very successful, and I hoped and believed they would bear the severer test of being printed. This, I was well aware, is not always the case; and I examined these manuscripts with the idea of possible inaptitude clearly in my mind. The result, however, was a conviction that the Lectures, or a portion of them, ought to be published. They contain, aside from their value as works of criticism, developments of the pure taste and gentle feeling of the author, which will interest, at least his friends, and be appreciated by all who value them exactly for what they were designed—not profound disquisitions, but popular lectures. In saying this, I must be understood as speaking with precision, and not in words either of real or affected disparagement. I wish to describe them as HE would do, were he alive to speak of his own modest work. There will be found on these pages, if I mistake not, hints and suggestions of philosophic criticism floating on the surface (or hidden not far beneath) of a most graceful and attractive current of thought and language.

It will be farther borne in mind that these Lectures are printed exactly as written, with scarcely a verbal alteration, and no change or modification of opinion. He wrote from a full mind, often with great rapidity, and without the opportunity or the necessity of revision. Knowing this to be his habit of composition, and that he never prepared himself specially for any one lecture, I have been much struck with the proof they afford of his long and habitual studiousness and rich and accomplished scholarship. His citations of authorities, or rather quotations, are purely incidental; and one of my duties has been to trace his studies to their sources, and, as far as possible, verify, by exact reference, the citations he has made. In this—for my own occupations have forced my ordinary reading into other channels—I have been aided by the only survivor (one still nearer to him than myself) to whom, before delivery and as he wrote them, he read these Lectures; and also by his and my friends,—to whom I am glad thus to make my acknowledgments,—Mr. George W. Hunter, Mr. Ellis Yarnall, and Mr. William Arthur Jackson.

In selecting this course of Lectures, I was guided by two

considerations,—one that it was a more complete and continuous course than others; another, that it was among the last delivered by him. The dates will be found noted in each lecture.

I have ventured not only to put, in the form of notes, some unconnected remarks by the author himself and marked with his initials, but to add a few of my own. These are very few, and are meant to be illustrative. Perhaps, in the analysis of my feelings, there may be another pardonable motive, in an affectionate desire, not diminishing, but growing with every hour of desolate separation, of connecting some work of mine with his. Now that it is done, I feel as if a mournful pleasure were over, and I was parting anew from him.

Should this volume be received with interest and favour, it is my wish to complete the series by two other courses on kindred subjects:

1. Lectures on Modern History down to the Period of the Reformation; and

2. Lectures on the History of England, as illustrated by Shakspeare's Historical Dramas.

If, then, (for I am dealing very candidly with the public,) sufficient interest be felt in the intellectual and moral developments of these volumes to justify such a tribute to his memory, I may venture—at least, this now is my purpose—to prepare a Memoir of my brother's gentle and tranquil life, and very interesting correspondence on both sides of the Atlantic. The life of a secluded American scholar may not be without interest to those near and at a distance.

With this hope clearly before me, and dreading, from observation in other cases, the effect of a preliminary memoir which affection so naturally exaggerates, I shall now simply note a few dates and incidents, by way of explanatory introduction, of his quiet life.

Henry Reed was born in Philadelphia on the 11th of July, 1808. He was christened by the name of Henry Hope, though the middle name was afterwards dropped. His early education was at the classical school, of high repute in its day, of Mr. James Ross. Here began a friendship, which lasted through life and survived in earnest sorrow for his premature death, with Mr. Horace Binney, (the younger,) whose name I venture to refer to in simple justice to the living and the dead, to us who grieve and to him for whom we mourn. This friendship was faithful and affectionate to the end.

Mr. Reed entered the Sophomore class at the University of Pennsylvania in September, 1822, and was graduated as Bachelor of Arts in 1825. He began the study of the law under the general guidance of Mr. Sergeant, then at the heighth of his professional fame, and was admitted to practice in the District Court of the City and County of Philadelphia in 1829.

In September, 1831, he relinquished the practice of his profession, and was elected Assistant Professor of English Literature in the University. In November of the same year, he was chosen Assistant Professor of Moral Philosophy. In the service of the College he continued for twenty-three years, faithful, I am sure I may say, to his duties, however irksome; and never in all that period, until his visit to Europe, absent for any length of time from his post, except when compelled by sickness. In 1835, he was elected Professor of Rhetoric and English Literature.

Mr. Reed was married, in 1834, to Elizabeth White Bronson, who, with three children, now survives him.

It had long been his wish to visit Europe, but his professional duties and other claims had always prevented it. In the spring of 1854, the Professorship of Moral Philosophy, which he had once filled as Assistant Professor, being vacant, Mr. Reed became a candidate for the chair, but was not elected. Although no personal disparagement was intended, so earnest and so reasonable was his ambition for what he considered a high academical distinction, that his disappointment was most keen and depressing. His secluded mode of life, exempt from the world's rough competitions; his modest wishes; his consciousness of services rendered and duties performed; his natural pride in the affection of his students; and, above all, his conviction that moral science, in its highest and holiest sense, as elevated by religious truth, was a department of education which he was peculiarly competent to take charge of, combined to render the disappointment very poignant. His friends and family never saw him more depressed. I certainly never saw him so deeply wounded. He asked for leave of absence, which was granted by the Trustees; and early in May, 1854, accompanied by his sister-in-law, Miss Bronson, he sailed for Europe.

No American, visiting the Old World as a private citizen,

ever received a kinder or more discriminating welcome. The last months of his life were pure sunshine. Before he landed in England, his friends, the family of Dr. Arnold, whom he had only known by correspondence, came on board the ship to receive him; and his earliest and latest hours of European sojourn were passed under the roof of the great Poet whose memory he most revered, and whose writings had interwoven themselves with his intellectual and moral being. "I do not know," he said in one of his letters to his family, "what I have ever done to deserve all this kindness." And so it was throughout. In England he was *at home* in every sense; and scenes, which to the eye were strange, seemed familiar by association and study. His letters to America were expressions of grateful delight at what he saw and heard in the land of his forefathers, and at the respectful kindness with which he was everywhere greeted; and yet of earnest and loyal yearning to the land of his birth—his home and family and friends. It is no violation of good taste here to enumerate some of the friends for whose kind welcome Mr. Reed was so much indebted; I may mention the Wordsworths, Southeys, Coleridges, and Arnolds, Lord Mahon, Mr. Baring, Mr. Aubrey De Vere, Mr. Babbage, Mr. Henry Taylor, and Mr. Thackeray—names, one and all, associated with the highest literary or political distinction.

He visited the Continent, and went, by the ordinary route, through France and Switzerland, as far south as Milan and Venice. returning by the Tyrol to Inspruck and Munich, ana thence down the Rhine to Holland. But his last associations were with the cloisters of Canterbury, (that spot, to my eye, of matchless beauty,) the garden vales of Devonshire, the valley of the Wye, and the glades of Rydal. His latest memory of this earth was of beautiful England in her summer garb of verdure. The last words he ever wrote were in a letter of the 20th September to his venerable friend, Mrs. Wordsworth, thanking her and his English friends generally for all she and they had done for him.

The rest is soon told.

On the 20th of September, 1854, Mr. Reed, with his sister embarked at Liverpool for New York, in the United States steam-ship Arctic. Seven days afterward, at noon, on the 27th, when almost in sight of his native land, a fatal collision occurred, and before sun-down, every human being left upon the ship had sunk under the waves of the ocean. The only survivor who was personally acquainted with my brother, saw him about two o'clock P.M.; after the collision, and not very long before the ship sank, sitting, with his sister, in the small passage aft of the dining saloon. "They were tranquil and silent, though their faces wore the look of painful anxiety." They probably afterwards left this position, and repaired to the promenade deck. For a selfish struggle for life, with a helpless companion dependent upon him, with a physical frame unsuited for such a strife, and, above all, with a sentiment of religious resignation which taught him in that hour of agony, even with the memory of his wife and children thronging in his mind, to bow his head in submission to the will of God,—for such a struggle he was wholly unsuited;

and his is the praise, that he perished with the women and children.

Nor can I conclude this brief narrative without the utterance of an opinion, expressed in no asperity, and not, I hope, improperly intruded here—my opinion, as an American citizen, that, in all the history of wanton and unnecessary shipwreck, no greater scandal to the science of navigation, or to the system of marine discipline, ever occurred than the loss of the Arctic and her three hundred passengers. There is but one thing worse, and that is the absence of all laws of the United States either to prevent the recurrence of such a catastrophe; to bring to justice those, if there are any such, who are responsible; or, at least, to secure a judicial investigation of the actual facts.

The news of Mr. Reed's death was received with deep and intense feeling in the city of his birth, his education, and active life. Philadelphia mourned sincerely for her son; and no tribute to his memory, no graceful expression or act of sympathy to his family, was withheld. For them all there are no adequate words of gratitude.

Returning with renewed health and refreshed spirits, with a capacity not only for intellectual enjoyment, but professional usefulness, enlarged by observation of other institutions and intercourse with the wise and good of the Mother country, especially those who had made education in its highest branches the study and business of their lives, Professor Reed, we may well believe, would have resumed his American duties with new zeal and efficiency. Not that I for one moment imagine he had become infected with the folly of fancying that a system of foreign University education, in any of its forms, could or ought to be transplanted here; but, I have no doubt, that observation of thorough training and accurate scholarship, the combination of moral and intellectual discipline such as is seen abroad, and especially in Great Britain, would have raised still higher in his mind the aims at which American students and American institutions of learning should be directed.

By his early death—for he was but forty-six years of age—all these hopes were doomed to disappointment. The most that can now be done is to give to the world these fragmentary memorials of his studious life; and for them I beg an indulgent and candid criticism.

WILLIAM B. REED.

PHILADELPHIA, *February 1st*, 1855.

Henry Reed.

For many days our eyes have seaward wander'd,
As if to search the Ocean o'er and o'er,
The while our hearts have sorrowfully ponder'd,
"Shall we behold his gentle face no more?"
The silent Sea no glad response returning,
We cry, "O Sun! that lightest nature's face,
Dost thou not shine upon some favour'd place
Where he is tost for whom our souls are yearning?"
No answering voice allays our trembling fears,
And long anxiety gives way to tears.
Beneath the waves o'er which great ships go flitting,
He waits the day when Ocean yields her dead;
And loving sighs and bitter drops are shed
By desolate ones around his hearthstone sitting;
And, while they mourn the gifted and the good,
The general grief shows holy brotherhood.

Thos. MacKellar.

LECTURES

ON

ENGLISH LITERATURE.

LECTURE I.—INTRODUCTORY.*

Principles of Literature.

Object, to assist and guide students—Necessity of systematic study—Judicious criticism—True aims and principles of literature—Choice of books—Its difficulties—Aim of this course of lectures to remove them—All books not literature—Accurate definition of literature—Its universality—Izaak Walton—Addison—Charles Lamb—Lord Bacon—Clarendon—Arnold—Spenser and Shakspeare—Southey and Wordsworth—Belles-lettres not literature—Literature not an easy, patrician pleasure—Its danger as to practical life—Its influence on character—De Quincey's definition—Knowledge and Power—Influence on female character—True position of woman—Tennyson's Princess—Novel-reading—Taste, an incorrect term—Henry Taylor—Cowper—Miss Wordsworth—Coleridge's philosophy.

THIS course of lectures is prepared in the hope of doing some service in connection with the abundant and precious literature which lies about us in our English speech. The plan has been, in some measure, prompted to my thoughts by applications not unfrequently made to me for advice and guidance in English reading. There is a stage

* Delivered in the Chapel Hall of the University, January 3, 1850.

in mental culture when counsel seems to be intended to take the place of exact tuition, and when, looking altogether beyond the period and the province of what is usually called "education," hints and suggestions, criticism, literary sympathies, and even literary antagonism, become the more expanded and freer discipline, which lasts through life. We cannot tell how much of good we may thus do to one another. We cannot measure the value of unstudied and almost casual influences. A random word of genuine admiration may prove a guide into some region of literature where the mind shall dwell with satisfaction and delight for years to come. But there is a demand for something more systematic than such chance culture as I have alluded to; and the mind that craves such knowledge of the literature of his own language as will make it part of his thoughts and feelings, has a claim for guidance and counsel upon those whose duty it is to fit themselves to bestow it. It is a claim that well may win a quick and kindly response, for the sense of delight is deepened the wider it is spread, or when it opens the souls of others to share in its own enjoyment.

There is perhaps no one, to whom the intercourse with books has grown to be happy and habitual, who cannot recall the time when, needing other counsel than his own mind could give, he felt some guidance that was strength to him. One can recall, in after years, how it was, that an interest was first awakened in some book—how sympathy with an author's mind was earliest stirred—how sentiments of admiration and of love had their first motion in our souls toward the souls of the great poets. We may perhaps remember, too, how the chastening influence of wise and genial criticism may have won our spirits away from some malignant fascination that fastened on the unripe intellect only to abuse it. But these kindly and healthful agencies exist not alone in the memory—gratefully retained as benefits received in the period of intellectual immaturity and inexperience. Even the student of literature whose range of reading is most comprehensive—whose habit of reading is most confirmed —whose culture is most complete—will tell you that it is still in his daily experience to find his choice of books not an arbitrary and lawless choosing, but a process open to the influences of sound and congenial criticism; he will tell how, by such influences, the activity of his thoughts is quickened—how his judgment of books is often the joint product of his own reflections, and the contact of the wisdom and experience of others. To him who wanders at will through the vast spaces of literature, with the sorry guidance of good intentions and inexperience, most needful are the helping hand and the pointing finger; to him who has travelled long in that same domain, pursuing his way with purposes better defined, and who has gained a wider prospect and farther-reaching views—even by him, guidance, if not so needful, still may be welcomed from some fellow-traveller. We marvel often at finding how, under the light of wise criticism, new powers and new beauties are made visible to our minds in books the most familiar.

I have thus alluded, at the outset, to the importance of the guidance which we may receive in our intercourse with the world of books, assuming at the same time that there is no call upon me to dwell upon the value of that intercourse itself. I take for granted that there is no one, even among those least conversant with books, wh(

could deny the value of an intelligent habit of reading. I need not occupy a moment of either your time or mine in discussing any such question as that. It is, however, proper to consider, by way of introduction, some of those aims and principles of literature which, though least generally appreciated, give it its highest value—noticing, in the first place, some of the difficulties which present themselves to a mind willing, at least, if not zealous, for such culture.

The first inquiry that presents itself is, "What books does it behoove me to know?" The docile question is, "What am I to read?" A world of volumes is before us. Poetry, science, history, biography, fiction, the multiform divisions of miscellaneous literature, each and all rise up in their vast proportions to assert their claims. Secular literature, in its various departments, and sacred literature, casting its lights into the life beyond, both are at hand with the boundless exuberance of their stores. There is the great multitude of books in our own English words; there is the host as large, which, in the kindred dialects of the North, the mind of Germany has given to mankind. The literature of France and of Italy, of Spain, the South of Europe, have their respective claims and attractions. Besides the modern mind, there is all that, venerable with the age of thousands of years, has come down to us from Greece, and Rome, and Palestine. Then, too, in the whole extent of modern literature, there is the daily addition of the illimitable issues from the press in our day: so that when the student's thoughts turn to the accumulation of the printed thoughts of past ages, and to the never-ending and superadded accumulation which is poured forth from day to day, and from year to year; and when these vast stores are seen to have been made part of the scholarship of men and become a portion of their intellectual and moral nature, one is appalled at the first approach, and may shrink from all effort, in despondency or hopelessness. It is a bewildering thing to stand in the presence of a vast concourse of books—in the midst of them, but feeble, or uncertain, or helpless in the using of them. It is sad to know that in each one of these volumes there is a spiritual power which might stir some kindred power in our own souls, which might guide, and inform, and elevate; and yet that it should be a power all hidden from us. It is oppressive to conceive what a world of human thought and human passion is dwelling on the silent and senseless paper, how much of wisdom is ready to make its entrance into the mind that is prepared to give it welcome. It is mournful to think that the multitudinous oracles should be dumb to us.

Furthermore, there is this difficulty, that, in the multitude, mingled in the indiscriminate throng, are evil books; or, if not evil, negative and worthless books. Thus the companionship is not only difficult, but it may be dangerous; the difficulty of making wise and happy choice, and the perilous presence of what is vicious in the guise of books.

Such are some of the difficulties which beset us, when we would bring the influence of books into the culture of our spiritual nature. These lectures are intended to present some thoughts and suggestions with a view to the surmounting of these difficulties, and to guidance into the department of English literature. I propose now to consider the general principles of literature, and in the next lecture to trace some of the applications of these principles in the formation of our habits of reading.

The discouraging effect which is produced by the present and perpetually increasing multitude of books is, in some degree, lessened by the thought that all are not literature. A vast deal of paper is printed and folded and shaped into the outward fashion of a book, that never enters into the literature of the language. What (it may be asked) is Literature? This is a question not enough thought of; the answer to it is important, but by no means, I think, difficult, when once we see the necessity of making the discrimination. Books that are technical, that are professional, that are sectarian, are not literature in the proper sense of the term. The great characteristic of literature, its essential principle, is that it is addressed to man as man; it speaks to our common human nature; it deals with every element in our being that makes fellowship between man and man through all ages of man's history and through all the habitable regions of this planet. According to this view, literature excludes from its appropriate province whatever is addressed to men as they are parted into trades, and professions, and sects—parted, it may be, in the division for mutual good; or, it may be, by vicious and unchristian alienation. It is the relation to universal humanity which constitutes literature; it matters not how elevated, whether it be history, philosophy, or poetry, in its highest aspirations; or how humble, it may be the simplest rhyme or story that is level to the unquestioning faith and untutored intellect of childhood: let it but be addressed to our common human nature, it is literature in the true sense of the term. No man can put it aside and say, "*It concerns not me:*" no woman can put it aside and say, "*It concerns not me.*" The books which do not enter into the literature of a language are limited in their uses, for they hold their intercourse with something narrower than human nature, while that which is literature has an audience-chamber capacious as the soul of man—enduring as his immortality. It has a voice whose rhythm is in harmony with the pulses of the human heart. It is this, and this alone—this *universality*—which places a book in a Nation's literature. It matters not what the subject, or what the mode of treating—be there but one touch of nature to make the whole world kin—it is enough to lift it into the region of literature. A London linen-draper writes a treatise on Angling, with no other thought, perhaps, than to teach an angler's subtle craft, but infusing into his art so much of Christian meekness, so deep a feeling for the beauties of earth and sky, such rational loyalty to womanhood, and such simple, child-like love of song, the songs of bird, of milk-maid, and of minstrel, that this little book on fishing has earned its life of two hundred years already, outliving many a more ambitious book, and Izaak Walton has a place of honour amid British authors, and has the love even of those who have learned the poet-moralist's truer wisdom,

> "Never to blend our pleasure or our pride
> With sorrow of the meanest thing that feels."*

I speak of this instance to show how a subject which is indifferent to many, and even repulsive to not a few, may be redeemed and animated by the author's true human-

* Wordsworth's Poems, Hart Leap Well. Collective edition, p. 152.

heartedness. How much deeper then must be the interest of all the subjects, in the vast variety, with which there is universal sympathy! How much mightier must be the agency of literature as it passes beyond and above that which is local and limited, temporary or conventional, into the region of the spiritual and the eternal, when it enters into the very soul of man, admonishing it of its weakness, and of its strength, and of its immortality!

Now, whether we look at the simpler and humbler aims of literature—healthful, innocent recreation—the recuperative influences which blend so happily with the severer functions of life, or whether we contemplate its elevating and chastening power on the minds of men, we cannot mistake that its just and great attribute is its universality. It speaks to every ear that is not deaf to it. It asks admission into every heart. The books that are not literature have the professional, the technical, but not the human stamp: some, the law-books for instance, put on an outward garb of their own, as if to warn all but one class of readers away from them. But observe the books which are Literature, how they speak to a people—to a whole nation—to scattered nations over the earth linked together by community of speech, above all such glorious community as our English speech; nay, more, so far as the Babel barriers which make the partitions of the earth are overleaped, a literature addresses itself to all mankind. This is true of even the light and more perishable literature, recreating and gladdening the hearts of men, if but for a season; and it is more lastingly true of the higher literature—for instance, our abundant and varied English essay-literature, philosophy, history with all its kindred themes, and poetry. Is it not for every fellow-being speaking the English tongue, that Addison and Charles Lamb, the "Spectator" and "Elia," have written? Is it not for every one who is willing to be lifted up to the high places of philosophy, that Bacon's words of wisdom were recorded? It is for all, that Clarendon's pictured page displays its great gallery of historic portraits: it is for all, that Arnold, in our own day, has shown how a mighty historian can throw a sacred light over profane history, by tracing God's providence in the annals of a pagan people. It is every man and every woman whom Spenser leads into the sunny and the shadowy spaces of his marvellous allegory; and Shakspeare into that more wondrous region, the soul of man, with its depths of goodness and of evil, brighter and darker than aught in the region of romance. In our own times, it was for all his race that Byron gave utterance to his passionate poetry: it was for all Christian readers that Southey, in his "Eastern Epics," interwove, with the heathen fable, bright threads of the glory of Christian faith; and it is for every one who takes thought of the deep things of his nature, the mysteries of his being, memories of early innocence and yearnings for eternity, that Wordsworth struck his lofty lyric, the most sublime ode in this and, perhaps, any language, on the birth—the life—the undying destiny of the soul of man.

I have dwelt upon this prime quality of literature, its universality, because, simple as it is, it is practically lost sight of, in the propensity to identify all things in the shape of books with literature. Whatever is meant to minister to our universal human nature, either in the nature of the subject or the handling of it, takes its place, in some range or other of literature: and nothing else is so entitled. And here let me step aside for a moment to notice an unworthy and very inadequate term, which, in its day has had some currency as a substitute for the term "literature." I refer to that vapid, half-naturalized term "*belles-lettres*," which was more in vogue formerly than now, getting currency, I suppose, during a period of shallow criticism not very remote from our day, when Doctor Blair and Lord Kames were great authorities. I have never met with anybody who could tell me what precise meaning it is meant to convey. The term had an appropriateness for much in the literature of France, but translate the words and transfer them to English literature, and how inane is such a title, so applied! Doctor Johnson has given it a place in the English vocabulary, and tells us it means "polite literature," which does not help the matter much. I should not have thought it worth while to stop to comment on this term, if I did not believe it to be not only vague and inadequate, but also mischievous; and it is well known what power of mischief there may be in a word. "Belles-lettres"—fine letters—polite literature—what thought do these terms convey but of luxuries of the mind, a refined amusement, but no more than amusement, confectionaries (as it were) of the mind, rather than needful, solid, healthy, life-sustaining food. If the term "*belles-lettres*" excludes the weighty and sublime productions of the mind, then is it a miserable substitute for what should be comprehended in such a term as "*literature:*" if it includes them, then is it a pitifully inapposite title. Now the mischief is just here: this dainty, feeble term leads people to suppose that literature is an easy, indolent cultivation, a sort of passive, patrician pleasure, instead of demanding dutiful and studious and strenuous energy. It lowers the great works of genius, as if they could be approached indolently, thoughtlessly, and without preparatory discipline. When the term was most in use, it was meant for that which is essential literature, and yet how meanly inadequate and injurious is it now in the department of poetry, if applied to the Fairy Queen, Paradise Lost, The Excursion! We might call the fanciful things in The Rape of the Lock, creations; but who will so speak of Milton's ruined Archangel, or Lear, or Hamlet? It is to be noticed that as the term "*belles-lettres*" was introduced in a feeble age of the British mind, so it has been in a great measure cast out by the deeper philosophy of criticism which has arisen in this century.

I have adverted to this subject, because the term detracts from that which is the prime characteristic of literature—its universality—its appeal to man as man. In this simple, elementary principle, we may unfold some of the manifold powers and uses of a literature: it would not thus address itself to all human beings, whose minds can be open to it, unless it had some great purpose—some worthier end than pastime. It is one of the countless and varied influences under which man's spiritual being passes through this mortal life. It is one agency amid many, only *one* among many, for we must not exaggerate its importance. We are dwelling amid the things of sight and sound in this inanimate world; and that has its influences on the soul of man: we are dwelling in the social world of kindred human beings, giving and receiving from one another impressions to last, it may be, through eternity: we are living amid the spiritual agencies which are vouchsafed to redeemed man: and our life is also in the world of books.

> And books, we know,
> Are a substantial world, both pure and good:
> Round these, with tendrils strong as flesh and blood,
> Our pastime and our happiness will grow.*

I have spoken of literature as only one of the powers from which the mind of man is to receive culture and discipline, for although the common danger lies in another direction, it may encroach upon other powers to our grievous spiritual injury. It may win us too much away from the discipline of actual life into an intellectual luxuriousness: it may withdraw us too much from all of earth and sky that for wise purposes is sensible to us, and we may thus lose that contemplative spirit, which can "find tongues in trees, books in the running brooks, sermons in stones, and good in every thing." We must not be unmindful how exquisitely the individual man and the external world are fitted to each other, so that it is scarce a poetic exaggeration, that

> One impulse from a vernal wood
> May teach you more of man,
> Of moral evil and of good,
> Than all the sages can.†

My present purpose is to consider this one agency—literature—as a means of culture of character, manly and womanly; but, at the same time, let it be borne in mind that nothing conduces more to the well-being and strength of the soul than to keep it open to all the healthful influences which are provided for it, and to hold them all

* Wordsworth. Sonnet, "Personal Talk," p. 186.
† Wordsworth. "The Tables Turned," p. 337.

in true adjustment. There is a time for the eye to dwell on the printed page, but there is also a time to gaze "on earth, air, ocean, and the starry sky;" there is a time to look into the faces of our fellow-beings, the bright and laughing face, or the sad and sorrowing one; there is a time too for silent, solitary, spiritual looking inward into the soul itself; and thus by no one function, but by many, does man build up his moral being. Such is education, in its large and true significancy. Looking to literature as our present subject, and having ascertained that its prime quality is its power of addressing itself to man as man, let us now see for what purpose it so deals with our common humanity, that we may have a principle to guide us in our choice of books. One of the most acute and logical minds of our time, that of him who has coupled his name with a morbid and ill-omened title—I refer to Mr. De Quincey, the English opium-eater—has drawn a distinction between two species of literature. "There is," he says, "first, the literature of *knowledge*, and, secondly, the literature of *power*. The function of the first is to *teach;* the function of the second is to *move*. . . . The very highest work that has ever existed in the literature of knowledge is but a provisional work; a book upon trial and sufferance. Let its teaching be even partially revised, let it be but expanded, nay, even let its teaching be but placed in a better order, and instantly it is superseded. Whereas the feeblest work in the literature of power, surviving at all, survives as finished and unalterable among men. For instance, the *Principia* of Sir Isaac Newton was a book *militant* on earth from the first. In all stages of its progress it would have to fight for its existence: first, as regards absolute truth; secondly, when that combat is over, as regards its form or mode of presenting the truth. And as soon as a La Place or anybody else builds higher upon the foundations laid by this book, effectually he throws it out of the sunshine into decay and darkness; by weapons even from this book he superannuates and destroys it, so that soon the name of Newton remains as a mere *nominis umbra*, but his book, as a living power, has transmigrated into other forms. Now, on the contrary, the Iliad, the Prometheus of Æschylus, the Othello or King Lear, the Hamlet or Macbeth, and the Paradise Lost are not militant, but triumphant power as long as the languages exist in which they speak or can be taught to speak. They never *can* transmigrate into new incarnations. . . . All the literature of knowledge builds only ground-nests, that are swept away by floods, or confounded by the plough; but the literature of power builds nests in aerial altitudes, of temples sacred from violation, or of forests inaccessible to fraud. *This* is a great prerogative of the *power*-literature. . . . The *knowledge*-literature, like the fashion of this world, passeth away. . . . But all literature, properly so called, . . . for the very same reason that it is so much more durable than the literature of knowledge is . . . more intense and electrically searching in its impressions. The directions in which the tragedy of this planet has trained our human feelings to play, and the combinations into which the power of this planet has thrown our human passions of love and hatred, of admiration and contempt, exercises a power bad or good over human life that cannot be contemplated when seen stretching through many generations, without a sentiment allied to awe. And of this let every one be assured, that he owes to the impassioned books which he has read many a thousand more of emotions than he can consciously trace back to them. Dim by their origination, these emotions yet arise in him, and mould him through life like the forgotten incidents of childhood."*

The distinction thus drawn between the literature of knowledge and the literature of power is, however, of uncertain application to many books in which, while the chief object is to impart information of some kind, power is given also; but this is certain that in all literature of a high order—a nation's purest literature, it is *power* that is given, and not *knowledge*. But what, it may be asked, is this Power which literature creates in the spirits of men? what is this soul-engendered energy? The knowledge-literature is measurable, and we can judge of the utility of this or that branch of it, its aptness to this or that man, this or that woman: but the power-literature is immeasurable, because it partakes of the infinite, and passing through and beyond the mere intellect, it dwells in the deep places of the soul. The common products of education are tangible and temporal, but there is a higher education that lifts you into the region of things eternal, "Truths that wake to perish never." There is an education which deals with acquirements, accomplishments, learning it may be, and, in all this, there may be vast variety and a huge profit, but there will be a transitoriness and withal weariness and vexation of spirit in it. There is a higher education, which is akin to religion, for it is a ministry of the soul, and deals not so much with what we know as with what we are, what we can do and what we can suffer, and what we may become here and hereafter.

* Essay on Pope, pp. 149, 152. American edition.

Thus it is that there are books of knowledge, and of power—books that make us more knowing, and books that make us wiser, and, in that wisdom, better.

This great distinctive principle gives good guidance to us, and it may be made most practical if a little thoughtful discrimination be bestowed in our intercourse with books; instead of apathy on the one hand, or on the other the voracious appetite that takes no heed of the various uses of books. A book may be read merely to talk about, and that is perhaps the meanest thing to read it for: it may be read for amusement, and that may be seasonable and salutary; but it also may be read for happiness, rather than for mere pleasure, for a perpetual rather than a passing joy: it may give health of mind, vigour, and vision: the heart may beat all the truer for it; the mind's eye may see all the clearer for it. As you close a book, ask yourself what it has done for you; and better, perhaps, than criticism or any outer counsel, shall the silent communings of your heart tell you whether the oracle was a good or an evil one.

I have thus sought to show how, amid the hundreds of thousands of books which are accumulating in the world, we may select as "*literature*" those which are characterized by the universality of being addressed to man as man; and how, in the next place, we may contract it to a more essential literature, in the books which strengthen rather than store the mind—giving it power rather than apparel; and then, how we may raise it to a purer and higher literature, in the books which, by calling forth the good elements in our being and by chastening the evil ones, give spiritual health, and innocence, and moral power. Let these principles be taken to heart, and let there be some thoughtful and genial intercourse with books, and there comes by degrees what seems almost an instinct to guide us in our companionship with them—leading to the good and truthful, and turning us away from the foolish, the false, and the pernicious. Even moderate experience, let it only be docile, thoughtful, and affectionate, will win for you an almost intuitive sense in judging what books you may take to your heart as friends, and friends for life: it will give also that confidence, most valuable in the days of multitudinous publications, the confidence in determining what books, and they are very many, it is good to be immutably ignorant of.

Reflecting on what a book can do and ought to do for you—how it may act on your mind, and your mind react on it—and thus holding communion, you can travel through a wilderness of volumes onward, onward through time, wisely and happily, and with perfect vision of your way, as the woodman sees a path in the forest—a path to his home, while the wanderer, whether standing or staggering, is lost in blind and blank bewilderment.

Literature, according to this conception of it, is to be employed for culture of character—manly character and womanly character. I speak of them separately, not because it is necessary so to do with reference to that which is essential literature, but because attention has lately been drawn to the subject of the social position of woman, and there is heard at least a sound of conflicting opinions and opposing theories. It is a discussion into which I mean not to enter, but only to touch upon in its connection with my present subject. Let me say, in the first place, that I question whether it is proper, or even practicable, so to detach womanhood from our common human nature as to make it a topic of distinct disquisition; it seems to me a little too much like a naturalist's study of some subject in zoology—the form and habits of some other species of created things. Again, as to all controversies respecting the equality of the sexes, or relative superiority or inferiority, I have only to say, that to me they are simply odious,—wrong, I believe,—in faith, in philosophy, and in feeling. Why should our minds be perplexed with modern speculations on this subject, when we have inspired teaching, which, in a few words, if we will but look at them, will show us the whole truth: "And the Lord God said, It is not good that the man should be alone; I will make him an help meet for him." "God doth not say," observes an old English divine, "it is not good for man to be alone," "he doth not say it is not good for this or that particular man to be alone; but it is not good in the general, for the whole frame of the world, that man should be alone."* Thus we find the creation of woman, and that providential law which preserves the equal numbers of the sexes, resting on the divinely-instituted principle of *companionship*, not alone of marriage, not alone of mother and child, but the manifold companionship of woman, single or married, companionship involving, of necessity, reciprocal dependence, but having nothing to do with equality or superiority or inferiority on one side or the other. There is a law of companionship far deeper than that of uniformity, or equality, or similarity, the law which reconciles similitude and dissimilitude, the harmony of contrast, in which

* Donne, vol. iv. p. 19.

what is wanting on the one side finds its complement on the other, for,

> Heart with heart and mind with mind,
> Where the main fibres are entwined,
>   Through Nature's skill,
> May even by contraries be joined
>   More closely still.*

Such was the exquisite companionship of the sexes as they were represented in our first parents, and so, however since disturbed, it remains as the ideal for all the generations of men and women. There was adduced another law, when the words were pronounced to the woman, "Thy desire shall be to thy husband, and he shall rule over thee;" and thus dominion was mingled with companionship—dominion of one sex over the other, which no sophistry can evade, for it is divine and to endure with the earth and the race. Having its origin in evil, it grows with evil, and the woman sinks down into the slave, and the man into her more imbruted tyrant; but goodness can still find the beauty of the primeval law of companionship undefaced by the element of dominion; for the penalty of dominion may, like the curse of labour, be converted into a blessing. As willing, dutiful labour brings gladness more than sorrow with it, so shall the fulfilment of the law of obedience win a glory of its own, brighter than any achievement of power. It is not by clamouring for rights, it is not by restless discontent, but it is by tranquil working out of the heaven-imposed law of obedience, that woman's weakness is transmuted into strength—a moral, spiritual power which man shall do homage to. Ambition, pride, wilfulness, or any

* Wordsworth. The Grave of Burns.

earthly passion will but distort her being; she struggles all in vain against a divine appointment, and sinks into more woful servitude, and the primeval curse weighs a thousand fold upon her, and the primeval companionship perishes. But bowing beneath that law which sounded through the darkening Paradise, she wins for her dower the only freedom that is worthy of woman—the moral liberty which God bestows upon the faithful and obedient spirit. It is from the soil of meekness that the true strength of womanhood grows, and it is because it has its root in such a soil that it has a growth so majestic, showering its blossoms and its fruits upon the world. Her influence follows man from the cradle to the grave, and the sphere of it is the whole region of humanity. We marvel at the might of it, because its tranquil triumphs are so placid and so noiseless, and penetrating into the deep places of our nature. It was the sun and the wind that in the fable strove for the mastery, and the strife was for a traveller's cloak; the quiet moon had naught to do with such fierce rivalry of the burning or the blast, but as in her tranquil orbit she journeys round the earth, silently sways the tides of the ocean.

There probably can be found no better test of civilization than the prevailing tone of feeling and opinion with regard to womanhood, and the recognition of woman's influences and social position. There may be the rude use of woman in barbaric life, or the frivolous uses of an over-civilized society. There may be the high-wrought adulation of an age of chivalry, which, so far as it is a sentiment of idolatry, is at once false and pernicious; or there may be that wise and well-adjusted sense of affectionate reverence of womanhood, which is thoughtful of the vast variety of human companionship—matronly, maidenly, sisterly, daughterly. In woman, there may be a true sense of sex, its duties and its claims, meekness with its hidden heroism; or there may be the unfeminine temper, fit to be rebuked by the Desdemona model.* Such a rebuke may be apposite where female character disfigures itself by obtrusiveness and self-sufficiency and pedantry. But, as far as my observation goes, that is not the state of society here; on the contrary, there is needed an effort much more difficult than repressing the froward; and that is, to lift modest, intelligent, sensitive womanhood above the dread of the ridicule of pedantry. Manly culture would gain by it as well as womanly. I heard lately from a woman's lips one of the finest pieces of Shakspeare criticism I ever met with; admirable in imagination and in the true philosophy of criticism, and yet uttered in conversation in the easy, natural intercourse of society.† Such should be the culture of woman, and such the tone of society, that these fine processes of womanly thought and feeling may mingle naturally with men's judgments.

There may be a social condition in which womanly

* With regard to the Desdemona model, it must also be remembered that it is not the only model of womanly character which the poet has left to the world; on the contrary, he has given others of equal worth and beauty, varied to the infinite variety of womanly duty. Indeed, what a woman ought to do often depends upon what man does, and very often, too, on what he leaves undone: so that, while it may be her duty to bow "like the gentle lady married to the Moor," man's wrongs or his omissions may call her to other duties—going forth, like Imogen, for womanly well-doing in the open and rude places of the earth. H. R.

† Mrs. Kemble.

culture is in advance of the manly, and then the woman is placed in the sad dilemma of either lowering the tone of her own thoughts, or of raising the minds of men and their habits of thought—a task that demands all of womanly sagacity and gentleness, and is a trial to womanly modesty. The companionship of the sexes is important in the culture of each, and by such communion the marvellous harmony of diverse qualities is made more perfect for the strength and beauty of their common humanity. One of the latest strains of English poetry has well proclaimed

"The woman's cause is man's: they rise or sink
Together, dwarf'd or godlike, bond or free:
* * * * *
(She must) "Live, and learn, and be
All that not harms distinctive womanhood,
For woman is not undevelopt man,
But diverse: could we make her as the man,
Sweet love were slain, whose dearest bond is this
Not like to thee, but like in difference:
Yet in the long years liker must they grow,
The man be more of woman, she of man;
He gain in sweetness and in moral height,
Nor lose the wrestling thews that throw the world;
She mental breadth, nor fail in childward care;
More as the double-natured poet each:
Till at the last she set herself to man
Like perfect music unto noble words;
And so these twain, upon the skirts of Time,
Sit side by side, full summ'd in all their powers,
Dispensing harvest;
Self-reverent each, and reverencing each,
Distinct in individualties;
But like each other, even as those who love:
Then comes the statelier Eden back to men."*

* I quote from that late poem of Mr. Tennyson's, "*The Princess,*" which has made a deep impression on the thoughtful criticism of his

I have been tempted further into this subject than I meant to be, but what I have said respecting the companionship of the sexes can have no better illustration than in the study of literature. All that is essential literature belongs alike to mind of woman and of man; it demands the same kind of culture from each, and most salutary may the companionship of mind be found, giving reciprocal help by the diversity of their power. Let us see how this will be. In the first place, a good habit of reading, whether in man or woman, may be described as the combination of passive recipiency from the book and the mind's reaction upon it: this equipoise is true culture. But, in a great deal of reading, the passiveness of impression is well nigh all, for it is luxurious indolence, and the reactive process is neglected. With the habitual

countrymen, and which has been described as having for its leading purpose the exhibiting the true idea and dignity of womanhood. I will not part from it without citing that other fine tribute to womanly influence—a manly acknowledgment full of deep thought and of true feeling, when he speaks of

———"One
Not learned, save in gracious household ways,
Not perfect, nay, but full of tender wants;
No angel, but a dearer being all dipt
In angel instincts, breathing paradise,
Interpreter between the gods and men,
Who look'd all native to her place, and yet
On tiptoe seem'd to touch upon a sphere
Too gross to tread, and all male minds perforce
Sway'd to her from their orbits as they moved,
And girdled her with music. Happy he
With such a mother! faith in womankind
Beats with his blood, and trust in all things high
Comes easy to him, and, though he trip and fall,
He shall not blind his soul with clay." H. R.

novel-reader, for instance, the luxury of reading becomes a perpetual stimulant, with no demand on the mind's own energy, and slowly wearing it away. The true enjoyment of books is when there is a co-operating power in the reader's mind—an active sympathy with the book; and those are the best books which demand that of you. And here let me notice how unfortunate and, indeed, mischievous a term is the word "taste" as applied in intercourse with literature or art; a metaphor taken from a *passive* sense, it fosters that lamentable error, that literature, which requires the strenuous exertion of action and sympathy, may be left to mere passive impressions. The temptation to receive an author's mind unreflectingly and passively is common to us all, but greater, I believe, for women, who gain, however, the advantages of a readier sympathy and a more unquestioning faith. The man's mind reacts more on the book, sets himself more in judgment upon it, and trusts less to his feelings; but, in all this, he is in more danger of bringing his faculties separately into action: he is more apt to be misled by our imperfect systems of metaphysics, which give us none but the most meagre theories of the human mind, and which are destined, I believe, to be swept away, if ever a great philosopher should devote himself to the work of analyzing the processes of thought. That pervading error of drawing a broad line of demarcation between our moral and intellectual nature, instead of recognising the intimate interdependence of thought and feeling, is a fallacy that scarce affects the workings of a woman's spirit. If a gifted and cultivated woman take a thoughtful interest in a book, she brings her whole being to bear on it, and hence there will often be a better assurance of truth in her conclusions than in man's more logical deductions, just as, by a similar process, she often shows finer and quicker tact in the discrimination of character. It has been justly remarked, that, with regard "to women of the highest intellectual endowments, we feel that we do them the utmost injustice in designating them by such terms as 'clever,' 'able,' 'learned,' 'intellectual:' they never present themselves to our minds *as* such. There is a sweetness, or a truth, or a kindness—some grace, some charm, some distinguishing moral characteristic which keeps the intellect in due subordination, and brings them to our thoughts, temper, mind, affections, one harmonious whole."

A woman's mind receiving true culture and preserving its fidelity to all womanly instincts, makes her, in our intercourse with literature, not only a companion, but a counsellor and a helpmate, fulfilling in this sphere the purposes of her creation. It is in letters as in life, and there (as has been well said) the woman "who praises and blames, persuades and resists, warns or exhorts upon occasion given, and carries her love through all with a strong heart, and not a weak fondness—she is the true helpmate."*

Cowper, speaking of one of his female friends, writes, "She is a critic by nature and not by rule, and has a perception of what is good or bad in composition, that I never knew deceive her; insomuch that when two sorts of expressions have pleaded equally for the precedence in my own esteem, and I have referred, as in such cases I

* The Statesman, by Henry Taylor, p. 70.

always did, the decision of the point to her, I never knew her at a loss for a just one."*

His best biographer, Southey, alluding to himself, and to the influence exerted on Wordsworth's mind by the genius of the poet's sister, adds the comment, "Were I to say that a poet finds his best advisers among his female friends, it would be speaking from my own experience, and the greatest poet of the age would confirm it by his. But never was any poet more indebted to such friends than Cowper. Had it not been for Mrs. Unwin, he would probably never have appeared in his own person as an author; had it not been for Lady Austen, he never would have been a popular one."

The same principles which cause the influences thus salutary to authorship, will carry it into reading and study, so that by virtue of this companionship the logical processes in the man's mind shall be tempered with more of affection, subdued to less of wilfulness, and to a truer power of sympathy; and the woman's spirit shall lose none of its earnest, confiding apprehensiveness in gaining more of reasoning and reflection; and so, by reciprocal influences, that vicious divorcement of our moral and intellectual natures shall be done away with, and the powers of thought and the powers of affection be brought into that harmony which is wisdom. The woman's mind must rise to a wiser activity, the man's to a wiser passiveness; each true to its nature, they may consort in such just companionship that strength of mind shall pass from each to each; and thus chastened and invigorated, the common humanity of the sexes rises higher than it

* Southey's Cowper, vol. ii. p. 35.

could be carried by either the powers peculiar to man or the powers peculiar to woman.

Now in proof of this, if we were to analyze the philosophy which Coleridge employed in his judgment on books, and by which he may be said to have made criticism a precious department of literature—raising it into a higher and purer region than was ever approached by the contracted and shallow dogmatism of the earlier schools of critics—it would, I think, be proved that he differed from them in nothing more than this, that he cast aside the wilfulness and self-assurance of the mere reasoning faculties; his marvellous powers were wedded to a child-like humility and a womanly confidingness, and thus his spirit found an avenue, closed to feeble and less docile intellects, into the deep places of the souls of mighty poets: his genius as a critic rose to its majestic height, not only by its inborn manly strength, but because, with woman-like faith, it first bowed beneath the law of obedience and love.

It is a beautiful example of the companionship of the manly and womanly mind, that this great critic of whom I have been speaking proclaimed, by both principle and practice, that the sophistications which are apt to gather round the intellects of men, clouding their vision, are best cleared away by that spiritual condition more congenial to the soul of woman, the interpenetrating the reasoning powers with the affections.

Coleridge taught his daughter that there is a spirit of love to which the truth is not obscured; that there are natural partialities, moral sympathies, which clear rather than cloud the vision of the mind; that in our communion with books, as with mankind, it is not true that *"love is blind."* The daughter has preserved the lesson in lines worthy of herself, her sire, and the precious truth embodied in them :

"Passion is blind, not love; *her* wondrous might
Informs with three-fold power man's inward sight;
To her deep glance the soul, at large displayed,
Shows all its mingled mass of light and shade :
Men call her blind when she but turns her head,
Nor scans the fault for which her tears are shed.
Can dull Indifference or Hate's troubled gaze
See through the secret heart's mysterious maze?
Can Scorn and Envy pierce that "dread abode"
Where true faults rest beneath the eye of God?
Not theirs, 'mid inward darkness, to discern
The spiritual splendours, how they shine and burn.
All bright endowments of a noble mind
They, who with joy behold them, soonest find;
And better none its stains of frailty know
Than they who fain would see it white as snow."*

I have in this introductory lecture attempted nothing beyond the exposition of a few broad and simple principles of literature, the importance of which will perhaps best be seen in the practical application of them to the guidance and formation of our habits of reading. It

* Biographia Literaria, of S. T. C. Vol. i. Part. 1. p. clxxxiv. Ed. 1847. This daughter was Mrs. Sara Coleridge, who died in 1852. I do not know where I can more appositely note the fact, that, when after years of constant literary correspondence with different members of the Coleridge family, Mr. Reed visited England in 1854, the welcome he received from them was most cordial and affectionate. He was greeted as an old friend and taken home to their very hearts. Since his death, no more earnest and affectionate tributes to his memory, no more accurate appreciation of his character, have been paid than by this circle of his kind English friends. Especially I will venture to refer to Mr. Justice Coleridge and his kinsman, the Rev. Derwent Coleridge of St. Mark's College, Chelsea. W. B. R.

was my intention to have worked those principles out to their application, but I have already consumed more of your time than I desire to do during one evening. It seemed necessary to show, in the first place, that I appreciated the difficulties which are caused by the multiplicity of books; and then to set forth these essential principles of literature, as distinguished from mere books, that it is addressed to our universal human nature, and that it gives power not to the intellect alone, but to our whole spiritual being; and that if it be true to its high purpose, it gives power of wisdom and happiness. I felt it to be important also, with a view to some applications to be made in subsequent lectures—to consider the reciprocal relations of the manly and womanly mind.

I propose in the next lecture to consider the application of these principles to habits and courses of reading; reserving for the third lecture the subject of the English language, to which I am anxious to devote an entire lecture.

LECTURE II.

Application of Literary Principles.*

Narrow and exclusive lines of reading to be avoided—Catholicity of taste—Charles Lamb's idea of books—Ruskin—Habits of reading comprehensive—Ancient Literature—Foreign languages—Different eras of letters—English essay-writing—Macaulay—Southey—Scott and Washington Irving—Archdeacon Hare—Lord Bacon's Essays—Poetic taste—Influence of individual pursuits—Friends in Council—Serious and gay books—English humour—Southey's ballad—Necessity of intellectual discipline—Disadvantage of courses of reading—Books not insulated things—Authors who guide—Southey's Doctor—Elia—Coleridge—Divisions of Prose and Poetry—Henry Taylor's Notes from Books—Poetry not a mere luxury of the mind—Arnold's habits of study and taste—The practical and poetical element of Anglo-Saxon character—The Bible—Mosaic Poetry—Inadequacy of language—Lockhart's character of Scott—Arnold's character of Scipio—Tragic Poetry—Poetry for children—Robinson Crusoe and the Arabian Nights—Wordsworth's Ode to Duty—Character of Washington.

In my last lecture I sought to show how, amid the multitude of books, we must in the first place seek guidance for our choice by laying down in our minds certain general principles respecting the essential properties and uses of literature. I endeavoured to show that nothing but what is addressed to man as man is literature, and that that is more appropriately and eminently literature which gives power rather than knowledge, and that that is worthy literature which gives power for good, healthful strength

* January 10, 1850.

of mind, wisdom, and happiness. Now let us see how we can follow the principles out to practical uses. It might be thought that such a definition of literature was too narrow a one; that it was too high and serious a view of the subject; and that it would exclude much inoffensive and agreeable reading. When I speak of a book giving moral power and health, or even if I should use words of graver import, spiritual strength and health, I employ these expressions in their largest sense, as comprehending the whole range of our inner life, from the lonely and loftiest meditations down to casual, colloquial cheerfulness, so that literature, in its large compass, shall furnish sympathy and an answer to every human emotion, and to all moods of thought and feeling. It is important, in the first place, having settled in one's mind an idea of the general properties of literature, to give to it a large and liberal application: in other words, to avoid narrow and exclusive lines in reading, to cultivate a true catholicity of taste. In so doing, you enlarge your capacities of enjoyment; you expand the discipline as well as the delights of the mind. It is with books as with nature, travel widely, and while at one time, you may behold the glories of the mountains, or the sublimities of the sea, you shall at another take delight as genial in the valley and the brook. We must needs be watchful of our habits of reading in this respect, for favourite lines of reading may come to be too exclusive. A favourite author may have too large an occupation. Women should remember that in all that is essentially literature, they have a right in common with men, because the very essence of it is, that it addresses itself to no distinctive property of sex, but to human nature. They wrong themselves in shrinking from any portion of the literature of their race, and they wrong man by not fulfilling in this respect the duty of companionship. For man and woman, alike, liberal communion with books is needed. I have known a person acquire late in life a hearty and healthful enjoyment of books, by this simple principle of opening the mind to docile and varied intercourse with them. I have known, on the other hand, that power of enjoyment lost, after years of intelligent and habitual reading, by giving way to a narrow bigotry in the choice of books. Daintiness, let it be always remembered, is disease, and fastidiousness is weakness. The healthy appetite of mind or body is strength for all healthful food. There was wisdom under the humour when Charles Lamb said, "I have no repugnances. Shaftesbury is not too genteel for me, nor Jonathan Wild too low. I can read anything which I call a *book*."* And a living writer, who has, with high power and eloquence, treated man's sense of enjoyment of nature and art, remarks: "Our purity of taste is best tested by its universality, for if we can only admire this thing or that, we may be sure that our cause for liking is of a finite and false nature. But if we can perceive beauty in every thing of God's doing, we may agree that we have reached the true perception of its universal laws. Hence false taste may be known by its fastidiousness, by its demands of pomp, splendour, and unusual combination, by its enjoyment only of particular styles and modes of things, and by its pride also, for it is forever meddling, mending, accumulating, and self-exulting; its eye is always upon itself, and it tests all things

* Lamb's Prose Works, vol. 3, p. 45. "Detached Thoughts on Books and Reading."

around it by the way they fit it. But true taste is forever growing, learning, reading, worshipping, laying its hand upon its mouth because it is astonished, casting its shoes from off its feet because it finds all ground holy, lamenting over itself, and testing itself by the way it fits things."* This finely-conceived contrast between the catholicity of true taste, and the narrowness of a false taste, is equally true as applied to literature. Indeed, it is matter of the highest moment in the guidance of our habits of reading to make them large and comprehensive; it is essential to a just judgment of books, and also to a full enjoyment of them. We form a truer estimate of things, when we rise to a high point, and get a larger field of vision. A knowledge of *ancient* literature, gives a deeper insight into the modern; if we see to what point, and in what manner, the pagan mind struggled, we can the better comprehend the higher destiny of the Christian mind. Acquaintance with *foreign* literature may help to a better estimate of our own. I shall have occasion hereafter, more than once, to trace the influences of the continental literature of Europe upon English literature. Let me here remark, that while the study of foreign languages and literature, along with many other advantages, may help us the better to understand and feel our own, it never can be made a substitute without great detriment. I make this remark, because in the education of the day, and especially in the education of women, there is a tendency to give to the mind a direction too much away from the literature of our own speech. This arises partly, perhaps, from one of the misdirected aims of education, looking to the showiness of accomplish-

* Ruskin's Modern Painters, vol. I, p. 23.

ments, rather than to more substantial and all-pervading good. If a man or a woman be ambitious of applause, and great or small celebrity, one's native literature is a much less effective weapon than a foreign literature; and the more remote that is, the more effective it is for ostentation. But if there be a better purpose than feeding vanity, then, for all the best and most salutary influences, nothing can take the place of the vernacular—the literature identified with the mother-tongue, with which alone our thoughts and feelings have their life and being.

Further, an expanded habit of reading is most important, as giving familiarity with different eras of our own literature. I hope to show in this course that the succession of those eras has a relation to each other much more life-like than a mere sequence of time. There is a continuity in a nation's literary as well as political life; and no generation can cast off the accumulated influences of previous ages without grievous detriment to itself. There are many readers who dwell altogether in their own times, busy with what one day produces after another. This is a great error; and they are the less able to gain a rational knowledge of that very literature, because exclusive familiarity with it gives no vision beyond, and, consequently, no capacity of comparison.

Now just in proportion as one enlarges his reading into different periods, does his taste grow more enlightened and wiser, and his judgment more assured. Let us take a practical example; and I turn for the purpose to the department of English *Essay-Writing*, in which the mind of our race has found utterance in several centuries. During the last few years there has been a large multitude of readers for Mr. Macaulay's Essays—brilliant, showy, attractive reading. But what assurance can any one of that multitude, who is unacquainted with other productions in the same class of books, have, in his admiration of these essays? How can he be assured that they are going to endure in our literature, and that their attractions are rightful attractions? I myself believe that they will prove perishable, because the pungency of a period, and the dazzling effects of declamation are, to Mr. Macaulay, dearer at least than faith and charity. The admirer of his Essays may think otherwise, but whether he be right or wrong, he is not entitled to form a judgment unless he has disciplined his power of judging by the reading of other works of a kindred nature—kindred, I mean, in form, not in spirit. Let him, therefore, turn to the other Essay-writing of our own times, (and it has been a large outlet for the contemporary mind,) the essays of Southey, of Scott, of Washington Irving, the inimitable "Elia" of Charles Lamb, or that thoughtful and thought-producing miscellany, the "Guesses at Truth." Then going back into other periods, and making choice of some of Dr. Johnson's Essays in the latter part of the eighteenth century, and of Addison's or Steele's in the "Spectator" and the "Tatler," in the early part of it, he will find his judgment enlarged by seeing how those generations dealt with this same branch of letters. Travelling back a century earlier, let him take the single volume of Lord Bacon's Essays, in which thoughts and suggestions of thought move in such solid phalanx that every line is a study. This is a simple rule for reading, and it may readily be practised: then bringing his acquaintance with the

English essays of the last two hundred years, and the power of judgment he has at the same time been unconsciously gaining, back to the Macaulay Essays, and he will perceive that they are not what they used to be to him—that the brilliant essayist "'gins to pale his ineffectual fire." A sense of enjoyment will indeed have passed away, but it will be because the reader has discovered elsewhere a deeper wisdom, a more tranquil beauty of thought and feeling, and of expression, a fuller beat of the human heart. The flashing of the will-o'-the-wisp shall no longer mislead him, who turns his looks to the steady cottage candle-light quietly shining out into the darkness, or to the still safer guidance of the slow-moving stars.

The principle which I have thus endeavoured to exemplify, is important in all the divisions of literature. It is needful to lift us out of the influences which environ us, to raise us above prejudices and narrow judgments which are engendered by confinement to contemporaneous habits of opinion. I hope to show at another part of the course how we may enlarge and elevate our Sunday occupations, and fortify our judgment of the sermons we read and hear, by acquaintance with the earlier sacred and devotional literature, especially that of the seventeenth century.

In nothing is familiarity with the literature of various periods more important than in the culture of poetic taste, our judgments and feelings for the poets. One meets perpetually with a confident partiality for some poet of the day, or a confident antipathy to another; and, all the while, such confidence may be entirely unequal to that which is the simplest test—the capacity to comprehend and enjoy the poetry of other ages. The merits of the living poets must be more or less in dispute; and he alone has any claim to venture on a prediction, as to which shall be immortal and which ephemeral, who has cultivated his imagination by thoughtful communion with the great poets of former centuries. Let him, who is quick to condemn, or slow to admire, ask whether the fault may not be in himself:—it may be the caprice or the apathy of uncultivated taste: he, and he alone, whose capacity of admiration has grown by culture ample enough to know and to feel the power of the poetry of the past, is qualified to speak in judgment of the poetry of the present. That this or that poem pleases him, who knows the present only, proves nothing: but he, whose imagination responds to the Chaucer of the fourteenth century, the Spenser and Shakespeare of the sixteenth, and the Milton of the seventeenth century, can see truly the poets of the nineteenth century, foreknowing which light shall pass away like a conflagration or a meteor, and which is beginning a perpetual planetary motion with the great lights of all ages.

I have spoken of the value of acquaintance with the literature of different eras, and the influence is reciprocal—the earlier upon the later, and the later upon the earlier. But with regard to the elder literature, there is an agency for good in the added sentiment of reverence. The mind bows, or ought to bow to it, as to age with its crown of glory. It is as salutary as for the youthful to withdraw for a season from the companionship of their peers, and to sit at the feet of the old, listening in reverential silence. In the elder literature, the perishable has passed away, and that is left which has put on its immortality.

A true catholicity of taste in our intercourse with books is in danger of being counteracted not only by the incessant and clamorous demand which the current literature makes upon us, but also by the impulses which we may be exposed to in consequence of our individual pursuits and personal positions. This point has been wisely touched in a passage, which I would commend to the reflection of every one, in the recent volume of that thoughtful book, "*Friends in Council*"—an admirable specimen of the essay-writing of our day. "There is," it is remarked, "a very refined use which reading is put to; namely, to counteract the particular evils and temptations of our callings, the original imperfections of our characters, the tendencies of our age, or of our own time of life. Those, for instance, who are versed in dull, crabbed work all day, of a kind which is always exercising the logical faculty and demanding minute, not to say, vexatious criticism, would, during their leisure, do wisely to expatiate in writings of a large and imaginative nature. These, however, are often the persons who particularly avoid poetry and works of imagination, whereas they ought to cultivate them most. For it should be one of the frequent objects of every man who cares for the culture of his whole being, to give some exercise to those faculties which are not demanded by his daily occupations and not encouraged by his disposition."*

In order to guard our habits of reading from the narrowing influences, which arise either from outward or inward temptations, it is necessary to cultivate in our choice of books a large variety, remembering, however,

* Arthur Helps: "Friends in Council." Part II., p. 15.

that the variety must be a healthful variety, and not that mere love of change, which, owning no law, is capricious, restless and morbid—at once a symptom and a cause of weakness, and not of health. To the mind that cultivates a thoughtful and well-regulated variety in its reading, this reward will come, that, where before, things seemed separate and insulated, beautiful affinities will reveal themselves; you will feel the brotherhood, as it were, that exists among all true books, and a deeper sense of the unity of all real literature, with its infinite variety.

In adjusting a diversified course of reading, we must keep in mind that it is not alone the serious literature which gives us power and wisdom, for Truth is often earnest in its joyousness as in its gravity: and it is a beautiful characteristic of our English literature, that it has never been wanting in the happy compound of pathos and playfulness, which we style by that untranslateable term "*Humour*"—that kindly perception of the ridiculous which is full of gentleness and sympathy. It is a healthful element: it chastens the dangerous faculty of Wit, turning its envenomed shafts into instruments of healing: it comes from the full heart, and it dwells with charity and love of the pure and the lofty: it holds no fellowship with sarcasm or scoffing or ribaldry, which are issues from the hollow or the sickly heart, and are fatal to the sense of reverence and of many of the humanizing affections. A sound humourous literature may be found throughout English language, in prose and verse, from its earliest periods down to our own times,—from Chaucer to Southey and Charles Lamb; and it behooves us to blend it with graver reading, to bring it, like the innocent and happy face of childhood, in the presence of hard-thinking, self-occupied, care-worn, sullen men, a pensive cheerfulness to recreate despondency and dejection. It is, therefore, not only variety, but a cheerful variety, that should be cultivated. "No heart," it has been well said, "would have been strong enough to hold the woe of Lear and Othello, except that which had the unquenchable elasticity of Falstaff and the 'Midsummer Night's Dream.'"* As in the author, so in the reader—it is the large culture which gives the more equal command of our faculties, whereas if we close up any of the natural resources to the mind, there follows feebleness or disproportioned power, or moodiness and fantastic melancholy, and, in extreme cases, the crazed brain. If the statistics be accurate, it is an appalling fact that in that region of the United States in which the intellect has been stimulated to most activity, insanity prevails to an extent double that in sections of the country less favourably situated. It would seem that the activity of the intellect had been too much tended, and its health too little. It is a common peril of humanity, with all its grades of danger, from the fitfulness of an ill-regulated mind up to the frenzy of the maniac.†

* Hare's Guesses at Truth. Part I., p. 319.

† This theory was no doubt founded on the assumption that the census statistics of insanity were correct; but my friend, and my brother's friend, Doctor Thomas J. Kirkbride, the superintendent of the Pennsylvania Hospital for the Insane, to whom I showed this passage, says, in a letter now before me:

"It has been shown conclusively that there can be no dependence placed on the census returns, and, except Massachusetts, I know of no state that has instituted inquiries for the special purpose of ascer-

There is a short poem of Southey's, which, in this connection, has a sad interest. Having written one of those humourous ballads drawn from his acquaintance with Spanish legendary history, he added an epilogue telling of its impressions on his household audience, especially the wondering and delighted faces of his children: he turns to his wife,

But when I looked at my mistress' face
  It was all too grave the while;
And when I ceased, methought there was more
  Of reproof than of praise in her smile.

That smile I read aright, for thus
  Reprovingly said she,
"Such tales are meet for youthful ears,
  But give little content to me.

"From thee far rather would I hear
  Some sober, sadder lay
Such as I oft have heard, well pleased,
  Before those locks were gray."

"Nay, mistress mine," I made reply,
  "The autumn hath its flowers,
Nor ever is the sky more gay
  Than in its evening hours.

*   *   *

---

taining how many insane are to be found within her limits. Your brother's views correspond with those of most persons who have paid attention to the subject, and are probably correct; but it must also be remembered that there is apparently, at least, most insanity where the largest provision is made for the treatment; for large numbers of cases then come before the public notice which previously had been kept out of observation. New England being a pioneer in providing State Hospitals, the number of insane is better known than in those states which have just commenced the erection of institutions of that character." W. B. R.

"That sense which held me back in youth
From all intemperate gladness,
That same good instinct bids me shun
Unprofitable sadness.

"Nor marvel you if I prefer
Of playful themes to sing:
The October grove hath brighter tints
Than summer or than spring;

"For o'er the leaves before they fall
Such hues hath nature thrown,
That the woods wear in sunless days
A sunshine of their own.

"Why should I seek to call forth tears?
The source from whence we weep
Too near the surface lies in youth,
In age it lies too deep.

"Enough of foresight sad, too much
Of retrospect have I:
And well for me that I sometimes
Can put those feelings by;

"From public ills, and thoughts that else
Might weigh me down to earth,
That I can gain some intervals
For healthful, hopeful mirth."*

This is a poet's wise pleading, and there is warning in the fact that this wife's shrinking from her husband's healthful, hopeful mirth, was the precursor of insanity: and it is sad to know that the poet's own lofty and richly stored mind sank, not, as has been supposed, from the exhaustion of an over-tasked brain, but under the wasting watchings over the wanderings of the crazed mind of the wife. This deepens the pensive humour of the lesson he has left

* Southey's Poetical Works, vol. vi. p. 282.

us—to find joyous, or at least cheerful companionship, as well as serious, in books.

Assuming that this catholicity of taste, the value of which I have endeavoured to present, is acquired, it then becomes a matter of much moment to have some principles to guide one through the large spaces of which the mind has vision. The capacity for extended and various reading may lose much of its value, if undisciplined and desultory. Indeed, if a large and varied power of reading be indulged in a desultory and chance way, it is likely to be lost: there is no genuine and permanent catholicity of taste for books but what is guarded by principles, and has a discipline of its own. That discipline is twofold: it is guidance we get from other minds, and that which we get from our own; and as these are well and wisely combined, we may secure ample independence for our own thinking, and ample respect for the wisdom of others.

It is not unfrequently thought that the true guidance for habits of reading is to be looked for in prescribed courses of reading, pointing out the books to be read, and the order of proceeding with them. Now, while this external guidance may to a certain extent be useful, I do believe that an elaborately prescribed course of reading would be found neither desirable nor practicable. It does not leave freedom enough to the movements of the reader's own mind; it does not give free enough scope to choice. Our communion with books, to be intelligent, must be more or less spontaneous. It is not possible to anticipate how or when an interest may be awakened in some particular subject or author, and it would be far better to break away from the prescribed list of books, in order to follow out that interest while it is a thoughtful impulse. It would be a sorry tameness of intellect that would not, sooner or later, work its way out of the track of the best of any such prescribed courses. This is the reason, no doubt, why they are so seldom attempted, and why, when attempted, they are apt to fail.

It may be asked, however, whether every thing is to be left to chance or caprice, whether one is to read what accident puts in the way—what happens to be reviewed or talked about. No! far from it: there would in this be no more exercise of rational will than in the other process; in truth, the slavery to chance is a worse evil than slavery to authority. So far as the origin of a taste for reading can be traced in the growth of the mind, it will be found, I think, mostly in the mind's own prompting; and the power thus engendered is, like all other powers in our being, to be looked to as something to be cultivated and chastened, and then its disciplined freedom will prove more and more its own safest guide. It will provide itself with more of philosophy than it is aware of in its choice of books, and will the better understand their relative virtues. On the other hand, I apprehend that often a taste for reading is quenched by rigid and injudicious prescription of books in which the mind takes no interest, can assimilate nothing to itself, and recognises no progress but what the eye takes count of in the reckoning of pages it has travelled over. It lies on the mind, unpalateable, heavy, undigested food. But reverse the process: observe or engender the interest as best you may, in the young mind, and then work with that—expanding, cultivating, chastening it.

It matters little from what point, or with what book a young reader begins his career, provided he brings along that thoughtful spirit of inquiry in which activity and docility are justly balanced. No good book is an insulated thing; you can always, if you will but look for them, discover leadings on to something else—other books on the same or kindred subjects—or other books by the same author. You acquire an affection for an author, and that may be made to embrace the books of his affection. I know of no more practical or safer principle in the guidance of one's reading, than thus to follow an author in whom you feel that your confidence is well placed. There are what may, in this respect, be called *guiding* authors, whose genial love of letters was not only a light to their own lives, but still shines, a lamp to show the path to others. You feel that what they loved may fitly be loved by you; that what stirred their spirits may have a power over yours. And so shall we find perpetual guidance, following it with freedom and loyalty, and extending our acquaintance with books just in the way in which we do with our acquaintance with living men and women. We use books for instruction or amusement, but hardly enough for guidance. Let me rapidly exemplify this principle, the value of which is, perhaps, in danger of being overlooked only from its simplicity. Take such a book as Southey's Life of Cowper, and you shall perceive the mind of Cowper and of his biographer so touching in various ways upon other authors, as to attract you to a large and admirable variety of the best literature in the language. Taking that remarkable work "*The Doctor*," in which Southey poured forth the vast abundance of his fine scholarship, or the Elia Essays, you will find guidance into many of the beautiful and secluded spots in English literature Or again, what countless suggestions for life-long reading, and what wise guidance to profitable studies may not be found in the several works of Coleridge! I mention these as eminently "guiding authors," and it would be easy to add to the list others of the same class in their degree. This is a use of books which combines healthful independence of judgment with healthful reverence for authority, giving safety from the two extremes—carelessness and servility of opinion.

It affords a communion of thought which is, in some respects, better than mere formal criticism. It is free from some of the temptations of such criticism, which we must be careful not to use too much of, in these times of many reviews and magazines, and when we turn to them for guidance, we must shun as a pestilence, all heartless criticism, all uncongenial criticism, such especially as unimaginative handling of subjects of imagination, and all malignant criticism. The criticism, which may well be followed and commenced with is that of which it has been said, "It may almost be called a religious criticism, for it holds out its warnings when multitudes are mad; and there is a criticism founded upon patient research and studious deliberation, which, even if it be given somewhat rudely and harshly, cannot but be useful. And there is the loving criticism, which explains, elicits, illumines; showing the force and beauty of some great word or deed, which, but for the kind care of the critic, might remain a dead letter or an inert fact; teaching the people to understand and to admire what is admirable."

In following out the general principle presented in the last lecture, that literature—that which is essentially literature in the highest sense of the term—is meant to give power rather than information, and in cherishing a catholicity of taste for books, it is a good practical rule to keep one's reading well proportioned in the two great divisions, prose and poetry. This is very apt to be neglected, and the consequence is a great loss of power, moral and intellectual, and a loss of some of the highest enjoyments of literature. It sometimes happens that some readers devote themselves too much to poetry: this is a great mistake, and betrays an ignorance of the true uses of poetical studies. When this happens, it is generally with those whose reading lies chiefly in the lower and merely sentimental region of poetry, for it is hardly possible for the imagination to enter truly into the spirit of the great poets, without having the various faculties of the mind so awakened and invigorated, as to make a knowledge of the great prose writers also a necessity of one's nature.

The disproportion usually lies in the other direction—prose reading to the exclusion of poetry. This is owing chiefly to the want of proper culture, for although there is certainly a great disparity of imaginative endowment, still the imagination is part of the universal mind of man, and it is a work of education to bring it into action in minds even the least imaginative. It is chiefly to the wilfully unimaginative mind that poetry, with all its wisdom and all its glory, is a sealed book. It sometimes happens, however, that a mind, well gifted with imaginative power, loses the capacity to relish poetry simply by the neglect of reading metrical literature. This is a sad mistake, inasmuch as the mere reader of prose cuts himself off from the very highest literary enjoyments; for if the giving of power to the mind be a characteristic, the most essential literature is to be found in poetry, especially if it be such as English poetry is, the embodiment of the very highest wisdom and the deepest feeling of our English race. I hope to show in my next lecture, in treating the subject of our language, how rich a source of enjoyment the study of English verse, considered simply as an organ of expression and harmony, may be made; but to readers who confine themselves to prose, the metrical form becomes repulsive instead of attractive. It has been well observed by a living writer, who has exercised his powers alike in prose and verse, that there are readers "to whom the poetical form merely and of itself acts as a sort of veil to every meaning, which is not habitually met with under that form, and who are puzzled by a passage occurring in a poem, which would be at once plain to them if divested of its cadence and rhythm; not because it is thereby put into language in any degree more perspicuous, but because prose is the vehicle they are accustomed to for this particular kind of matter, and they will apply their minds to it in prose, and they will refuse their minds to it in verse."*

The neglect of poetical reading is increased by the very mistaken notion that poetry is a mere luxury of the mind, alien from the demands of practical life—a light and effortless amusement. This is the prejudice and error of ignorance. For look at many of the strong and largely cultivated minds which we know by biography and their own works, and note how large and precious an element of strength is their studious love of poetry. Where could

* Taylor's Notes from Books, p. 215.

we find a man of more earnest, energetic, practical cast of character than Arnold?—eminent as an historian, and in other the gravest departments of thought and learning, active in the cause of education, zealous in matters of ecclesiastical, political, or social reform; right or wrong, always intensely practical and single-hearted in his honest zeal; a champion for truth, whether in the history of ancient politics or present questions of modern society; and, with all, never suffering the love of poetry to be extinguished in his heart, or to be crowded out of it, but turning it perpetually to wise uses, bringing the poetic truths of Shakspeare and of Wordsworth to the help of the cause of truth; his enthusiasm for the poets breaking forth, when he exclaims, "What a treat it would be to teach Shakspeare to a good class of young Greeks in regenerate Athens; to dwell upon him line by line and word by word, and so to get all his pictures and thoughts leisurely into one's mind, till I verily think one would, after a time, almost give out light in the dark, after having been steeped, as it were, in such an atmosphere of brilliance!"*

This was the constitution not of one man alone, but of the greatest minds of the race; for if our Anglo-Saxon character could be analyzed, a leading characteristic would be found to be the admirable combination of the practical and the poetical in it. This is reflected in all the best English literature, blending the ideal and the actual, never severing its highest spirituality from a steady basis of sober, good sense—philosophy and poetry

* Arnold's Life, p. 284, (American Edition,) in a letter to Mr. Justice Coleridge.

forever disclosing affinities with each other. It was no false boast when it was said that "Our great poets have been our best political philosophers;"* nor would it be, to add that they have been our best moralists. The reader, then, who, on the one hand, gives himself wholly to visionary poetic dreamings is false to his Saxon blood; and equally false is he who divorces himself from communion with the poets. There is no great philosopher in our language in whose genius imagination is not an active element: there is no great poet into whose character the philosophic element does not largely enter. This should teach us a lesson in our studies of English literature.

For the combination of prose and poetic reading, a higher authority is to be found than the predominant characteristic of the Saxon intellect as displayed in our literature. In the One Book, which, given for the good of all mankind, is supernaturally fitted for all phases of humanity and all conditions of civilization, observe that the large components of it are history and poetry. How little else is there in the Bible! In the Old Testament all is chronicle and song, and the high-wrought poetry of prophecy. In the New Testament are the same elements, with this difference, that the actual and the imaginative are more interpenetrated—narrative and parable, fact and poetry blended in matchless harmony; and even in the most argumentative portion of holy Writ, the poetic element is still present, to be followed by the vision and imagery of the Apocalypse.

Such is the unquestioned combination of poetry and

* Preface to Henry Taylor's Notes on Books.

prose in sacred Writ—the best means, we must believe, for the universal and perpetual good of man; and if literature have, as I have endeavoured to prove in the previous lecture, a kindred character, of an agency to build up our incorporeal being, then does it follow that we should take this silent warning from the pages of Revelation, and combine in our literary culture the same elements of the actual and the ideal or imaginative.

But, as it is the poetic culture which is most frequently discarded, let me follow out this high authority in that direction. You will recall how, when it was the divine purpose to imprint upon the memory of the chosen race what should endure from generation to generation, the minister of the divine will was inspired to speak, not in the language of argument or law, but in the impassioned strains of the imagination. The last tones of that voice which had roused his countrymen from slavery and sensuality in Egypt, and cheered, and threatened, and rebuked them during their wanderings, which had announced the statutes of Jehovah, had proclaimed victory to the obedient and judgment on the rebellious—the last tones, which were to go on sounding and sounding into distant ages, were the tones of poetry. The last inspiration which came down into the soul of Moses burst forth in that sublime ode which was his death-song. And why was this? "It shall come to pass," are the words, "when many evils and troubles are befallen them, that *this song* shall testify against them as a witness, for it shall not be forgotten out of the mouth of their seed." Well may we conceive how, in after times, when Israel was hunted by the hand of Midian into caves and dens—when, smitten by the Philistine, the ark of God was snatched away—when, after Jerusalem had known its highest glory, the sword of the King of the Chaldees smote their young men in the sanctuary, and spared neither young man nor maiden, old man nor him that stooped for age, or when the dark-browed Israelite was wandering in the streets of Nineveh or Babylon, an exile and a slave,—how must there have arisen on his sad spirit the memory of that song, with its sublime images of God's protection, now forfeited, "as an eagle stirreth up her nest, fluttereth over her young, spreadeth abroad her wings, so the Lord alone did lead him, and there was no strange god with him!"

I know that there is a way in which some people turn a deaf ear to this, saying that it is Oriental imagery, an Asiatic fashion of speech. Yes, but none the less, in the all-foreseeing purposes of Him who inspired it, was it meant for all after time and all after generations of men—in the West no less than in the East. The ancient and the Hebrew song had a modern and a larger destiny; it was to pass into a body of English words, and so come unto us.

This proof of the value of poetic culture is fortified when you reflect how that which may be reverenced as the very ideal of poetry—I mean that which flowed from direct divine inspiration—has always proved its adaptation to the hearts of men in all ages, in the Christian as well as in the Jewish church, in all their conditions of joy and of woe. The Holy City was given over to the fearful fulfilment of prophecy by the bloody sword of the Chaldean and the Roman—its temple and town razed to the ground, to be for a weary length of centuries trodden on by the infidel foot of the Saracen; and yet the sounds that issued from the harp of Jerusalem's king, silenced in the desecrated city, have never been hushed elsewhere, but to this day are heard, and their never-ending echoes will rise up to heaven from every side of the round earth as long as this planet of ours shall roll glittering in the sunlight through the boundless spaces of the sky. And thus it is that in all true worship there is incorporated forever the large influence of imagination.

Now, I have spoken of the combination of the practical and the poetical as a character of our English race, of the greatest English minds, and above all, as observable in Holy Writ; and such authority might be all-sufficient; but let us further seek a reason why this combination should be cherished, and prose and poetry studied in well-adjusted proportion. I speak of them as distinct, but let it be remembered that they are not contra-distinguished, for the best prose and the best poetry are but varied forms of uttered wisdom. The perfection of a literature is in the true combination of its poetry and prose, which bear to each other a relation which has been imaged with equal truth and fancy in these simple stanzas:

> I looked upon a plain of green
> That some one called the land of prose,
> Where many living things were seen
> In movement or repose.
>
> I looked upon a stately hill,
> That well was named the mount of song,
> Where golden shadows dwelt at will,
> The woods and streams among.
>
> But most this fact my wonder bred,
> Though known by all the nobly wise—
> It was the mountain streams that fed
> The fair green plain's amenities.*

* Anonymous.—"Poetry, Past and Present," p. 194.

The prose literature leads us along into the region of actual truth, that which has manifested itself in action, in deeds, in historic events, in biographic incidents. It tells us what men have done, and said, and suffered, or it reasons on the capacity for action and for passion, and so it gives power to the mind, in making us the better know ourselves and our fellow-beings. But most inadequate are his conceptions of truth, who thinks it has no range beyond the facts and outward things which observation and research and argument ascertain. Beneath all the visible and audible and tangible things of the world's history, there lies the deeper region of silent, unseen, spiritual truth—that which was shadowed forth in action, and yet the action, which to some minds seems every thing, is but the shadow, and the spirit is the reality. The experience of any one's own mind may teach the inadequacy of mere actual truth: has not every one felt, at the time when any deep emotion stirred him, or any lofty thought animated him, what imperfect exponents of such emotion or thought, his words or actions are? Nay, the more profound and sacred the affection, how it shrinks from any outward shape, as too narrow and superficial for it! Is it not in your daily consciousness to recognise the presence of emotions, yearnings, aspirations of your spiritual nature, which baffle expression, even if you wished to bring them forth from the recess of silence—motions of the soul, which word nor deed do justice to? Do you not know that there are sympathies, affinities with our fellow-beings, and with the external world of sight and sound, which pass beyond the reach of argument or common speech? So true is it, that there are powers,

"That touch each other to the quick—in modes
Which the gross world no sense hath to perceive,
No soul to dream of."*

This whole range of subjects, of deepest moment in the science of humanity, belongs to the imaginative portion of literature, toward which the prose literature is always tending, whenever it approaches the deep and spiritual and mysterious parts of human nature. When Mr. Lockhart, at the conclusion of his admirable biography of Sir Walter Scott, devotes a chapter to a delineation of Scott's character, with all his familiarity with his subject and his powers as an author, he prefaces his attempt with this remark: "Many of the feelings common to our nature can only be expressed adequately, and some of the finest can only be expressed at all, in the language of art, and more especially in the language of poetry."† When Arnold, in his History of Rome, portrays the character of Scipio, and especially that deep religious spirit in it which baffled the ancient historians—feeling the inadequacy of his effort in dealing with character, which, like Scipio's and the Protector Cromwell's, "are the wonders of history," he adds, "the genius which conceived the incomprehensible character of Hamlet would alone be able to describe with intuitive truth the character of Scipio, or of Cromwell."‡ Now observe how two authors, of the finest powers in these two high departments—biography and history—after carrying those powers to the farthest, profess their sense of how much remains unaccomplished; and, moreover, their conviction that all of higher or deeper achievement which lies beyond is left to poetry, or left to

* Wordsworth's "Address to Kilchum Castle," collective ed. p. 242.
† Lockhart's Scott, vol. x. p. 22. ‡ History of Rome, vol. iii. p. 385.

silence; not that it is less true or less real, but because there is truth which prose can never reach to—truth to which a form can be given only by imagination and art, whether using the instrument of words, the pencil, or the chisel—the hand of poet, of painter, or of sculptor. We ought to remember, then, that when we let imaginative studies drop out of our habits of reading, we neglect a whole region of truth and reality which the highest prose authority acknowledges itself unequal to.

The propensity to partial prose reading is attended with further loss, inasmuch as it not only separates us from much of the highest truth human nature can hold communion with, but it makes one lose the finest and deepest-reaching discipline our spiritual being is capable of. Two thousand years ago, the great philosopher of criticism gave his well-known theory of tragic poetry, that it purifies our feelings through terror and pity. But in the large compass of its power, poetry employs also other and kindlier agencies of good. It deals with us in the spirit of the most sagacious morality: it does not single out this or that faculty, and tutor the one till it grows weary or stubborn, or stupid under the narrow teaching and the dull iteration, but it addresses good sense, (which true poetry is never heedless of,) the intellect, the affections, and what has been well called "the great central power of imagination, which brings all the other faculties into harmonious action."* Instead of ministering to the mind diseased or the mind enfeebled one drug, or hard, unvaried food, it carries poor suffering humanity to the seaside, or up to the mountain-tops, for the larger contemplation which

* Talfourd's Literary Sketches and Letters, being the Final Memorials of Charles Lamb, p. 255.

leads to infinity, and for the health and strength and life of sublimer and purer thoughts and feelings. Were it possible to fathom the mystery which dwells in the serious eyes of infancy, we should learn, I believe, that nature leads the young spirit on to its sense of truth through wonderment and faith; and we do know how the imagination of childhood puts forth its powers into the region of the marvellous, the distant, the shadowy, and the infinite, —Robinson Crusoe's lonely island, the Arabian wonders, fairy fictions, fables without the "morals," which are skipped with better wisdom than they were put there, or travels in far-off lands. These things wear away as the work of life comes on, and, unhappily, the loving, faithful, imaginative spirit wears away too. The imagination is suffered to grow torpid, instead of being cultivated into a wiser activity, and our souls become materialized and sophisticated. There is enough in life to make us practical, but what we more need is to study how to be wisely visionary, to carry the freshness and feelings of childhood (and this has been said to be a characteristic of genius) into the mature reason, for

> We live by admiration, hope, and love;
> And, even as these are well and widely fixed,
> In dignity of being, we ascend.
>
> *Excursion*, collective ed.—587.

This is the poetic process of our spiritual growth, and when the poet teaches or chastens, he, at the same time, elevates and brings forth into life and light all of great and good that lies hidden in our nature. "Wouldst thou," says that earnest but rigid writer, Carlyle, "plant for eternity, then plant into the deep, infinite faculties of man his fantasy and heart; wouldst thou plant for year and day, then plant into his shallow, superficial faculties, his self-love, and arithmetical understanding."* The poet's planting is the deep planting, and his teaching becomes a ministry within our inmost being, so that the oracle without and the response within are in marvellous unity. It is not like the lessons which, remaining outward to us and unrecognised by our deep sympathies, are easily intercepted by chance or blown away from us, but it is made part of our very life and taste, to give perpetual strength or welcome warning. I would rather a child of mine should know and feel the high, imaginative teachings of Wordsworth's "*Ode to Duty*," than any piece of uninspired prose morality in the language, because the heart that will truly take that lofty lesson unto itself, however it may falter with frailty or fall short in the fulfilment, will fain not cast it out; it is teaching, that tempers the pride and wilfulness of manhood, showing how much more of moral beauty and strength and happiness there is in the spirit of willing obedience than in that of power or of liberty; nay, that the only genuine liberty is that which is in harmony with law and self-control; it is teaching fitted to give to womanhood a star-like life and motion, obedient to her orbit, and kindling the firmament of humanity with bright and benignant influences, radiant from that orbit alone; for the poet, better than the prose moralist, by throwing the consecration of his art around the sense of duty, discloses its hidden power for suffering or for action, so that, if need be, the woman will bow, like "the gentle lady married to the Moor," beneath the doom of some dark tragedy of home, or, if man's wrongs

* Sartor Resartus, p. 228. Am. Ed.

or his omissions should call her to other duties—for what a woman ought to do often depends on what man does or leaves undone—she will go forth, like Imogen, for womanly well-doing in the rude places of the open and unroofed world.

When that accomplished lady, whose genius, with no ther instruments than the poet's text and her own voice, so finely illustrated the genius of Shakspeare, read in a neighbouring city, to an audience of teachers, some selections of English literature, she gave that eloquent tribute to the character of Washington, which occurs in the historical lectures of Professor Smyth, of the English University of Cambridge,* and also Wordsworth's Ode to Duty, to which I have made allusion. I was struck with I will not say the felicity of the choice, but with the wisdom of it—the one selection portraying the might and glory of duty as actualized in the life of the moral hero of modern times; the other showing them idealized by the imagination of the poet. I refer to this as an admirable combination of the deep teachings of prose and poetry.

In order to receive the true benefit of the discipline of poetry, and also the full enjoyment of it, there must be given to it much more of thought, of strenuous activity of the reader's own imagination, more caution of mind, than most people think it worthy of. It must be studied, and not merely read. There are some books which I wish to commend to you with a view to the proper culture and discipline of the imagination. I will

* Smyth's Lectures, vol. ii. p. 486.

take occasion to give an opportunity to those who desire to do so to take a note of them, on the next evening, before I proceed to the lecture for that evening;—the subject of which will be "The Study of the English Language, considered as a source of enjoyment from its powers in prose and verse."

LECTURE III.

The English Language.*

Medium of ideas often forgotten—Witchery of English words—Analysis of good style difficult—The power of words—Our duty to the English language—Lord Bacon's idea of Latin—Milton—Hume's expostulation with Gibbon—Daniel's Lament—Extension of English language—French dominion in America—Landor's Penn and Peterborough—Duty of protecting and guarding language—Degeneracy of language and morals—Age of Charles II.—Language part of character—Arnold's Lectures on Modern History—Use of disproportionate words—Origin of the English language in the North—Classical and romantic languages—Saxon element of our language—Its superiority—The Bible idiom—Structure of sentences—Prepositions at the end of most vigorous sentences—Composite sentences, and the Latin element—Alliteration—Grandeur of sentences in old writers—Modern short sentences—Junius—Macaulay—No peculiar poetic diction—Doctor Franklin's rules—Shakspeare's matchless words—Wordsworth's sonnet—Byron—Landor—Coleridge's Christabel—"The Song in the Mind"—Hood—The Bridge of Sighs.

THE subject which I propose for this evening's lecture is the study of the powers of the English language in prose and verse. My desire to say something on this subject has been prompted by the conviction that some attention to it will increase our enjoyment of books, and will in fact give the reader a superadded pleasure. In our reading, we are very apt to content ourselves with the reception of such thoughts and feelings as pass into our minds from the silent page, unheeding the medium through which

* January 17, 1850.

they reach us; indeed, often, the purer and more excellent the style, the less conscious are we of its merits, so transparently does it let the writer's thoughts and emotions pass through it. We think of what is said or written, and feel it, but not *how* it is said or written: while the power which an author's meaning has upon our minds is intimately blended with the power his language exercises over us, of the latter we scarce have a conscious recognition. Does not every one know how differently the same thing said in different ways affects us? We welcome it, perhaps, in one case, and we repel it in the other. There shall be in one man's language an air of truth, of earnestness, and reality, which will gain assent to what he tells us, while the same thing told in other words will sound vain and unreal. There is wondrous agency of power and beauty in language, a winning witchery in words—grandly and beautifully so in our English speech. I desire to consider some of the elements of this, regarded as a source of intellectual enjoyment. In all intercourse with the best writers, whether in prose or verse, our minds have, no doubt, an unconscious perception of the goodness of the style, just as we have unconscious freedom of breath in a pure atmosphere; but if the perception of style be made reflective, it may come to have too much of consciousness in it: we may come to think too much of the instrument, and too little of the music; to be too critical of our own emotions of delight. I have, therefore, some apprehensions that in attempting any thing like an analytical exposition of the enjoyment of language, considered simply as an organ of expression, it may prove a little too much like *parsing* our pleasure. The happy, healthful-breathing asks for no analysis of the air; the mountain-spring is quaffed without thought of what science can tell of its components. In treating the powers of the English language in prose and verse, I should like, without vexing it with comment, or criticism, or analysis, but simply sounding it, to show what an instrument it has been in the hands of its great masters.

I wish, however, to accomplish something more. At the same time, on an occasion like this, and within the limits of one lecture, it would not be practicable to enter into technical details of either the history or the philology of our language. I propose, therefore, to give a didactic character to this lecture, rather by making it suggestive of the interest which is to be found in the study of the language, by noticing some of its characteristics, and the applications of the philosophy of language which it serves to illustrate. Avoiding technical and recondite points of philology, I aim at treating the subject according to the universality of the interest it has, so as to show how the culture of it comes home to everybody, and how it is in the power of each one of us to awaken it into more action.

The history of the language, its origin and progress, the principles of English philology, and the laws of English metre, are subjects of deep interest and demand careful study, and a different kind of attention from what I have any right to ask from you. I propose, therefore, rather to notice and exemplify some of the leading characteristics of the language, so as to awaken into more active and intelligent consciousness our enjoyment of it, so as to form this, among our other habits of reading; to have an eye and a feeling for the fitness of the words, their power, their beauty, their simplicity, and truthfulness; to find ourselves, in reading a wise and good book, often pausing, in silent thankfulness and delight, as we think and feel what glorious apparel the author's wise thought or good feeling hath arrayed itself in—with what majesty or loveliness of speech or song the mind makes music for itself in the words in which it is embodied—so that the thought and the words receive strength and beauty from each other. Of that connection which exists between our thoughts and feelings, and the words we clothe them in, of their mutual relation and reaction, I cannot now speak further, than to say that the more we reflect on our own inner nature, and on the wondrous powers of words, the better we shall feel and understand that relation, perceiving how words seem to dwell midway between the corporeal and incorporeal—a connection between our spiritual and material being.

The simple suggestion of this deep significancy of language, and its relation to man's spiritual nature, may perhaps, in some measure, correct, or, at least, startle that error of looking upon this whole subject as a mere matter of rhetoric and grammar, a superficial study of style, and therefore having claim upon the rhetorician rather than on the man—on art rather than on humanity, not reflecting on the divine origin of language; that speech, even more than reason, distinguishes man from the brute; and that the two powers, in their mysterious union, lift him out of barbarism. Whatever it may be, whether the rude and imperfect speech of the savage, articulate words with no help of written language, or whether it be the copious and refined language of civilized nations, there is, all the earth over, the duty of loyalty, thoughtful loyalty if possible, to the mother-tongue.

The universal duty rests on us, and let us see what special obligations are due to our ENGLISH speech. That speech runs the career of the race that uses it, and the speed and the spread of that career have, perhaps, had more help from the speech than philosophy has dreamed of. Little more than two hundred years ago, Lord Bacon, speaking of his Essays, said, "I do conceive that the Latin volumes of them, being in the universal language, may last as long as books last." He seems to have had no such assurance for his insular English language. Somewhat later, it needed Milton's filial and loyal affection for his mother-tongue to give it a share with the Latin in his prose-writings.* A poet, a contem-

* As recently as the middle of the last century, Hume expostulated with Gibbon on his use of the French instead of the English language: "Why," said he to him, "why do you compose in French, and carry fagots to the wood, as Horace says with regard to those Romans who wrote in Greek? I grant that you have a like motive to those Romans, and adopt a language more generally diffused than your own native tongue; but have you not remarked the fate of those two ancient languages in following ages? The Latin, though then less celebrated and confined to more narrow limits, has, in some measure, outlived the Greek, and is now become generally understood by men of letters. Let the French, therefore, triumph in the present diffusion of their tongue. *Our solid and increasing establishments in America, where we need less dread the inundation of barbarians, promise a superior stability and duration to the English language.*"—Burton's Life of Hume, vol. ii. p. 411. H. R.

Yet Hume, in the second edition of his "History of the Stuarts," expunged the following passage. Speaking of America, he had said, "The seeds of many a noble state have been sown in climates kept desolate by the wild manners of its ancient inhabitants, and an asylum (is) secured in that solitary world for liberty and science, if ever the spreading of unlimited empire or the inroad of barbarous nations should again extinguish them in this turbulent and restless hemisphere."—*Id.* vol. ii. p. 74. W. B. R.

porary and friend of Shakspeare, feelingly lamented the limits of the English language:

> "Oh that the Ocean did not bound our style
> Within these strict and narrow limits so,
> But that the melody of our sweet isle
> Might now be heard to Tiber, Arne, and Po,
> That they may know how far Thames doth outgo
> The music of declined Italy!"*

Such was the lament of him, the purity and simplicity of whose style won for him the title of the "well-languaged Daniel." In one mood, he speaks of England as

> "This little point, this scarce-discovered isle,
> Thrust from the world, with whom our speech unknown
> Made never traffic of our style."

Again, however, with truer and more hopeful vision, he exclaims,

> ——"Who knows whither we may vent
> The treasure of our tongue? To what strange shores
> This gain of our best glory will be sent
> T' enrich unknowing nations with our stores?
> What worlds in the yet unformed occident
> May come refined with th' accents that are ours?"

This was the poet's vision, larger than even the imaginative reason of the philosopher Bacon counted on. This was not three centuries ago, and now the Island-language girdles the earth. Soon after the poet's heart gave forth its hope, English words began to find a home in the West, close begirt, however, with the fierce discords of the Indian-tongues: for years and years their home was hemmed in within a narrow strip along the Atlantic, the English and the French languages hav-

* Dedication of Cleopatra to the Countess of Pembroke.

ing a divided sway, when the Bourbon was strong enough to hold the Canadas, and proud enough to adventure that magnificent scheme of colonial dominion which was to stretch from the St. Lawrence to the Ohio and the Mississippi, leaving the Briton his scant foothold between the mountains and the sea. The might of the race broke this circumscription; and, in our own day, we have seen this language of ours span the continent, and now it gives a greeting on the shores of the Pacific as well as of the Atlantic. An earnest English author does not fear to predict that the time will come when the language will occupy the far South on each side the Andes; Rio, and Valparaiso, holding rivalry in the purity of the English speech.* But, without venturing into the uncertainties of the future, see how our language has an abode, far and wide, in the islands of the earth, and how, in India, it has travelled northward till it has struck the ancient but abandoned path of another European language—one of the great languages of the world's history—the path of conquest along which Alexander carried Greek words into the regions of the Indus.

---

* In Landor's Imaginary Conversations, written some twenty years ago, William Penn is made to say, "Whenever I see a child before me in America, I fancy I see a fresh opening in the wilderness, and in the opening, a servant of God, appointed to comfort and guide me, ready to sit beside me when my eyes grow dim, and able to sustain me when my feet are weary. Look forward, and behold the children of that child. Few generations are requisite to throw upon their hinges the heavily-barred portals of the vast continent . . . Who knows but a century or two hence we may look down together on those who are journeying in this newly-traced road toward the cities and marts of California, and who are delayed upon it by meeting the Spaniards driven in troops from Mexico?" H. R.

Our language at this day has a larger extent of influence than the Greek, the Latin, or the Arabic ever had, and its dominion is expanding.

When we contemplate the spread of the language, we may conceive the vast power which is coupled with it and we should remember that, commensurate with the power is the responsibility, the duty of cultivating and guarding it as a possession and inheritance, and a trust. Reflect, too, upon this, that along with national or individual degradation, there is sure to come corruption of the language—an accompaniment more than a mere consequence of that degradation. The language was vitiated—worse then than ever—when the court of Charles the Second scattered the poison of its licentionsness and ribaldry. The wicked and debased, who are banded together in the fellowship of crime, disown the common language of their fellow-men, and delight in a strange vocabulary of their own; for when they break bond with the moral elements that link them to society, they cast off the language as one of the links. Words which serve the wise and good become to the silly and the sensual a burden, because they are associated with wise and good uses, such as couple our English speech with so much good sense, lofty imaginings, deep philosophy, ministrant in the cause of freedom, of duty, and of truth. Hence it has been well said that "A man should love and venerate his native language as the first of his benefactors, as the awakener and stirrer of all his thoughts, the frame and mould and rule of his spiritual being; as the great bond and medium of intercourse with his fellows; as the mirror in which he sees his own nature, and without which he could not even commune with himself; as the image in which the wisdom of God has chosen to reveal itself to him."* And it is a deep feeling of the perpetual power of the associations of our language, which prompts the poet's words

> We must be free or die, who speak the tongue
> That Shakspeare spake.

Now how is the language to be guarded and cultivated? By the thoughtful and conscientious use of it by every one who speaks it. It is not by authors alone, but by each man and woman to whom it is the mother-tongue, that the language is to be preserved in its purity and power; by each one in his sphere and according to his opportunities. This is a duty, and the fulfilment of it is of deeper moment than many are aware of. It is not enough thought of, that "accuracy of style is near akin to veracity and truthful habits of mind," and to sincerity and earnestness of character.† "Language," observes a great master of it—"Language is part of man's character."‡ You may, I believe, easily prove the truth of this by familiar observation, discovering the physiognomy that is in speech as well as in the face. You will find one man's words are earnest of sincerity, straightforwardness of character, fair dealing, genuine and deep feeling, true manliness, true womanliness, symbolized in the words. You will perceive in another man's speech signs of a confused habit of thought, of vagueness and indirectness of purpose. What before was a beautiful and transparent atmosphere, through which earthly objects

* Guesses at Truth, Part i. p. 296.

† Coleridge's Literary Remains, vol. i. p. 241.

‡ Landor's Imaginary Conversations. First Series. Demosthenes and Eubulides, vol. i. p. 232.

could be distinctly seen, or the stars were brightly shining, is turned into murkiness and mist. Again, there are men whose words, volubly uttered and with ample rotundity of sound, come to us like sounds, and nothing more, suggesting the unreality and hollowness of the speaker's character; and sometimes, too, to the thoughtful observer, the falsity of character will betray itself in the fashion of the speech. Dr. Arnold, in his Lectures introductory to Modern History, (the best guide-book in our language to historical reading generally,*) has shown how we must judge of an historian's character by his style. "If it is very heavy and cumbrous, it indicates either a dull man or a pompous man, or at least a slow and awkward man; if it be tawdry and full of commonplaces enunciated with great solemnity, the writer is most likely a silly man; if it be highly antithetical and full of unusual expressions, or artificial ways of stating a plain thing, the writer is clearly an affected man. If it be plain and simple, always clear, but never eloquent, the writer may be a very sensible man, but is too hard and dry to be a very great man. If on the other hand, it is always eloquent, rich in illustrations, and without the relief of simple and great passages, we must admire the writer's genius in a very high degree, but we may fear that he is too continually excited to have attained to the highest wisdom, for that is necessarily calm. In this manner the mere language of an

* Mr. Reed's edition of Arnold's Lectures, with notes, appeared in America in 1845; and for the memory of that remarkable man he felt and expressed—as will be often seen in these Lectures—an almost filial respect. Some of the happiest hours of the last months of Mr. Reed's life were passed at Foxhow, in the society of Mrs. Arnold, her children, and grandchildren. W. B. R.

historian will furnish us with something of a key to his mind, and will tell us, or at least give us cause to presume, in what his main strength lies, and in what he is deficient." The same method of observation, let me add, will not unfrequently furnish us with a key to the characters of other authors beside the historians, and also of men and women who are not authors, but our ordinary companions in life.

According to this view of the subject, the first study of style begins not with the words, as the tongue articulates them or the hand writes them, but it begins *here*, at the heart, and works upward and outward from that. The philosophy and art of language come afterward. Supposing the moral qualifications to exist—I mean sincerity, truthfulness, freedom from affectation or vanity, earnestness—then in the next place it is important to associate a certain conscientiousness in the use of speech, so that it shall correspond to something within us. I do not mean that we are to sacrifice the naturalness of speech to a perpetual pedantry; that we should be ambitious of being such rigid purists as to break the liberty and spirit of a living language by the weight of too much authority; that we should fetter the easy grace of colloquial speech with sad formality, as Charles Lamb complains of in the conversation of the Scotch, when he said, "Their affirmations have the sanctity of an oath." But there may be somewhat more of heed in our use of language than we do pay to it, without running into any thing so odious as pedantry; and indeed cultivated conversation not unfrequently turns to these topics of language, and in a casual and familiar way will treat them most agreeably and intelligently, sò that we may correct an inaccuracy of diction or of pronunciation, which we might have remained unconscious of, but for an interchange of views in such companionship. In this way, we may do much for one another by a fellowship of loyalty to the language.

Besides the vice of using words without thoughts or feelings to correspond to them, there is another fault which would be chastened by a little more conscientiousness in our expressions; I mean a propensity very common—somewhat more so, perhaps, to one sex (I will not say which) than the other—to employ words of force disproportionate to the occasion, especially in the expression of feelings either agreeable or the reverse. Something which is simply pleasing is described as "delightful" or "charming;" or that which is disagreeable or unsightly or discordant, is spoken of as "dreadful," "terrible," "horrible," or "awful."* This, no doubt, is often merely the exaggeration of innocent exuberance of spirits, and the words are received, therefore, with large allowances. It in some measure comes of poverty or carelessness of speech, or both, somewhat in the way that oaths are uttered sometimes, (we may charitably believe,) not as a purposed profanity, but for lack of words that are strong without the stain of wickedness upon them. But besides being alien from accuracy and a truthful habit of mind, the habitual use of disproportioned language is attended with this disadvantage, our strong words are all wasted before they are wanted; if, for instance there comes an occasion calling for deep and hearty hatred, and also for

* In another relation, one sees the constant misuse of this word, in its strict employment by Barrow, when he speaks of "a devout affection of heart, an *aweful sense of mind.*" Barrow, vol. v. p. 605. W. B. R.

an earnest expression of it, our vocabulary is exhausted; our armory is despoiled by our own extravagance; we have been shooting our arrows in the air, and when we truly need them, our quiver is empty.*

Let us now look at some of the characteristics of the English language as an instrument of expression for those who recognise the duty of the thoughtful use of it. He will the better understand and use it who keeps in mind that it belongs to the family of the Northern languages. Our English speech is to be traced beyond England into the forests of Germany and to the shores of the Northern Ocean; the dialect, that was in time to grow into our English language, was carried fourteen hundred years ago to the island from the Teutonic region of the continent.† Our speech holds not its genealogy from the cultivated languages of the South; they had done their appointed work—the languages of Greece and Rome—and the English language, for the fulfilment of its destiny, had another birth, and was long kept aloof from them. It was to have a fresher and purer spring than in the languages

---

* There is an opposite fault, which we have caught from England, but which an English writer, mindful of the language, has condemned "as that stupid modern vulgarism, by which we use the word '*nice*' to denote almost every mode of approbation for almost every variety of quality, . . . from sheer poverty of thought," or fear of "saying any thing definite." Julius Charles Hare, Philological Museum. H. R.

† It was a slow and various transmission which carried the language which was to grow into modern English over from the continent to the island; for there are reckoned six several migrations of different divisions of the Saxon race, extending through almost exactly a century, bearing with them their various dialects for future formation into one great language. H. R.

which were identified with the degeneracy of the nations that spoke them. It was to become the voice of another form of national character, and of a different and deeper spirituality, than that which belonged to the sunny regions of the south. The contrast between what has been called the "*classical* mind" and the "*romantic* mind," is traceable in the respective languages, and has been beautifully illustrated by the names of "good omen," which the Greeks delighted in, and the names of "dark mystery," which were congenial to those who dwelt in the gloom of the North.

The sunny wisdom of the Greeks
  All o'er the earth is strewed:
On every dark and awful place,
  Rude hill and haunted wood,
The beautiful, bright people left
  A name of omen good.

They would not have an evil word
  Weigh heavy on the breeze;
They would not darken mountain side
  Nor stain the shining seas,
With names of some disastrous past;
  The unwise witnesses.

* * * *

Unlike the children of romance,
  From out whose spirit deep
The touch of gloom hath passed on glen,
  And mountain lake and steep;
On Devil's Bridge and Raven's Tower
  And lovelorn Maiden's Leap.

Who sought in cavern, wood, and dell,
  Where'er they could lay bare

The path of ill, and localized
  Terrific legends there;
Leaving a hoarse and pondrous name
  To haunt the very air.

Not so the radiant-hearted Greeks,
  Who hesitated still
To offend the blessed Presences
  Which earth and ocean fill;
Whose tongues, elsewhere so eloquent,
  Stammered at words of ill.

All places, where their presence was
  Upon the fruitful earth,
By kindly law were clasped within
  The circle of their mirth,
And in their spirits had a new
  And consecrated birth.

O bless them for it, traveller!
  The fair-tongued ancients bless!
Who thus from land and sea trod out
  All footmarks of distress;
Illuminating earth with their
  Own inward cheerfulness.*

In other ways it might also be shown that the genius of the Northern character gave utterance to itself differently from the races of the South. The beginning of a just knowledge of the English language is an accurate sense of its Northern origin. The date of that origin cannot be fixed; but certainly the language is a growth out of the Anglo-Saxon speech, however important may be the additions it has received elsewhere. Of the 38,000 words, of which it is reckoned the English language consists, 23,000 are of Saxon origin—near five-eighths of it;

* Faber's Styrian Lake and Other Poems, p. 318.

a proportion which must needs control, to a great extent, the grammatical laws of the language; that is, along with the multitude of Northern words, there must be much of Northern method, and in that method, baffling, as it often does, the technical systems of grammar, we are to look for the idioms. It is a remark of one of the most nervous authors of our day, Walter Savage Landor: "Every good writer has much idiom; it is the life and spirit of language; and none ever entertained a fear or apprehension that strength and sublimity were to be lowered and weakened by it. . . . Nations in a state of decay lose their idiom, which loss is always precursory to that of freedom."* And Coleridge exclaimed, "If men would only say what they have to say in plain terms, how much more eloquent would they be!" But it is the simple Saxon-English words, and the Saxon way of putting them together, that people will not be content with. There is forever a pushing away from the purest English, and from the genuine idioms; and, what is noticeable, it is the half-educated who are always most ambitious of long words and high-sounding combinations of them. There is not pomp enough for them in our short, often one-syllable Saxon speech. Observe what a propensity there is to substitute the word "individual," (and unfitly too) for such a clear, simple, short word as "man." It seems to be employed as a sort of midway expression between "*man*" and "*gentleman*," between "*woman*" and "*lady*," as if there was not quite courtesy enough in the words "*man*" and "*woman*," and a little more than was wanted in the other

* Imaginary Conversations, First Series. Conversation xiv., vol. i p. 244.

words. It is in this way that there may be a false refinement, a mistaken delicacy, that is fatal to the primitive simplicity and nervousness of language. From being too dainty in our choice of words, we come at last to forfeit the use of some of the best of them. Again, I do verily believe, that the good word "*begin*," is in danger of becoming obsolete, so that, after a while, it will sound quaint and antiquated; and yet it is both as old as the language, and as fresh as to-day's talk, known in all the eras of the language, sanctioned by all possible authority, grave and formal as well as familiar and homely, and expressive of all that is needed. Really some people seem to shun it as much as if it were indelicate, or, at the least, a vulgarism. Listen almost where you will, and now-a-days nobody hardly is heard of as "*beginning*," for everything is "*commenced.*" But what a shock would our instinct of language and some of our best associations receive, if this change could creep on to the pages of our English version of the Bible, instead of reading "In the *beginning* God created the heavens and the earth"—"the fear of the Lord is the *beginning* of wisdom"—"In the *beginning* was the Word." Truly did Coleridge say, that "Intense study of the Bible will keep any writer from being vulgar in point of style."* And an eloquent living divine has asked, "Who can estimate the grandeur, the depth, the expansive power, which our language and the German have derived from the national liturgical offices, as well as from the national translation of the Scriptures?" Let those who crave a statelier word than "begin," learn that even Milton, with all his

* Table Talk, vol. i. p. 177.

erudite diction, never, throughout all his poems, I believe, uses the words "*commence*" or "*commencement*;" and let them observe how Shakspeare perpetually makes his beautiful uses of the simple English word, and is even content to make it shorter and simpler yet, as in the touching line that tells so much of the guilt-wasted soul of Macbeth—

> "I 'gin to grow a-weary of the sun."

Let me exemplify this tendency away from the native character of the language in the structure of sentences as well as in the choice of words. I refer to the frequent abandonment of that peculiarly characteristic arrangement which puts a preposition at the end of a sentence. This is eminently an English idiom, and nothing but prejudice arising from misapplied analogy with the Southern languages, and the propensity to make style more formal and less idiomatic, could ever have led any one to suppose this construction to be wrong. The false fastidiousness which shuns a short particle at the end of a sentence, is fatal often to a force which belongs to the language with its primal character. The superiority of the idiom I am referring to, could be proved beyond question by examples of the best writing in all the eras of the language. As the error is pretty wide spread, let me cite a few of these. Lord Bacon says, "Houses are built to live in, and not to look on;" and again, "Revenge is a kind of wild justice, which the more a man's nature runs to, the more ought law to weed it out." Any attempt to transpose these separable prepositions would destroy the strength and the terseness of the sentences. Even a stronger example occurs in a passage in one of the great English divines, a contemporary of Bacon's: "Hath God a name to swear by? . . . Hath God a name to curse by? Hath God a name to blaspheme by? and hath God no name to pray by?"* The opening sentence of one of Mr. Burke's most celebrated speeches is—"The times we live in have been distinguished by extraordinary events;" Dr. Franklin's phrase, with its twenty-five Saxon and four Latin words: ". . . William Coleman, then a merchant's clerk about my age, who had the coolest, clearest head, the best heart, and the exactest morals of any man I ever met with." And observe such a sentence as this of Arnold's, "Knowledge must be worked for, studied for, thought for; and, more than all, it must be prayed for."† I really think that people, in writing and speaking, might get over their fear of finding a preposition at the end of their sentences.

But it is not only the Saxon side of the language that is to be prized and cultured: its glory is, in fact, its wonderfully composite character, the Anglo-Norman element, as well as the Anglo-Saxon, contributing to its copiousness and power; and there is no more pleasing study in language, than to observe how, in all the best writers, these elements are harmoniously combined. One of the boldest instances of this has been noticed in these lines in Macbeth, in which two very long words are blended with short ones with singular effect:

"Will all great Neptune's ocean wash this blood
Clean from my hand? No! this, my hand will rather
The multitudinous sea incarnardine,
Making the green—one red."‡

---

* Donne's Sermon on the Penitential Psalms, vol. vi. p. 380.

† Arnold's Miscellaneous Works, p. 234. On the Education of the Middle Classes. Also, Hallam's Literature of Europe, vol. iv. 535.

‡ A less familiar line occurs to me where, at the end of a series of

A well-known line in the same tragedy reminds me of another antique quality which has been curiously retained, long after the formal practice of it has been disused, and now prevails peculiarly in all vigorous English prose, as well as poetry: I refer to the use of *alliteration*, as derived from some of the forms of early poetry in England. If you will take the pains to observe it, you will probably be surprised to find to what an extent it is employed in English literature, both now and formerly. It is a curious study of the language to trace the power that lies in the repetition of a letter in a succession of words; as when Macbeth says,

"Ay, now, I see, 'tis true:
For the blood-boltered Banquo smiles upon me,
And points at them for his.*

In the versions attached to Retsch's Outlines in French, Italian, Spanish, and German, no one of the languages attempts this tremendous alliteration. I cannot pause upon this quality of style further than to remark, that he who studies the language, will find an interest in observing how beautiful and striking, and, indeed, how natural, this apparently artificial process becomes in the hands of a master

---

Saxon words, a Latin word is brought in with singular power. In the second part of Henry VI., Suffolk says to Queen Margaret,

"For where thou art, there is the world itself
With every several pleasure in the world;
And where thou art not, *desolation*." W. B. R.

* Or in the incantation,

"the salt-sea shark;
Root of hemlock digg'd; i' the dark,
Finger of birth-strangled babe,
Ditch-delivered by a drab." W. B. R.

of the language. The mere affinity of initial letters is also one of the mental associations which not unfrequently gives the fittest word to be found.*

In describing the English language as a *composite* language, we get, perhaps, a wrong notion of its being made up by the union of two dialects, the Saxon and the Norman. The truth rather seems to be, that the Anglo-Saxon language has displayed the same powers of acquisition as have distinguished the race, and has thus enlarged the domain by conquest, and appropriation, and annexation, retaining, however, withal, its essentially Teutonic character. Its early acquisitions from abroad were words of French or Southern birth, which became part of the natural spoken language, the copiousness and power of which were thus admirably increased. A single specimen will show that this is a copiousness giving not

---

* "The Northern languages," remarks Mr. Henry Taylor, (Notes on Books, p. 132,) "have often been reproached for their excess in consonants, guttural, sibilant, or mute, and it has been concluded, as a matter of course, that languages in which vowels and liquids predominate must be better adapted to poetry, and that the most mellifluous language must be also the most melodious. . . This is but a rash and ill-considered condemnation of our native tongue. . . In dramatic verse, more particularly, our English combinations of consonants are invaluable, not only for the purpose of reflecting grace and softness by contrast, or accelerating the verse by a momentary detention, but also in giving expression to the harsher passions, and in imparting keenness and significancy to the language of discrimination, and especially to that of scorn. In Shakspeare for instance, what a blast of sarcasm whistles through that word, "*Thrift, thrift,* Horatio!" with its one vowel and five consonants, and then how the verse runs on with a low, confidential smoothness, as if to give effect to the outbreak by the subsequent suppression,

"the funeral-baked meats
Did coldly furnish forth the marriage tables." H. R.

merely duplicate words, but distinct expressions for delicate shades of meaning. The words "*apt*" and "*fit*" might be thought to differ only in this, that the former is of Latin derivation; but "*apt*" has an active sense, and "*fit*" a passive sense—a distinction clearly shown by Shakspeare, when the poisoner in the play in Hamlet says, "hands *apt*, drugs *fit*," and by Wordsworth

"Our hearts more apt to sympathize
With heaven, our souls more fit for future glory."*

While the early additions to the language were fairly absorbed into it, and have proved so valuable, the later introductions of words of Latin or French formation have never, in like manner, become natural and national; and their presence has, therefore, been often injurious as an element not divested of its foreign tone.

In our reading of English prose, it is well worth while to study what has become almost a lost art. I mean what may be called the architecture, as it were, of a long and elaborate sentence, with its continuous and well-sustained flow of thought and feeling, and, however interwoven, orderly and clear. This is to be sought chiefly in the great prose-writers of former centuries. "Read that

* The composite character of the language thus provides us with a large class of words not strictly synonymous, but serving to express the most delicate shades of meaning: we have, for instance, the words "*feelings*" and "*sentiments*," at first sight apparently mere duplicate words; but it has been observed that there is a certain idea of passiveness connected with the *feelings*, which contrasts with the idea of activity in the word "*sentiments*," and that the former came down to us from the ruder and simpler Saxon, and the latter from the more refined and cultivated Norman. H. R.

page," said Coleridge, pointing to one of them; "you cannot alter one conjunction without spoiling the sense. It is a linked strain throughout. In your modern books, for the most part, the sentences in a page have the same connection with each other that marbles have in a bag: they touch without adhering."* Junius, waging his fierce, factious war, fought with these short, pointed sentences, piercing his foes with them; and it has been said that nothing but Horne Tooke and a long sentence were an overmatch for him; and in our day, Macaulay, waging his larger and more indiscriminate war, deals so exclusively with the same fashion of speech, that if you undertake to read his history aloud your voice will crave a good old-fashioned, long sentence, as much as your heart may crave more of the repose and moderation of a deeper philosophy of history. This fashion of short sentences is mischievous, not only as a temptation to an indolent habit of reading, (for it asks a much less sustained attention,) but it is fatal to the fine rhythm which English prose is capable of. As I cannot pause to consider especially the nature of our prose rhythm, I will give what

---

* Coleridge's Table Talk, vol. ii. p. 185.

One of the grandest long sentences in our modern English is the opening passage of Mr. Brougham's speech in defence of Queen Caroline. It extends through twenty-seven lines. If I were asked to select a sentence of perfect English formation, I should take the following from Miss Sewell's History of Greece. It dwells in my mind like music:

"There is little now to be seen in the plains of Olympia but a few ruins of brick. The mountains stand as they did in the old times, and trees flourish upon them year after year, and the rivers flow in the same track; but all the great buildings and statues have crumbled to dust, and the valley is silent and deserted." W. B. R.

is better, a sentence from the pen of a living divine, which is an example of true prose rhythm, and all pure English words:

"The land that is very far off—it can be no other than the heavenly country, for love of which God's elect have lived as strangers in the earth—a land far away, over a long path of many years, up weary mountains, and through deep broken ways, full of perils and of pit-falls; through sicknesses and weariness, sorrows and burdens, and the valley of the shadow of death; world-worn and foot-sore, they have been faring forth, one by one, since the world began, 'going and weeping.'"*

There is no appearance of art in this sentence; but the highest art could not more truly make choice and combination of its words.

I must hasten to the powers of the language in verse; and, in the first place, let me say that it is a happy trait in our literature that it has no peculiar *poetic diction.* Words that are used in good prose are not excluded from poetry, and words which the poets employ belong also to our prose uses of speech and writing; and hence the poets are the better enabled to exert a perpetual influence in the fulfilment of their high function of conservators of the purity of the language. Our prosody, taking accent rather than quantity for its principle, seldom if ever, disqualifies words on account of their sound, whereas in the Latin, as has been ascertained, one word out of every eight is excluded from its chief metres by the rules of its prosody. An analysis of a passage from Cicero, the elevated prose of the language, for this purpose, has proved

* Manning's Sermons, vol. iii. p. 432.

that, in fifty lines, thirty words are impossible words for the most usual forms of Latin verse.

The study of English poetry, being in closer affinity with the prose, admits of an important use in the formation of a good prose style. A mind as earnestly practical as Dr. Franklin's observed this, and he recommended the study of poetry and the writing of verse for this very purpose: it was one of the sources of his own excellent English. It is a species of early training for prose-writing which he recommended, having recognised it in his own case as having given a genuine copiousness and command of language. This certainly is worth reflection, too, that all the great English poets, Chaucer, Spenser, Shakspeare, Milton, Dryden, Cowper, Byron, Southey, and Wordsworth, have displayed high power as prose-writers.

It is sometimes supposed that the laws of metrical language must, of necessity, produce a style more or less artificial, and therefore alien from prose uses; but the very opposite is the fact. The true poet is always a true artist, and words are the instruments of his art. The laws of metre are no bondage to him, but genial self-control; he asks less license of language than any one, and the constraint of rhyme will often increase and not lessen the precision and clearness of expression. It is, in truth, one of the cases which prove the great moral truth, that willing obedience gains for itself unwonted power: submitting to the control of his art, bowing to its laws with happy loyalty, the poet's reward is the endowment of an ampler command of expression and of the music of the language. Verse and metre are wings, and not fetters, to the true poet.

Observe the matchless English everywhere in Shakspeare—how free it is with all the art that is to be discovered in it; how true it is, and full of beautiful and almost familiar simplicity! If, in the recollection of any passage, a word shall escape your memory, you may hunt through the thirty-eight thousand words in the language, and no word shall fit the vacant place but the one that the poet put there. Take that exquisite lament of the banished Norfolk over his native English: the words are all simple, homely words, such as anybody might use, (for Shakspeare never made his language "too bright or good for human nature's daily food.") Notice, too, if you can do so without impairing the general effect, that there are in the passage no fewer than eight alliterations:

"A heavy sentence, my most sovereign liege,
And all unlook'd for from your highness' mouth;
A dearer merit, not so deep a maim
As to be cast forth in the common air,
Have I deserved at your highness' hand.
The language I have learn'd these forty years,
My native English, now I must forego:
And now my tongue's use is to me no more
Than an unstringed viol or a harp;
Or like a cunning instrument cas'd up,
Or, being open, put into his hands,
That knows no touch to tune the harmony.
I am too old to fawn upon a nurse,
Too far in years to be a pupil now."

Or turn to those beautiful sentences in Coriolanus, where the Roman hero, returning with wounds and victory, is met by his exulting mother and his silent, weeping wife:

"My gracious silence, hail!
Would'st thou have laugh'd, had I come coffin'd home,
That weep'st to see me triumph? Ah, my dear,
Such eyes the widows in Corioli wear,
And mothers that lack sons."

Or, to take what is not so much used by Shakspeare, the rhymed poetry in Love's Labour's Lost:

"These earthly godfathers of heaven's lights,
That give a name to every fixed star,
Have no more profit of their shining nights
Than those that walk, and wot not what they are."

How true is it what Coleridge said, "that you might as well think of pushing a brick out of a wall with your forefinger, as attempt to remove a word out of any of the finished passages of Shakspeare."*

To show the wonderful power of expression that belongs to poetry, under even the most severe laws of verse, what mere prose-writer or reader would suppose it possible, within the narrow limit of fourteen lines, and with all the complex structure and redoubled rhymes of the sonnet, for a poet to speak of no fewer than seven of the illustrious poets of modern Europe, and to touch upon their characters and the story of their lives; and yet this has been achieved, apparently without effort—so natural is the flow of the language—in that well-known sonnet of Wordsworth, wherein he at once defends and illustrates that form of composition :—

"Scorn not the Sonnet; Critic, you have frowned,
Mindless of its just honours; with this key
Shakspeare unlock'd his heart; the melody
Of this small lute gave ease to Petrarch's wound;

* Table Talk, vol. ii., p. 211.

A thousand times this pipe did Tasso sound;
With it Camoens soothed an exile's grief;
The Sonnet glittered a gay myrtle-leaf
Amid the cypress with which Dante crowned
His visionary brow; a glow-worm lamp,
It cheer'd mild Spenser, called from Faëry-land
To struggle through dark ways, and when a damp
Fell round the path of Milton, in his hand
The thing became a trumpet; whence he blew
Soul-animating strains—alas, too few!"

It is the poets who have best revealed the hidden harmony that lies in our short Saxon-English words—the monosyllabic music of our language. This was one of the secrets of the charm and the popularity of Lord Byron's poetry—his eminently English choice of words. Two short passages of Mr. Landor's Poems will serve to show the metrical effect of simple words of one syllable. In the sentence I am about to quote, out of thirty such words, there is but one long latinized word—the rest are nearly all monosyllables, the last line wholly so:

"She was sent forth
To bring that light which never wintry blast
Blows out, nor rain, nor snow extinguishes—
The light that shines from loving eyes upon
Eyes that love back, till they can see no more."*

The next will better exemplify the harmonious combination of the simple English and the classical or Southern words.

"Crush thy own heart, Man! but fear to wound
The gentler, that relies on thee alone,
By thee created, weak or strong by thee;

* Landor's Works, vol. ii. p. 480. Hellenics viii.

Touch it not but for worship; watch before
Its sanctuary; nor leave it till are closed
The temple-doors, and the last lamp is spent."

The combination of the various elements of the language will be found most abundantly illustrated in the poems of Milton, but from such a theme, too large for me to venture on now, let me pass to a few other illustrations more readily to be disposed of.

The poetry of our own times has done high service to the language by expanding its metrical discipline, opening a larger freedom and variety, and yet keeping aloof from mere license. Observe, for instance, in these lines, the effect produced at the close by a change in the structure of the stanza and the single long line with which, at the end, the imagination travels forth;

"O! that our lives, which flee so fast,
In purity were such,
That not an image of the past
Should fear that pencil's touch!

Retirement then might hourly look,
Upon a soothing scene;
Age steal to his allotted nook,
Contented and serene;

With heart as calm as lakes that sleep
In frosty moonlight glistening;
Or mountain rivers, where they creep
Along a channel smooth and deep
To their own far-off murmurs listening."*

One of the most exquisite studies of the beautiful freedom of English verse is to be found in that poem, the music of which so fascinated the spirit of Sir Walter Scott and of Lord Byron, as to prompt them both to some of

* Wordsworth.

their own finest effusions; I refer to Coleridge's Christabel, in which a variety of line and rhyme, and even blank verse is wrought into a marvellous unity—nowhere more than in that passage picturing Christabel in the forest, when she hears the moaning of the witch.

"Is the night chilly and dark!
The night is chilly, but not dark.
The thin gray cloud is spread on high,
It covers but not hides the sky.
The moon is behind, and at the full,
And yet she looks both small and dull.
The night is chilly, the cloud is gray,
'Tis a month before the month of May,
And the Spring comes slowly up this way.
The lovely lady Christabel,
Whom her father loves so well,
What makes her in the woods so late,
A furlong from the castle-gate?
She had dreams all yesternight
Of her own betrothed knight:
And she in the midnight wood will pray
For the weal of her lover that's far away.

She stole along, she nothing spoke,
  The sighs she heav'd were soft and low;
And naught was green upon the oak
  But moss and rarest mistletoe;
She kneels beneath the huge oak-tree,
And in silence prayeth she.

The lady sprang up suddenly,
  The lovely lady, Christabel!
It moan'd as near as near can be,
  But what it is, she cannot tell;
On the other side, it seems to be
Of the huge, broad-breasted old oak-tree.

The night is chill, the forest bare:
  Is it the wind that moaneth bleak.

There is not wind enough in the air
  To move away the ringlet curl
From the lovely lady's cheek;
  There is not wind enough to twirl
The one red leaf, the last of its clan,
That dances as often as dance it can,
Hanging so light, and hanging so high
On the topmost twig that looks up to the sky.
Hush, beating heart of Christabel!"

There is one more principle in the study of language in poetic literature which I wish to notice, and that is the beauty of the adaptation in all true poetry of the metrical form to the subject and feeling of the poem. "Every true poet," it has been well said, "has *a song in his mind*, the notes of which, little as they precede his thoughts—so little as to seem simultaneous with them—do precede, suggest and inspire many of these, modify and beautify them."* How this connection exists between the poet's thought and passion, and their apt tune in language, is more, perhaps, than philosophy can discover; but there is an interest in observing the fact; and this also is to be thought of, that the true poet awakens this spiritual song in the mind of his reader.

Even the same form of verse is very different in the hands of different poets, and has great and characteristic variety of excellence—the blank verse of Milton, of Cowper, and of Wordsworth, having each a beautiful melody of its own. It adds to our knowledge of our language and its powers, and also greatly to the cultivated enjoyment of poetical reading, if we take the pains to observe and appreciate the harmonious relation of the measure and

* Darley's Introduction to Beaumont and Fletcher, as quoted in "Chaucer Modernized," p. 48.

the subject. I will give an illustration of this relation, by quoting two pieces by the same poet, and then will detain you but a few minutes longer. The contrast between the pieces is a refined one, because in each there is an adaptation to deep pathos, but exquisitely varied to different forms of pathos, the emotion at the aspect of death in its gentleness, and of death in its terrible tragedy.

"We watched her breathing through the night,
  Her breathing soft and low,
As in her breast the wave of life
  Kept heaving to and fro.

So silently we seemed to speak,
  So slowly moved about,
As we had lent her half our powers
  To eke her living out.

Our very hopes belied our fears,
  Our fears our hopes belied;
We thought her dying when she slept,
  And sleeping when she died.

For when the morn came dim and sad
  And chill with early showers,
Her quiet eyelids closed—she had
  Another morn than ours."*

What perfect tranquillity and sense of resignation there is in these purely simple English words and their gentle flow. Turn from them to that other poem of the same author, "*The Bridge of Sighs*,"—a poet's feeling rebuke of the vice and inhumanity of a great metropolis, and of sympathy with its poor, degraded victims, driven to suicide in the midnight waters of the city's river. The tranquil, soul-subduing music of the former piece is

* Collected Edition of Hood's Poems, vol. ii., p. 98, and vol. i., p. 264.

changed to a short and abrupt measure, in which the passions of pity, bitter anger, and grief are stirring for utterance.*

It is thus in a nation's poetry (that is, of course, when it is really poetry of a high and worthy kind) that the language will be found in its highest perfection, in its truest cultivation; for a poet can never suffer his style to fall short of a well-sustained purity. It is, therefore, in the poetry that a language may best be studied, even for prose uses; that is, when any one would know to what state of excellence the language may be carried, he must look to that chiefly, but, of course, not exclusively, in the poetical literature.

We are living at a period when the language has attained a high degree of excellence, both in prose and verse,—when it has developed largely, for all the uses of language, its power and its beauty. It is one of the noblest languages that the earth has ever sounded with; it is our endowment, our inheritance, our trust. It associates us with the wise and good of olden times, and it couples us with the kindred peoples of many distant regions. It is our duty, therefore, to cultivate, to cherish, and to keep it from corruption. Especially is this a duty for US, who are spreading that language over such vast territory; and not only that, but having such growing facilities of intercommunication, that the language is perpetually speeding from one portion of the land to another

* I have not thought it worth while to reprint at length a poem so familiar as the "Bridge of Sighs;" but those who heard this lecture will not easily forget the beautiful and tearful manner—his own gentle nature agitated by uncontrollable sympathy—in which HE recited its beautiful stanzas. W. B. R.

with wondrous rapidity, equally favourable to the diffusion of either purity or corruption of speech, but, certainly, calculated to break down narrow and false provincialisms of speech.

In the culture and preservation of a language, there are two principles, deep-seated in the philosophy of language, which should be borne in mind. One is, that every *living* language has a power of growth, of expansion, of development; in other words, its *life*—that which makes it a *living* language, having within itself a power to supply the growing wants and improvements of a living people that uses it. If by any system of rules restraint is put on this genuine and healthful freedom, on this genial movement, the native vigour of the language is weakened.

It may be asked whether, by this principle of the *life* of a language, it is meant that the language has no law. Very far from it. The other principle (and with which the first is in perfect harmony) is, that every language, living or dead, has its laws. Indeed it has been wisely said that, "whatever be the object of our study, be it language, or history, or whatsoever province of the material or spiritual world, we ought, in the first instance, to be strongly impressed with the conviction that every thing in it is subject to the operation of certain principles, to the dominion of certain laws; that there is nothing lawless in it, nothing unprincipled, nothing insulated or capricious, though, from the fragmentary nature of our knowledge, many things may possibly appear so."

Now this willing, dutiful belief in the existence of the laws of a language, however concealed they may be under apparent anomalies, will not unfrequently evolve some beautiful principle of speech, some admirable adaptation of words to the thoughts and feelings, in what otherwise is, too often, carelessly and ignorantly dismissed as an irregularity. Permit me to illustrate briefly my meaning, by an example. In expression of the *future* time, there is employed that curious mixture of the two verbs "*shall*" and "*will*," which is so perplexing to foreigners, and inexplicable, though familiar, to many who are to the language born. Upon this subject it has been observed, there is in human nature generally an inclination to avoid speaking presumptuously of the future, in consequence of its awful, irrepressible, and almost instinctive uncertainty, and of our own powerlessness over it, which, in all cultivated languages, has silently and imperceptibly modified the modes of expression with regard to it. Further, there is an instinct of good breeding which leads a man to veil the manifestation of his own will, so as to express himself with becoming modesty. Hence, in the use of those words, "*shall*" and "*will*," (the former associated with compulsion, the latter with free volition,) we apply, not lawlessly or at random, but so as to speak submissively in the first person, and courteously when we speak to or of another. This has been a development, but not without a principle in it; for, in our older writers, for instance, in our version of the Bible, "*shall*" is applied to all three persons. We had not then reached that stage of politeness which shrinks from even the appearance of speaking compulsorily of another. On the other hand, the Scotch, it is said, use "*will*" in the first person; that is, as a nation, they have not acquired that particular shade of good-breeding which shrinks from thrusting itself forward.

I have cited this theory of the English future tenses, to show how that which is often dismissed as a caprice—a freak in language—may have a law, a philosophy, a truth of its own, if we will but thoughtfully and dutifully look for it.

In conclusion, let me say that he will gain the best knowledge of our language who shall seek it, not so much in mere systems of grammar, as in communion with the great masters of the language, in prose and verse. He will best appreciate and admire this English language of ours—our mother-speech—who learns that the genius of it is as far removed from mere lawlessness, on the one hand, as from any narrow set of rules which would cramp it to what has been called "grammar-monger's language." In the variety of our idioms, the free movement of the language, there is, as in the race that speaks it, Saxon freedom—freedom that is not license, but law.

LECTURE IV.

Early English Literature.*

Early English prose and poetry—Sir John Mandeville—Sir Thomas More's Life of Edward the Fifth—Chaucer's Tales—Attempted paraphrases—Chaucer Modernized—Conflict of Norman and Saxon elements—Gower—Reign of Edward the Third—Continental wars—Petrarch—Boccacio—Froissart—The church—Wyclif—Arts and Architecture—Statutes in English—Chaucer resumed—His humour and pathos—Sense of natural beauty—The Temple of Fame—Chaucer and Mr. Babbage—The flower and the leaf—Canterbury Tales—Chaucer's high moral tone—Wordsworth's stanza—Poet's corner and Chaucer's tomb—The death of a Language—English minstrelsy—Percy's Reliques—Sir Walter Scott—Wilson—Christian hymns and chaunts—Conversion of King Edwin—Martial ballads—Lockhart—Spanish ballads—Ticknor's great work—Edom of Gordon—Dramatic power of the ballad—The Two Brothers—Contrast of early and late English poetry.

I PROCEED now to some general considerations of the chief eras into which my subject may be, without difficulty, divided. The whole period of our literature may be determined with more precision than might at first be expected, considering the gradual development of the language out of its Anglo-Saxon original. It is a literature covering the last five hundred years; for, while

---

* Thursday, Jan. 24, 1850. Prefixed to this lecture, in manuscript, are some desultory hints as to authorities to be consulted by students of English literature. As they were but hints, though very interesting as illustrative of Mr. Reed's views on this subject, and formed no part of the regular course, I may print them in an appendix. W. B. R.

Sir John Mandeville, whose book of travels has gained for him the reputation of the first English prose-writer, flourished in the first part of the fourteenth century, the first great English poet died in the year 1400. The early English prose possesses, however, little, if any, purely literary interest; its value is antiquarian, and chiefly as showing the formation of the language. It is worthy of remark, that the prose powers of a language, and, consequently, that division of literature, are more slowly and laboriously disclosed than the poetic resources. Though the history of English prose begins about 1350, with what is considered the first English book—Sir John Mandeville's Travels—a century and a half more was required to achieve any thing like the excellence of later English prose. It is not until about 1509, that Mr. Hallam finds in Sir Thomas More's Life of Edward V. what he pronounces "the first example of good English language; pure and perspicuous, well chosen, without vulgarisms or pedantry."* There is, therefore, a period, and that of considerable length, during which, for all that makes up the essential and high value of literature, the prose of the period has very little claim upon us. It is not so, however, with the poetry of early English literature; for, as Mr. De Quincy has remarked, "At this hour, five hundred years since their creation, the tales of Chaucer, never equalled on this earth for tenderness and for life of picturesqueness, are read familiarly by many in the charming language of their natal day."† And Coleridge said: "I take increasing delight in

* Hallam's Literature of Europe, vol. i. p. 232.

† Essay on Pope, p. 154.

Chaucer. His manly cheerfulness is especially delicious to me in my old age. How exquisitely tender he is, and yet how perfectly free from the least touch of sickly melancholy or morbid drooping! The sympathy of the poet with the subjects of his poetry, is particularly remarkable in Shakspeare and Chaucer; but what the first effects by a strong act of imagination and mental metamorphosis, the last does without any effort, merely by the inborn kindly joyousness of his nature."*

The present poet-laureate of England has said, "So great is my admiration of Chaucer's genius, and so profound my reverence for him as an instrument in the hands of Providence for spreading the light of literature through his native land, that I am glad of the effort for making many acquainted with his poetry who would otherwise be ignorant of every thing about him but his name"† Another eminent living man of letters has expressed his admiration of the old poet, by saying that he rather objected to any attempts to remove the difficulties of the antique text, inasmuch as he wished "to keep Chaucer for himself and a few friends."

Unfortunately, the obsolete dialect in which Chaucer wrote is such an obstacle, that it is far easier to keep him for oneself than to recover for him now the hearing of his fellow-men, which he once commanded, and which can never cease to be the due of his genius. I know of nothing in literary history like the fate of Chaucer in this

---

* Table Talk, vol. ii. p. 297.

† This is an extract from a letter from Wordsworth to Mr. Reed, dated January 13, 1841, sending a copy of a little volume published in London, called "The Poems of Geoffrey Chaucer Modernized." The work is by different hands. W. B. R.

respect. His poems are not in a dead language; they cannot be said to be in a living language. They are not in a foreign tongue, and yet they are hardly in our own. There is much that is the English still in use, and there is much that is very different. A reader not accustomed to English so antiquated, opens a volume of Chaucer, and he meets words that are familiar and words that are uncouth to him. In this, there is something repulsive to the eye and the ear, especially in finding words strangely syllabled and accented. He is not prepared to apply himself to it as he might to a poem in a foreign or dead language, to be toilsomely translated; and yet he cannot approach it as the literature of his own living speech. The use of glossaries and explanatory vocabularies cannot be dispensed with; but, to most readers, this is a wearisome process, for there is something thwarting and vexatious in finding ourselves at fault in dealing with our own mother-tongue. It seems like encountering the curse of Babel in our own homes, on our own hearths; and that is a misery. In forming acquaintance with ancient or foreign literature, the student knows that a well-defined exertion is needed, and this he makes in working his way through ancient or foreign words and idioms; and thus he comes to know the literature of Greece and Rome, of France, or Italy, or Germany. But the antiquated dialect of his own language is a mingled mass of sunshine and shadow, with sharp and sudden changes from one to the other, so that the mind is distracted in the uncertainty how long the clearness will last, and how soon the obscurity will come again, going along, like Christabel, "now in glimmer and now in gloom." This proves a greater obstacle than the total separation of language which enforces the task of translation, and it has been remarked with truth that, "if Chaucer's poems had been written in Greek or Hebrew, they would have been a thousand times better known. They would have been translated."*

A process akin to translation has been attempted, the most noted of the paraphrases of Chaucer's poems being those by Dryden and Pope. Those versions are, however, of little avail for what should have been their chief purpose; for, while they serve to give the reader a notion of Dryden and Pope, the genius of Chaucer, with all its natural simplicity and power, is lost by being transmuted into the elaborate polish of the verse of the times of Charles the Second and of Queen Anne.

The only successful attempt to make the approach to the poetry of Chaucer more easy, by modifying his diction and metre, has been made within the last few years, in a small work entitled "*Chaucer Modernized.*" It may be recommended as a safe introduction to a knowledge of Chaucer's poetry, for the versions are from the pens of several distinguished living poets, combining in this service of filial reverence to the memory of the Father of English Poetry; and the versions are composed strictly on this principle, that the paraphrase is limited to such changes as are absolutely necessary to render the meaning and metre of the original intelligible; and thus the reader in the nineteenth century is placed in the same relative position as the reader of the fourteenth, communing with the imagination of the Poet, through verse which is readily and naturally familiar.

* Introduction to "Chaucer Modernized," p. 5.

Now, considering these difficulties of language, it is remarkable that the few readers of Chaucer's poetry should have had authority, from generation to generation, to sustain his traditionary fame; for if he is not known and felt to be the earliest of the great English poets, he is at least always named as such.

"That noble Chaucer, in those former times,
Who first enriched our English with his rhymes,
And was the first of ours that ever broke
Into the Muse's treasures, and first spoke
In mighty numbers; delving in the mine
Of perfect knowledge, which he could refine
And coin for current, and as much as then
The English language could express for men,
He made it do."*

Usually, in the history of a nation's literature, it may be observed that the language and the literature move forward together—the rude dialect being adequate to express the motives of the rude mind; so that what is handed down in an unformed language is commonly nothing more than the imperfect products of the early intellect or fancy. But the peculiarity of Chaucer's position in literary history is just this, that in the era of an unshaped language, we have an author of the very highest rank of poetic genius.

That Chaucer took the language of his own time, and in its best estate, (for language always makes gift of its best wealth to a great poet,) need not be doubted; but it is difficult to conceive the condition of the language during his time, in the fifty years' reign of Edward the Third. For the scholastic uses of the learned, and for

* Drayton's Elegy, "To my dearly-loved friend, Henry Reynolds, Esq., "Of Poets and Poesy." Anderson's Poets, vol. iii. p. 348.

ecclesiastical purposes, the Latin was still a living language. The French was the speech of the court, and in private correspondence had superseded the Latin. But with the great body of the people there was the great body of Anglo-Saxon words and forms of speech, with a living power in them which no foreign or ancient dialects could quench; and to that, the English language, imperfect, unformed, and changing as it was, this great poet gave his heart; showing, like his most illustrious successors, that the great poet is ever a true patriot also. "Let, then," said Chaucer, "clerkes enditen in Latin, for they have the propertie of science, and the knowing of that facultie; and lette Frenchmen in their French also enditen their queint termes, for it is kindly to their mouthes; and let us show our fantasies in such wordes as we learnden of our Dame's tongue." And when he wrote for the teaching of his little son, he used English, because, said he, "curious endityng and harde sentences are full hevy at once for such a childe to lerne," and bids the boy think of it as the King's English.*

It needed the large soul of a great poet to make choice of the People's speech rather than the dialects of the learned or the nobles. Chaucer's contemporary and senior brother-poet, honoured by him as the "moral Gower," ventured upon no such confidence in the language of the land. The legacy of his song was committed to Latin and to French words; and yet what might he not have achieved, had he oftener trusted the rude mother-tongue, as in that passage in which he pictures Medea

---

* Prologue to Testament of Love. Ed. 1542, cited in Pickering's Edition of Chaucer, vol. i. p. 202.

going forth at midnight to gather herbs for the incantations of her witchcraft? I give you without a change, the words and the metre, five hundred years old, of the poet Gower:

> "Thus it befell upon a night,
> Whann there was naught but sterre light,
> She was vanished right as hir list,
> That no wight but hirselfe wist:
> And that was at midnight-tide;
> The world was still on every side.
> With open head, and foote all bare
> His heare to spread; she gan to fare:
> Upon the clothes gyrte she was,
> And speecheles, upon the gras
> She glode forth, as an adder doth."

If Chaucer was unfortunate in the period of his country's language, he was happy in the era of his country's history. The Saxon and the Norman, the conqueror and conquered, had grown together into one people. It was Chaucer's fortune to be an eye-witness of that vast ambition which fired his sovereign in grasping at the diadem of France, to make the two great monarchies of Europe one; and how could the fire in a great poet's heart sleep, when he beheld his king and his prince, those proud Plantaganets, the third Edward and his heroic son, going forth like royal knights-errant in quest of majestic adventures. The reign was one of high monarchal pride, displayed, however, so as to animate a high national pride by lifting up the sense of the nation's dignity, and power, and magnificence. Kings were suppliant to England's princes for help—kings were captive in England's capital; and that ambitious noble, "old John of Gaunt," Chaucer's patron and kinsman, not content with his English dukedom, was proclaimed King of Castile. It was a period of high-wrought martial enthusiasm, and the early modes of warfare passed not away without fierce employment, as if the arrow could not cease to be a weapon of death without drinking its last deep draught of blood, when the air was darkened over the plains of Crecy and Poictiers, by the shafts from the hosts of English archers. With all the animating movements of the reign, Chaucer was in close and active sympathy; he was a courtier and a soldier, as well as a student. No poet has ever held such large and free communion with the world and his fellow-men. He stood in the presence of kings and nobles; and became versed in the lore of chivalry, its principles and its fashions: he went forth from the pomp of the court to do a soldier's service, and in the season of peace to muse in the fields, to look with loving eyes upon the flowers, to sympathize with the simple hearts of children and of peasants, to honour womanhood alike in humble or in high estate, and to commune with the faithful and the zealous of the priesthood. He travelled into foreign lands, an envoy or an exile, (so varied was his career,) happy, if the conjecture be not unfounded, in listening to words falling from the living lips of Italy's great poet, then the aged Petrarch, possibly meeting Boccacio and Froissart. When, near three hundred years later, the youthful Milton visited the shores of Italy, amid all the classical associations that were thronging into his heart, he found room for the proud memory that the father of English poetry had stood on the same soil.*

* In the Epistle to Manso, the friend of Tasso, a production which Mr. Hillard, in his charming book on Italy, calls "the most Virgilian of all compositions not written by Virgil," Milton says:

Ergo ego te, Clius et magni nomine Phœbi,
Manse pater, jubeo longum salvere per ævum,

The times in which Chaucer lived were momentous also as a period in which were first seen the forecast shadows of mighty changes in the Christian church; and we can well believe that his heart must have leaped up when he beheld the bold British hand of John Wyclif, a hundred years and more before the days of Luther, strike the first blow at ecclesiastical tyranny—the same hand which was an instrument of Providence in taking the seal from off the Bible, and spreading it in living English words throughout the land.

The last half of the fourteenth century, which was the period of Chaucer's manhood, (for he died, let it be remembered, an aged man, in the year 1400,) was an era in which the English mind was touched by many of its finest and most quickening influences. The impulse it received was manifest in various departments of human thought. The arts were cultivated, civic architecture especially, and chiefly that sacred form of it which has been the wonder of after ages. Painting was cultivated, and the more glorious sister art of poetry was taught by two poets more eminent than England had yet produced, John Gower and Geoffry Chaucer. It was fitting that in such an age the Parliament of England should decree that the statutes of the

---

Missus Hyperboreo juvenis peregrinus ab axe.
Nec tu longinquam bonus aspernabere musam,
Quæ nuper gelida vix enutrita sub Arcto,
Imprudens Italas ausa est volitare per urbes.
Nos etiam in nostro modulantes flumine cygnos
Credimus obscuras noctis sensisse per umbras,
Qua Thamesis late puris argenteus urnis
Oceani glaucos perfundit gurgite crines
Quin et in has quondam pervenit Tityrus oras."
Mitford's Milton, vol. 3, p. 317. W. B. R.

realm were no longer to be enrolled in a foreign dialect, but that the voice of British legislation should speak in the nation's own language.

The student of literature, who will take the pains to master the difficulties of Chaucer's antiquated poems—and they will quickly diminish before him—will find an abundant reward. His poems are as varied as they are voluminous, rich in original materials and in that which, drawn from foreign sources—the Latin, French, and Italian literature—bears in the transmutation the glory of a great poet's invention. What most distinguishes the genius of Chaucer is the comprehensiveness and variety of his powers. You look at him in his gay mood, and it is so genial that that seems to be his very nature, an overflowing comic power, or, rather, that power touched with thoughtfulness and tenderness—"humour" in its finest estate. And then you turn to another phase of his genius, and with something of wonder, and more of delight, you find it shining with a light as true and natural and beautiful into the deeper places of the human soul—its woes, its anguish, and its strength of suffering and of heroism. In this, the harmonious union of true tragic and comic powers, Chaucer and Shakspeare stand alone in our literature: it places these two above all the other great poets of our language, for such combination is the highest endowment of poetic genius.

The genius of Chaucer is manifest also in that other characteristic of the poetic spirit, wise and genial communion with the spiritual influences of the material world, "Earth, air, ocean, and the starry sky." All nature is with him alive with a fresh and active life-blood. His green leaves, it has been well said, are the greenest that were ever seen. His grass is the gladdest green; the cool and fragrant breezes he sings of seem to fan the reader's cheek; his birds pour forth notes the most thrilling, the most soothing, that ever touched mortal ear—

> "There was many and many a lovely note,
> Some singing loud, as if they had complained;
> Some with their notes another manner feigned;
> And some did sing all out with the full throat."

The earth and sky—his earth and sky—are steeped in brightest sunshine, and "all things else about him drawn from May-time and the cheerful dawn."*

---

* Introduction to Chaucer Modernized, p. xcvi., and Wordsworth's Version of the Cuckoo and the Nightingale, p. 41. I am tempted in this connection to make an extract from a most graceful tribute to my brother's memory in a private letter from Lady Richardson, the wife of Sir John Richardson of Arctic celebrity, and a lady of high intelligence and accomplishments. It is descriptive of the first impression of a bright May morning, with its gentle companionship of singing birds and flowers, among the English lakes and amid Wordsworth's haunts: "It must have been," writes Lady Richardson, "about the middle of May that we heard of Mr. Reed's arrival at Rydal Mount; on the next day he called. The day was so beautiful, that, fearing he might not see the valley of the Easedale again on so fine a day, I took him to Wordsworth's Wall and round the Terrace Walk for a first view. We had little time for more than to walk quickly round, I pointing out where "the Prelude" was composed, and where so many summer hours were passed. He did not say much; but the expression of his face showed me the deep delight he felt, both in the present beauty and in the associations the place recalled. As we returned, the "Wandering Voice" was peculiarly blythe and near to us on that May morning, and I remember he told me he had heard the cuckoo for the first time at Rydal Mount. He remarked on the beauty of the holly, which he did not seem to know before. He spoke of Southey's lines on the holly-tree, the loss of its thorns, and its smooth leaves as it grows high, compared to what old age should be. We paused to talk and sit and quote some of our favourite

A favourite form of imaginative composition of those times was the romantic allegory, and Chaucer, taking up the fashion, has perpetuated it, especially in two poems, which the life-giving power of genius yet preserves. One of these, the "House of Fame," is known to modern readers chiefly through Pope's paraphrase, bearing the statelier title—a characteristic alteration—of the "Temple of Fame." This poem is not one on which I need stop for criticism, and I am about to mention it for quite a different purpose. It contains a passage which has struck me as in curious anticipation of a scientific hypothesis suggested in our own days; poetic imagination foreshadowing the results of scientific reasoning. In the ninth Bridgewater Treatise, from the pen of Mr. Babbage, he propounded a theory respecting the permanent impressions of our words—spoken words—a theory startling enough almost to close a man's lips in perpetual silence: "That the pulsations of the air, once set in motion by the human voice, cease not to exist with the sounds to which they give rise; that the waves of the air thus raised perambulate the earth and

lines; and all that he said impressed me with the feeling of his being of that genial, elevated, and kindly stamp which Wordsworth most delighted in. On coming to a walk at the foot of some rocks which my husband had engineered during his last visit, Mr. Reed said, 'How pleasant it is, that one whose heroic character and sufferings interested me so much, as a boy, in America, can now be associated with this lovely scene!' We parted with a promise that they would come and see me in the South. This they were unfortunately prevented doing, and we never met again."—*MS. Letter*. I hope I violate no propriety in using a letter which never was intended for the public eye; but the temptation to give this glimpse of the last bright hours, the simple, natural tastes and pure imaginings, associated, like his great poetic models, with all that was beautiful in nature, of one whom it is now no flattery to praise, has been irresistible. W. B. R.

ocean's surface; and soon every atom of its atmosphere takes up the altered movement, due to the infinitesimal portion of the primitive motion which has been conveyed to it through countless channels, and which must continue to influence its paths throughout its future existence. Every atom," adds the philosopher, "impressed with good and with ill, retains at once the motions which philosophers and sages have imparted to it, mixed and combined, in ten thousand ways, with all that is worthless and base. . . . The atmosphere we breathe is the ever-living witness of the sentiments we have uttered, ... and (in another state of being) the offender may hear still vibrating in his ear the very words, uttered perhaps thousands of centuries before, which at once caused and registered his own condemnation."

Now I have no thought of intimating, in the most remote degree, that in this remarkable train of thought Mr. Babbage was under obligations to Chaucer. The passage has an air of absolute originality; and, besides, the writer of it is too strong-minded and manly to allow such obligations, if they existed, to pass unacknowledged. I have no sympathy with the spirit which delights in detecting plagiarisms in the casual and innocent coincidences which every student knows are frequently occurring. That there is such a coincidence worthy of notice, will be seen in these lines in The House of Fame:

"Sound is nought but air that's broken,
And every speeche that is spoken,
Whe'er loud or low, foul or fair,
In his substance is but air:
For as flame is but lighted smoke,
Right so is sound but air that's broke,
Eke where that men harpstrings smite

Whether that be much or lite,
Lo! with the stroke, the air it breaketh;
Thus wot'st thou well what thing is speech:
Now, henceforth, I will thee teach
How ever each speeche, voice or sown,
Through his multiplicion,
Though it were piped of a mouse,
Must needs come to Fame's House.
I prove it thus; taketh heed now
By experience, for if that thou
Throw in a water now a stone,
Well wot'st thou it will make anon
A little roundel as a circle,
Par venture as broad as a covércle,
And right anon thou shalt see well
That circle cause another wheel,
And that the third, and so forth, brother,
Every circle causing other,
Much broader than himselfen was:
Right so of air, my leve brother,
Ever each air another stirreth,
More and more and speech up beareth,
Till it be at the 'House of Fame.' "*

---

* That this was mere coincidence, Mr. Reed ascertained, in conversation with Mr. Babbage, on his visit to England, in 1854. "I mentioned to him," Mr. Reed writes to a friend in America, "that I had once in a public lecture quoted from his Bridgewater Treatise the startling passage about the perpetuity of sound, and that some of my audience used to say that it almost made them afraid for some days to speak, from the dread that the sounds were to last, and mayhap come back to them in the hereafter: on telling him I had cited the passage in a literary connection, as a curious parallelism with Chaucer, he expressed much surprise, and begged me to refer to the passage. It was all new to him."—*MS. Letter.*

A curious chapter on these perfectly innocent coincidences might be written—for literary history is full of them. In Lockhart's Scott, (vol. x. p. 208,) it is said, "Dr. Watson, having consulted on all things with Mr. Clarkson and his father, resigned the patient to them, and

One of the brightest dreams that poet ever fashioned out of shadowy imaginings, is the allegory, "*The Flower and the Leaf*," with its beautiful moral, and an exuberance of fancy seldom met with out of the region of early poetry. A gentlewoman, seated in an arbour, beholds a great company of ladies and knights in a dance on the grass, which being ended, they all kneel down and do honour to the daisy—some to the flower, and some to the leaf; and the meaning thereof is this: "They which honour the flower, a thing fading with every blast, are such as look after beauty and worldly pleasure; but they that honour the leaf, which abideth with the root, notwithstanding the frosts and winter storms, are they which follow virtue and during qualities, without regard of worldly respects."

The fame of Chaucer rests, however, chiefly on the

---

returned to London. None of them could have any hope but that of soothing irritation. Recovery was no longer to be thought of, but there might be *Euthanasia*." A hundred years before Arbuthnot wrote to Pope, "a recovery in my case and at my age is impossible: the kindest wish of my friends is *Euthanasia*." Haydon, in his strange journal, writing in 1826, says, "There is hardly any thing new. I never literally stole but one figure in my life (Aaron) from Raphael. Yet to-day I found my Olympias, which I had dashed in in a heat, exactly a repetition of an Antigone, and the first thing I saw in the Louvre was Poussin's Judgment of Solomon, with Solomon in nearly the same position as in my picture. Yet I solemnly declare I never saw even the print when I conceived my Solomon, which was done one night, before I began to paint, at nineteen, when I lodged in Carey Street, and was ill in my eyes. I lay back in my chair, and indulged myself in composing my Solomon. I will venture to say, no painter but Wilkie will believe this, though it is as true as that two and two make four." *Haydon's Memoirs*, vol. i. p. 488; see also *Wilmott's Pleasures of Literature*, p. 259. W. B. R.

great work of his matured powers, showing how genius carries forward the freshness of feeling for three-score years. I refer, of course, to the "*Canterbury Tales*," an unfinished poem, like the Faery Queen, and, like it, wonderful as a fragment, for the vast extent of what is achieved, as well as of what was planned. The design of this poem is one of the happiest thoughts that ever housed itself in a poet's heart. A chance-gathered company of pilgrims on their way to the shrine of St. Thomas à Becket at Canterbury, meet in a London inn, and the host proposes that they beguile the ride by each telling a tale to his fellow-pilgrims. Thus comes, with its large variety, the collection of the Canterbury Tales. The prologue, containing the description of the pilgrims, is better known, perhaps, than the rest of the work, partly, perhaps, from Stothard's well-known picture of the pilgrimage. From this prefatory poem of a few hundred lines, a truer and livelier conception of the state of society in England, five hundred years ago, can be got than from all other sources of information. It makes us more at home there in the distant years; carries us more into the spirit of the age; lets us see the men and the women of those times, be among them and know their ways of life, manners, and dress, far better than any unimaginative record can do. There are a hundred things—prime elements, too, in a nation's heart—that history never troubles itself with. The torch of a poet's imagination is held on high, and forthwith a light is thrown on the whole region round, and we see a multitude of objects which else would be lost in the distance or the darkness.

Among other matters, the poems of Chaucer are full

of testimony, unstudied testimony, on a momentous subject—the condition of the Church in those ages, when its abuses, looseness, and luxury roused the indignation of the first of the great Reformers. What an image of monastic voluptuousness is there in one of Chaucer's pictures, a full-length portrait in one line, when he describes the monk,

"Fat as a whale, and walked like a swan!"

Nor was the poet's bold satire of the corruptions which had crept into the Church the sarcasm of a licentious, irreverent temper, for he has bequeathed to all after-times a portrait of the pure clerical character, which, as an imaginative picture of holy life, of Christian piety, zeal, meekness, and self-sacrifice, still stands unequalled in English literature:

"A poor parson of a town:
* * * *
Wide was his parish—houses far asunder—
But he neglected nought for rain or thunder,
In sickness and in grief to visit all,
The farthest in his parish, great and small,
Always on foot, and in his hand a stave.
This noble example to his flock he gave:
That first he wrought, and afterward he taught;
Out of the gospel he that lesson caught,
And this new figure added he thereto,
That if gold rust, then what should iron do?"*

The prologue is curious, too, as representing the freedom and ease of intercourse between the characters, drawn, as they are, from different ranks of society—an absence of reserve and restraint remarkable in an age with which we are apt, falsely perhaps, to associate much of stateliness

* Prologue to Canterbury Tales, v. 479.

and ceremonial. We find here a little social drama, as it were, bearing strongly the stamp of nature and reality, and the parties are unreservedly communing with each other—riding, talking, laughing, eating together. Here is the knight, "a very perfect, gentle knight," newly returned from his adventures, and modest with the memories of many a battle on sea and land, fought with the Moors and the foes of the faithful far away. With him comes his son, full of gayety and gallantry, "wakeful as a nightingale with his amorous ditties;" and the rest of the company is made up of a demure prioress, a monk, a friar and other ecclesiastical functionaries; a merchant, a franklin, a sea-captain, the doctor of physic, "whose study was but little on the Bible;" the lawyer, "a very busy man, yet seeming busier than he really was;" the parson, drawing mankind to heaven by gentleness; the miller, crafty in cheating his customers; the ploughman, a good, constant, labouring man, living in peace and charity, working hard, and cheerfully paying his dues to the church, along with other hearty commoners, spruced up for the pilgrimage in holiday-dress. There is the frolicsome wife of Bath; and a very different character, not to be forgotten, the Oxford student, silent or sententious, thoughtful and thin by dint of hard study, riding on a lean horse:

"He had rather have at his bed's head
Some twenty volumes, clothed in black or red,
Of Aristotle and his philosophy,
Than richest robes, fiddle or psaltery.
But tho' a true philosopher was he,
Yet had he little gold beneath his key;
But every farthing that his friends e'er lent,
In books and learning was it always spent."

These various characters are brought into happy companionship; and indeed the spirit of all Chaucer's poetry shows that if his own lot was cast in the company of kings and nobles, his human heart had large spaces to hold his fellow-beings in. His sympathies were with freedom in all created things, as in a passage, which is enough, I think, of itself, to open the prison-door and give to liberty and life again any caged bird in the world.

> "Where birds are fed in cages,
> Though you should day and night tend them like pages,
> And strew the bird's room fair and soft as silk,
> And give him sugar, honey, bread, and milk:
> Yet had the bird, by twenty thousand fold,
> Rather be in a forest wild and cold:
> And right anon, let but his door be up,
> And with his feet he spurneth down his cup,
> And to the wood will hie, and feed on worms.
> In that new college keepeth he his terms,
> And learneth love of his own proper kind:
> No gentleness of home his heart may bind."

The poetry of Chaucer is distinguished also for what is an inseparable quality of all high poetry, its genuine and healthy morality, for true imagination is ever one of virtue's ministers. The indelicacy and grossness which stain some of his pages seem to belong rather to the colloquial coarseness of his times, than to fasten on the purity of his feelings. He pleads forgiveness for these blemishes, as not of evil intent, and it is easy to follow his advice when he bids his reader,

> "Turn over the leaf, and choose another tale;
> For he shall find enough, both great and smale,
> Of storial thing that toucheth gentilesse,
> And eke morality and holiness."

One of the purest and wisest of the great English poets

who have succeeded Chaucer, has said of him, "If Chaucer is sometimes a coarse moralist, he is still a great one."* The plain-spoken coarseness is a spot here and there, but the great body of his poetry is a poet's pure and lofty discipline, thoughtful and affectionate reverence of womanly worth, teaching of Christian well-doing, of heroic morality, and of the morality of every-day life. He moralizes in the poet's happiest mood, imaginatively, feelingly, humorously, as when he teaches us that much-neglected art, the art of living with one another, the social duty of mutual forbearance.

" One thing, sirs, full safely dare I say,
That loving friends each other must obey,
If they would long remain in company:
Love will not be constrain'd by mastery.
When mastery cometh, the God of Love, anon
Beateth his wings, and, farewell! he is gone.
Love is a thing as any spirit free:
Women, by nature, wish for liberty,
And not to be constrain'd as in a thrall;
And so do men—to speak truth—one and all.
Note well the wight most patient in his love:
He standeth, in advantage, all above.
That patience is a virtue high, is plain,
Because it conquers, as the clerkes explain,
Things that rude vigour never could attain.
Chide not for every trifle, nor complain;
Learn to endure, or, so betide my lot,
Learn it ye shall, whether ye will or not.
For in this world is no one, certain 'tis,
But that he sometimes doth or saith amiss.
Anger, ill health, or influence malign
Of planets, changes in the blood, woe, wine,

* Wordsworth, as quoted in the Introduction to Chaucer Modernized, p. xcviii.

Oft cause in word or deed that we transgress;
For, for every wrong we should not seek redress.
After a time there must be temperance
In every man that knows self-governance."

There is a deeper strain of poetic wisdom on a kindred subject, showing that indeed "we live by admiration, hope, and love," in that fine exposition of the moral influences of well-directed affection, when, speaking of dutiful love, he says:

"In this world no service is so good
For every wight that gentle is of kind,
For thereof comes all goodness and all worth;
All gentleness and honour thence come forth;
Thence worship comes, content, and true heart's pleasure,
And full-assured trust, joy without measure,
And jollity, fresh cheerfulness, and mirth:
And bounty, lowliness, and courtesy,
And seemliness and faithful company,
And dread of shame that will not do amiss."

The same spirit, connecting all true passion with its deeper moral associations, is to be traced in that stanza of Wordsworth's, conveying in a few lines at once the simplest and sublimest conception of the passion of Love:

"Learn by a mortal yearning, to ascend
Towards a higher object. Love was given,
Encouraged, sanctioned chiefly for that end;
For this the passion to excess was driven,
That self might be annulled: her bondage prove
The fetters of a dream, opposed to love."*

Such is the affinity between the souls of great poets, though centuries are between them.

It is now well-nigh four hundred and fifty years since

* Laodamia, Works, p. 142. Am. Edition.

the body of Chaucer was entombed in that corner of Westminster Abbey where, in after generations, the perishable remains of other of England's great poets were to be gathered round his. Four centuries pass not over the writings of any mortal without defacing and obliterating. Language is liable to undergo perpetual changes; any person may observe, in even a short space of years, new forms of expression coming into use, old ones growing obsolete. Time brings along with it new modes of life, of thought, and action. Opinions and feelings often grow old-fashioned—fall behind the times, as the phrase is; and, as these are things that enter so largely into the composition of books, it needs must be that they, too, grow old-fashioned, obsolete, obscure. Chiefly will this happen when it has fallen to an author's lot to write in an unformed language, when the speech of men is made up of various and unsettled dialects, and, therefore, most quickly perishes for want of that consistency which alone perpetuates it. Time is busy in the work of change with all that is upon the earth: the brow is furrowed, the voice is broken, and the sight fails; temple and tower moulder with its touch; empires and dynasties are varying and wasting; but the strangest work of mutability is that which is at work with language. The most wondrous mortality the world witnesses is the dying of language. It almost baffles human conception to speculate either upon the birth or the death of the multitude, or rather the family of words that make up a nation's speech; to think how thousands of mankind come to utter their thoughts and feelings in the same words and the same combinations of words; and then, that, in the course of time, as if the earth and all earthly things should be as changeful as the moon which lights it, such utterance is changed, and at length wholly lost from the living tongue. Its sound becomes an uncertain and disputed thing, for it is only seen on the pages of books, or it may be only in dim and dubious inscriptions on the broken column, the ruined arch, or the empty monument. I know of nothing which so teaches the transitoriness of things as that phrase of mournful significance, "*a dead language.*" How does it startle us in our pride, the bare apprehension of our English speech changing into a lifeless and mouldy record—something dark for scholars and antiquaries vainly to attempt to enlighten—something of a degenerate dialect, in which might be faintly traced the shadows of a mighty language. The curse of the confusion of tongues is an unending curse, like the sentence of labour, on rebellious man. From the time when the ambition of men brought down this penalty, and the whole earth ceased to be "of one language and one speech," nations have been scattered abroad upon the face of all the earth, no longer understanding one another's speech—one generation, too, becoming unintelligible to another. So must it ever be as long as a cloud of divine displeasure travels onward with the earth, casting down upon it a dark shadow; and hence no language, no matter how lofty its literature may be, can boast a privilege from decay:

> "Babylon,
> Learned and wise, hath perished utterly,
> Nor leaves her *speech* one word to aid the sigh
> That would lament her."

The Pyramids, mysterious in their unnumbered centuries, are standing almost as imperishable as the Nile, and yet not one word survives that was spoken by the tens of thousands who toiled in building them:

> "Egyptian Thebes,
> Tyre by the margin of the sounding waves,
> Palmyra, central in the desert, fell;"

and all their dialects are silent as the desert sands. That noble language, too, of antiquity, with which Athens sent forth her philosophy and poetry to the islands of the Ægean and the shores of Asia, and "fulmined over Greece with her resistless eloquence"—the language that Corinth, from her famous isthmus, spake over the eastern and western waves, has, for many ages, known no other existence than that which it holds on the pages of books. The speech of the Roman—the language of empire and of law, spread by consul and emperor till it was stayed by the ocean and the barbarian—how has it ceased to hold companionship with the voice, and learned men of modern times can only conjecture respecting its accent!

If I have been thus led into a digression on the changes which are the destiny of all languages, let me say, in excuse, that I could scarce check the train of thought, being forced to feel most painfully the perishable nature of speech by the reflection that it is that cause which has dimmed the glory of the earliest and one of the greatest of England's poets.

The student of early English literature must not omit that miscellaneous poetry, obscure in its origin, and indefinite in its period—the ancient Minstrelsy. It is poetry of native growth, and having the savour of the soil. Existing for a long time in a traditional state, it has suffered the waste which mere oral tradition is never safe from; and it is only within the last fifty years that pains have been taken to gather the rude strains of those half-civilized ages, and to place them on record at this long distance of time after they existed as a living poetry. This has been done chiefly in Percy's Reliques of Ancient English Poetry, and in Sir Walter Scott's Minstrelsy of the Scottish Border. It was a fine trait in Scott's literary career, the affectionate earnestness with which he laboured for the recovery of the ancient lays of his native land, and the preservation of them in some safer form than what they had in the memory of aged persons, in times when every year, perhaps, was casting them more and more into neglect. When Scott travelled over the country, highland and lowland, seeking in its secluded glens for such remains of the poetry of the olden times as might not yet be lost out of the recollections of an illiterate peasantry—snatches of song remembered by the aged, as having been chaunted by the old folks of an earlier generation—he was not only gathering materials to illustrate the literature of his country, but he was storing his own mind with those large resources which his genius afterward poured forth with a copiousness which was the world's wonder. When the authorship of Waverley was a secret vexing public curiosity, Professor Wilson exclaimed, "I wonder what all these people are perplexing themselves with: have they forgotten the *prose* of the Minstrelsy?"*

Of the minstrel poetry now extant, much belongs to a period later than the age of Chaucer; but there is also reason to believe that it had a traditional connection with a still earlier and ruder minstrelsy that has perished. A more distant influence is to be traced back to the hymns

* Lockhart's Scott, vol. ii. p. 132.

and spiritual songs of the Church which accompanied Christianity, as it made its spiritual inroads on the fierce idolatries of the races of the North. For, although the sacred services chaunted by the early Christians and those grand hymns of the Middle Ages were in the Latin language, still they accustomed the popular ear to metrical sounds, and opened the hearts of the people to the uses of poetry. While the ancient classical poetry was sleeping its long sleep, to waken in later ages, the sacred songs of the early Christians were never silenced, even in years of persecution; and it is to them, that the poetry of Christendom owes its first impulse.

At a remote age of Britain's history, religious houses were built there, and as the holy men who dwelt in them, amid aboriginal ferocities and the turmoil of successive invasions—the Saxon and the Dane—uttered their songs of adoration, those harmonies went forth over river and plain, soothing the fierce elements they touched, and charming the evil spirit of war which vexed the hearts of barbaric kings. The music of a good man's chaunted devotions could not float on the air, turbid and tumultuous though it be with wicked passions, without awakening some pure and gentle emotions. A single stanza of ancient Saxon song survives as a memorial of such influence. When that remarkable personage, the Danish King Canute, had overthrown the Saxon dynasty in England, and was making a progress through his newly-conquered realm, as with his queen and knights he approached by water the Abbey of Ely, there arose upon the air the voices of the monks, chaunting their stated services; and when the music fell upon the conqueror's ear with such a sweet solemnity, chiming both with the river's flow and his own placid emotions, the sword of his bloody conquest sheathed, the active sympathy of his imagination found utterance in a simple strain of Saxon song, of which but one stanza has been spared by time:

> "Sweetly sang the monks in Ely
> As Canute the king was rowing by:
> 'Knights, to the land draw near,
> That the monks' song we may hear.'"*

"This accordant rhyme" was the response of one of the mightiest of those Scandinavian monarchs, the "Sea-kings," who struck terror into central Europe; he, before whom the ancient Saxon dynasty quailed, and whose barbarian flatterers told him that his word had power to stay the surges of the Atlantic; but, in a happy moment of tranquillity, the saintly music passed through the turbulent passions of pride and power into the depths of his human heart.

The same influences doubtless touched the nation's heart, and like that rude royal strain, the popular song echoed the music of hallowed verse.

An earlier instance of the power of the imagination to impart truth, may be remembered in that beautiful image of the mystery of human life which led to the conversion of King Edwin. A Christian entered the hall of the unconverted Saxon, but the tidings he brought were strange to the pagan heart, and the king summons his chiefs and priests; at that moment a bird flitted through the council-hall, to call from the wise imagination of one

* Lectures on the History of England: by a Lady; p. 439. Wordsworth's Sonnet. Works, p. 295.

of the heathen councillors a lesson, recorded by an old historian, and preserved in modern verse:

"Man's life is like a sparrow, mighty king,
That while at banquet with your chiefs you sit,
Housed near a blazing fire, is seen to flit,
Safe from the wintry tempest. Fluttering,
Here did it enter; there, on hasty wing,
Flies out, and passes on from cold to cold;
But whence it came we know not, nor behold
Whither it goes. Even such, that transient thing,
The human soul, not utterly unknown,
While in the body lodged, the warm abode;
But from what world she came, what woe or weal
On her departure waits, no tongue hath shown.
This mystery, if the stranger can reveal,
His be a welcome cordially bestowed."*

Important as must have been the influence of the metrical services of the church, considered simply as a means of civilization, the rude ages needed poetry for other uses than devotion. They craved the minstrel's power to touch the stories of daring adventure, of wild justice and revenge, and the tragic incidents of the field and fireside. The earliest of the martial ballads commemorate the exploits of a body of bold outlaws, in whose lives there was the last struggle against Norman tyranny. The strong hand of the conqueror had seized large tracts of land for royal hunting-grounds, the ancient owners outcast; and well may the oppressed people have applauded the exploits of the hardy archers who claimed their own again within the forbidden limits, and thus Robin Hood became indeed "the English ballad-singers' joy," asserting,

* Wordsworth's Works, p. 290. The legend is in Fuller's Church History of Britain, vol. i. p. 109.

as he did, what, under a complicated tyranny of authority, seemed

> "The good old rule, the simple plan,
> That they should take who have the power,
> And they should keep who can."

The old songs have kept his name, but no historian, like Niebuhr with the Roman legends, has unwoven the tangled threads of fact and fiction.

It would be a study of much interest to compare the early British ballad poetry with the other ballad poetry most famous in European literature. I mean that of Spain. Mr. Lockhart's fine version of the Spanish ballads, and our countryman Mr. Ticknor's recent classic work on Spanish Literature would give facilities for the comparison.* The higher civilization in Spain, both Moorish and Christian, and the struggle for centuries between the two races, as the Saracen was driven slowly from his last foothold in the West of Europe, wars which had the dignity of the highest sentiments of religion and loyalty, the greater refinement of society—all these things would be found in strong contrast with the rudeness of a poetry, picturing the feuds of petty chieftains, and the mingled ferocity and frolic of the border warfare.

* To my friend, (for such he has been for many years,) Mr. Ticknor, is in some measure due the publication of these Lectures, for on his saying to me, in accidental conversation since my brother's death that his literary, and especially his poetical, judgments, were concurrent with his own, I felt the assurance that I might, with no further authority, give them to the reading world. I felt, too, that in publishing these lectures, I might do something to raise Philadelphia letters a little nearer to the high level to which such men as Prescott, and Ticknor, and Longfellow, and Hillard, have elevated the literature of a sister city. W. B. R.

Our early minstrelsy, with all its comparative rudeness, was not without its gentle elements; and we can conceive how it helped to civilize the people, when we observe how much of pathos is woven into it, how it tells of the tenderness and pity that are congenial with courage and with the love of fierce adventure, springing often out of the sternest heart: the pathos is social, too, so free from sentimentalism, and told so simply. When Edom of Gordon, in his fierce assault on the castle, adding the terrors of fire to those of the sword, not staying his spear's point from the little girl who is lowered over the wall: as his victim lies before him, the blood dripping over her yellow hair, remorse is in the words he said:

"You are the first that ere
I wish't alive again.
* * * *
I might have spared that bonny face,
To have been some man's delight."

He calls his men away from his fierce victory

"Ill dooms I do guess;
I cannot look on that bonny face,
As it lies on the grass."

This transition of feeling is sometimes given in these rude strains with deep effect: observe it, for instance, in the contrast between the opening and the close, in these few detached stanzas:

"Beardslee rose up on a May morning,
Called for water to wash his hands;
'Gar loose to me the good gray dogs,
That are bound wi' iron bands.'"*

---

* Edom of Gordon, Percy's Reliques, vol. i. p. 240. Johnie of Beardslee, Motherwell's Ancient and Modern Minstrelsy, vol. i. p. 169.

The outlaw's mother, with a presentiment of his fate, entreats him to give over what was to prove a woful hunting, but in vain; and in spite of her forebodings and the terrors of the forest-laws, he goes forth. The rude and animated strain continues:

"Beardslee shot, and the dun deer leap'd,
And he wounded her in the side;
But a'tween the water and the brae,
His hounds, they laid her pride.

And Beardslee has bryttled the deer so well,
That he's had out her liver and lungs;
And with these he has feasted his bloody hounds,
As if they had been Earl's sons."

The hunter and his dogs fall asleep, and are surprised by the foresters, who overpower him, and, after a desperate conflict, leave him dying in the lonely wood. The outlaw's breath passes away in a very gentle strain:

"O! is there no a bonny bird
Can sing as I can say,
Would flee away to my mother's bower
And tell to fetch Beardslee away.

There 's no a bird in a' this forest
Will do as mickle for me,
As dip its wing in the wan water,
And streak it on my e'e bree."

Another characteristic of this poetry is the remarkable *dramatic* power that pervades it, the vividness of the dialogue. This is shown in that, the finest specimen of all, which Coleridge called "the grand old ballad of Sir Patrick Spens."* It is a poem with a certain air of historical

* Coleridge's Poems, Dejection, an Ode, p. 282.

interest, heightened by the mysterious uncertainty of its incidents, and remarkable both for the power of description and its depth of passion. It has come down from a remote antiquity, and has manifestly escaped the tampering of modern hands. Let me mention, respecting it, that after I had quoted it in a lecture of a former course, I was told by one of my very kind friends that I had carried him back to the days of his childhood in the old country, when he had heard this very ballad chaunted by the old Scotch people, who must have been familiar with it only by tradition, and not by books. I mention this incident, because it brought home to my mind most distinctly the manner in which the minstrel literature has been perpetuated.*

When the earliest poetry of Greece, the mighty song of Homer, was a tradition from age to age, on the shores and the islands of the Ægean, with no surer abiding-place than the memories and the tongues of the Rhapsodists, the wisest of Athenian lawgivers, and one of the most politic of Athenian statesmen, made it a part of their wisdom and their policy to gather the scattered poetry into safer keeping for the good of all after generations. No British Solon, no British Pisistratus, took like heed for Britain's early popular poetry. Doubtless, much of it has perished, and the names of the minstrels, like the names

* "The very kind friend," to whom my brother refers, was the Reverend Doctor Wylie, for many years Vice Provost and Professor of Ancient Languages in the University of Pennsylvania, a man of great learning and eminent purity of character and feeling. He died in 1852. He was a native of the North of Ireland, and for many years pastor of the First Reformed Presbyterian Church in this city. He was a man beloved by all who knew him. W. B. R.

of the great church architects of the Middle Ages, have perished utterly. They did their appointed work in their day and generation; and again, when in the last century, (as I proprose to show at a later part of the course,) English poetry became artificial, feeble, unreal, and sophisticated, the early song was revived, to breathe into it again health, and strength, and truth.

LECTURE V.

Literature of the Sixteenth Century.*

Dawn of letters a false illustration—Intellectual gloom from Edward III. to Henry VIII.—Chaucer to Spenser—Caxton and the art of printing—Civil wars—Wyatt and Surrey—The sonnet naturalized in English poetry—Blank verse—Henry VIII.—Edward VI.—Landor's sonnet—Sternhold and Hopkins—Bishop Latimer—Goodwin Sands and Tenterden Steeple—"Bloody Mary"—Sackville—"The Mirror of Magistrates"—His career—Age of Elizabeth—Contrasts of her life—The Church as an independent English power—Shakspeare—His journey to London—Final formation of the English language—"The well of English undefiled"—The Reformation—Sir Philip Sydney—The Bishop's Bible—Richard Hooker—Spenser and Shakspeare—Wilson's Criticism—Sir Walter Raleigh—Shakspeare's Prose.

In approaching the early English literature in my last lecture, I stated that, in forming a general notion of the extent of it, we may regard the era of our literature as a period of five centuries, from about 1350 to the present time—the middle of the fourteenth century down to the middle of the nineteenth. The student would, however, be misled, were he to believe as he might naturally do, that, during those five centuries, there was a continuous and uninterrupted progress, that the light of literature was faithfully handed from sire to son, and that new fires were kindled, in due succession, to light the new ages as the world moved on. Looking to that little island of our forefathers, we shall see, in its history, how

* January 31, 1850.

it travelled on with other lights flashing over it than the quiet illumination that shines from the studious watch-towers of poets and scholars. Such tranquil beams were, in many a year, dimmed by the fierce and lurid fires which war in its worst form, civil strife, and ecclesiastical persecutions were casting over the land.

The familiar and well-known metaphor which has long designated Chaucer as the "Morning Star" of English poetry, while it is most apt in telling of that primal and fair shining in the eastern sky of our literature, is not so truthful in its relations to the later as to the earlier times. The light of day came on too slowly; and, indeed, a long night followed that early outbreak of the imagination of England's first great poet. Nearly two centuries passed before another arose worthy to take place beside him. Mr. Hallam's historical study of the progress of the European mind during the Middle Ages, has led him to remark, that "The trite metaphors of light and darkness, of dawn and twilight, are used carelessly by those who touch on the literature of the Middle Ages, and suggest, by analogy, an uninterrupted succession, in which learning, like the sun, has dissipated the shadows of barbarism. But, with closer attention, it is easily seen that this is not a correct representation; that taking Europe generally, far from being in a more advanced stage of learning at the beginning of the fifteenth century than two hundred years before, she had, in many respects, gone backward, and gave little sign of any tendency to recover her ground. There is, in fact, no security, as far as the past history of mankind assures us, that any nation will be uniformly progressive in science, arts, and letters; nor do I perceive, whatever may be the current language, that we can expect this with much greater confidence of the whole civilized world." *

One of the most remarkable relapses of the kind in intellectual advancement is the long interval between the death of Chaucer, in the year 1400, and the birth of the next of England's great poets, Edmund Spenser, in 1553, and the appearance of the earliest of the great English prose-writers in the latter part of the sixteenth century. This period of more than a century and a half is, comparatively, a desolate tract of time; and, parting with Chaucer in the era of the Middle Ages, we gain companionship with no other master-spirit until, crossing the threshold of modern times, the year 1500, we find ourselves in the domain of the later civilization which succeeds the thousand years that separate the Roman world from modern times. In this transition we pass, let it also be remembered, from the ages in which the thoughts of men and the oracles of God were recorded only by the slow labour of the pen—the stupendous toil which modern art may marvel at rather than despise—into the times which become, in some respects, a new intellectual era by the agency of printing. It was near a century after the death of Chaucer that the first of English printers died—the honoured William Caxton—whose life is to be thought of, like that of the Venerable Bede, as monitory of "perpetual industry;" for, as the aged Saxon expired dictating the last words of a translation of St. John's Gospel—

> "In the hour of death,
> The last dear service of his parting breath,"

---

* Literature of Europe, chap. ii. § 49, vol. i. p. 173.

so did the old printer carry forward his last labour, on a volume of sacred lore, to the last day of a life that bore its burden of four-score years.

Having alluded to the familiar figure which is so often used to typify the position of the earliest of the great English authors, I may correct the error which might unawares be connected with it by another metaphor, which the memory can easily keep hold on. With a beauty of illustration, which does not often adorn the pages of Warton's History of English Poetry, he happily compares the appearance of Chaucer in the language to a premature day in spring, after which the gloom of winter returns, and the buds and blossoms, which have been called forth by a transient sunshine, are nipped by frosts and scattered by storms.*

Difficult as it may be to discover in the history of the human mind why, at particular periods, it bursts forth with such power, and at other times lies so torpid, we may trace with some confidence causes which at least help to account for this long and dismal blank between the reign of Edward the Third and that of Queen Elizabeth—the whole of the fifteenth century, and a large part of the six-

* "I consider Chaucer as a genial day in an English spring. A brilliant sun enlivens the face of nature with an unusual lustre; the sudden appearance of cloudless skies, and the unexpected warmth of a tepid atmosphere, after the gloom and inclemencies of a tedious winter, fill our hearts with the visionary prospects of a speedy summer; and we fondly anticipate a long continuance of gentle gales and vernal serenity. But winter returns with redoubled horrors; the clouds condense more formidably than before; and those tender buds, and early blossoms, which were called forth by the transient gleam of a temporary sunshine, are nipped by frost and torn by tempests." Warton, vol. ii. p. 51. W. B. R.

teenth: seven reigns of disputed legitimacy, thirty years of civil slaughter, first brutalizing and then crushing the nation's heart, the bloody variance of a feudal nobility, a long series of battles, so fierce in their vengeance that the very flowers, the innocent flowers, were torn from the once peaceful gardens to be made the emblems of unrelenting warfare; and then, when these evils had passed away, there came the darker strife of a nation's distracted church-persecution and the fiery terrors of the stake.

Chaucer had outlived the superb reign of Edward the Third, with its half century of lofty dominion. He had seen the miserable ending of Edward's giddy grandson, the second Richard, thrust from his throne by "mounting Bolingbroke." The cycle of the fortune of these Lancastrian Plantagenets, reaching its highest splendour in the foreign victories of the fifth Henry, had its sad completion in the disasters of the next reign, and the tragic death of the last of the house of Lancaster. The heart of the nation was suffering the grievous wasting of all that might have been dear to it, by the evil passions engendered in that most deplorable of all political and social conditions, civil warfare; a strife always the fiercest and most unrelenting, for, the ties once broken, which had bound men together by the unconscious bonds of instinctive feelings, bewildered humanity looks on the once dearest friend as the direst foe. "The bells in the church steeples," writes an old church historian, "were not heard for the sound of drums and trumpets."* The learned were not listened to, or rather were hushed into silence, and the humanizing music of poetry was unknown. How could the intellect

* Fuller, vol. i. p. 54.

adventure any thing when the heart was appalled! How could the imagination aspire when overwhelmed by the dark and fearful pressure of the present!

Thus passed one hundred years of the century and a half which lies between that genial age in which Chaucer flourished, and the other more genial era, that of the Elizabethan literature.

In looking at the early part of the sixteenth century—nearly the first half of it occupied by the reign of Henry VIII.—it is pleasing to find some literary interest in a period which is associated chiefly with ecclesiastical change and the second Tudor's domestic tyranny. An abiding impression on the nation's literature was made at that time by two writers, whose names from early and long association are scarce separable—men of noble birth and character—Sir Thomas Wyatt, the lover of Anne Boleyn, and Henry Howard, the ill-fated Earl of Surrey. Surrey, especially, is esteemed as one of the improvers of English verse. Acquainted with the refinements of Italian verse, acquired either by personal intercourse or by study, he introduced important changes into that of England. The language was made at once more graceful and simple; and Italian forms of verse introduced. The Sonnet was naturalized into English poetry, to disclose in later times that wondrous variety of power and of beauty which has been proved, within its narrow limits, by Milton and by Wordsworth. The English versification was more exactly disciplined; and to Surrey is due the merit of having given the first example of *blank verse;* that form which has so eminently adapted itself to the language and to the English poet's desires, that it has been well said to deserve the name of "*the* English metre;" a construction which from time to time has been revealing the musical resources of its unexhausted variety, in the dramatic language of Shakspeare, the epic of the Paradise Lost, in the homelier strains of the Task, in the heroic romance of Roderic, and in the philosophy of the Excursion. Such is our English blank-verse, alike it may be to the eye, but wonderfully varied to the ear, and to that inner spiritual sense which seems, even more than the organ of hearing, to take cognizance of the music of poetry; and admitting, too, of some characteristic impress from the genius of every great poet that has used it.

There gathered round this noble poet all that could dignify and endear him to his own times and to after times—a lofty lineage, rank, genius, virtue, loyalty, faithful and honourable services; but for his bright career as scholar, courtier, soldier, there was a dark destiny of blood. In our earliest knowledge of English history, one of the first and most vivid impressions is that which we have of the household atrocities of the eighth Henry—to a child's fancy, the British Bluebeard—driving to divorce or death his wives, the mothers of his children, and devoting more than one fair neck, once fondly embraced, to the bloody handling of the headsman. What reign, in the range of history, more execrable! and the last act of it cast a shadow on the annals of English literature. Henry Howard had been in childhood an inmate of the palace, a playmate of royal children; and when he grew to manhood he was a loyal and honoured courtier, a brave and trusted soldier. But it was Surrey's crime, his only crime, to bear the name of Howard, a name which had newly grown hateful to the despot's ear. He was committed, on a charge of treason, to the Tower; and in the very week in which Henry VIII. died, the gallant Surrey, at the age of twenty-seven, laid down his head upon the scaffold.

Let me add a vivid description of the close of Henry's reign, and its connection with Howard's tragic end, to fix the memory of this early author by the help of the dread association.

"It is fearful," says the author from whom I quote, "but not unsalutary, to cast a parting glance at the vicious body of Henry VIII. after its work upon the earth was done. It lay, immovable and helpless, a mere corrupt and bloated mass of tyranny. No friend was near to comfort it; not even a courtier dared to warn it of its coming hour. The men alone it had gorged with the offal of its plunder, hurry back in affright from its perishing agonies, in disgust from its ulcerous sores. It could not move a limb nor lift a hand. The palace-doors were made wider for its passage through them; and it could only then pass by means of machinery. Yet to the last it kept its ghastly state, descended daily from bed-chamber into room of kingly audience through a hole in the palace ceiling, and was nightly, by the same means, lifted back again to its sleepless bed. And to the last, unhappily for the world, it had its terrible indulgences. Before stretched in that helpless state of horror, its latest victim had been a Plantagenet. Nearest to itself in blood of all its living kindred, the Countess of Salisbury was, in her eightieth year, dragged to the scaffold for no pretended crime, save that of corresponding with her son; and having refused to lay her head upon the block, (it was for traitors to do so, she said, 'and she was none,') but moving swiftly round, and tossing it from side to side to avoid the execution, she was struck down by the weapons of the neighbouring men-at-arms, and while her gray hairs streamed with blood, and her neck was forcibly held down, the axe discharged, at length, its dreadful office. The last victim of all followed in the graceful and gallant person of the young Lord Surrey. The dying tyranny, speechless and incapable of motion, had its hand lifted up to affix the formal seal to the death-warrant of the poet, the soldier, the statesman, and scholar, and on 'the day of the execution,' according to Hollinshed, was itself 'lying in the agonies of death.' Its miserable comfort, then, was the thought that youth was dying too; that the grave which yawned for abused health, indulged lusts, and monstrous crimes had, in the same instant, opened at the feet of manly health, of generous grace, of exquisite genius, and model virtue. And so perished Henry VIII."*

We pass on from the long and odious reign of the sire to the short rule of his innocent and tender-hearted son,

> "King, child, and seraph, blended in the mien
> Of pious Edward."†

As the mind passes from this detested father to his son—gentle Jane Seymour's gentle son—one cannot but think how it exemplifies the truth which Landor's lines have told:

> "Children are what the mothers are.
> No fondest father's wisest care
> Can fashion so the infant heart,
> As those creative beams that dart,
> With all their hopes and fears, upon
> The cradle of a sleeping son.

---

* Forster's Treatise on Popular Progress.

† Wordsworth's Coll. Ed. p. 301.

His startled eyes with wonder see
A father near him on his knee,
Who wishes all the while to trace
The mother in his future face;
But 'tis to her alone uprise
His wakening arms, to her those eyes
Open with joy, and not surprise."*

Another copartnership in letters, closer than that of Surrey and Wyatt, and suggesting another kind of associations, may be noticed in that part of the sixteenth century which belongs to the reign of Edward VI. I refer to the first version of the Psalms of David in English metre, produced by two writers—whose names have become the symbols of dulness and clumsy versification—Thomas Sternhold and John Hopkins. Undoubtedly the grandeur of the Hebrew Psalmody is very inadequately represented in the flat and prosaic diction and the awkward metres of these two good men; but it should be remembered that a worthy translation of the Psalms into English metre has never yet been achieved; and, indeed, the best judges make question of the possibility of such version. If this old version, three hundred

* Mr. Landor's poems are so scattered, and in their modes of publication so fugitive, that they must often be quoted at second-hand. I find these verses marked with my brother's pencil in a little French volume called, "La Petite Chouannerie, ou Histoire d'un Collége Breton sous l'Empire, par A. F. Rio," p. 296. I am tempted to put on these pages the following lines, by Landor, on Charles Lamb, which appeared during the present year in the Examiner newspaper:

"Candid old man! what youth was in thy years!
What wisdom in thy levity! what truth
In every utterance of that purest soul!
Few are the spirits of the glorified
I'd spring to earlier at the gates of heaven!" W. B. R.

years ago, is rude and uncouth, honourable testimony has been borne to its fidelity to the Hebrew original. The version of later times, now most in use, is at once tame and tawdry, (worse faults than rudeness,) taking, too, larger license with the original, and "generally," it is said, "sacrificing altogether the direct, lightning-like force of the inspired sentences."*

Much of Sternhold and Hopkins's version would certainly now so affect the dainty modern ear, as to give a sense of ridicule most incongruous to the theme; but the reproach that rests on the old version may be lightened a little, when we meet with a stanza like this:

"The Lord descended from above, and bowed the heavens most high,
And underneath his feet he cast the darkness of the sky;
On cherub and on cherubim full royally he rode,
And on the wings of mighty winds came flying all abroad."†

However rude this version was, it has a claim to respect as the first that fitted to English lips the music of the royal inspired singer; and as the homely verses were, years after, familiarized in the people's devotions, the imagery of the Hebrew poetry was sinking into the hearts of the men of England, and helping to form that sacred character which is the glory of all the highest inspirations of English poetry.

The progress of English prose, as it was slowly advancing to its best estate, appears, at the period I have been speaking of, in the sermons of him whose intrepid spirit and cheerful constancy sustained him in the hour of

* Keble.

† Psalm xviii. 9, 10. It is to be observed that more modern paraphrasers of the Psalms have generally shrunk from rendering these verses into their slender English. W. B. R.

martyrdom—Hugh Latimer, Bishop of Worcester. It was in a sermon preached before Edward VI. that he introduced, in accordance with the quaint pulpit-oratory of the times, the well-known illustration of the Goodwin Sands and Tenterden Steeple, in reply to a very common fallacy; and the passage may be quoted to show the character of the prose, which was then equal, at least, to simple purposes of natural narrative:

"Here was preaching," he says, "against covetousness all the last year in Lent, and the next summer followed rebellion; *ergo* preaching 'against' covetousness was the cause of rebellion. A goodly argument!

"Here, now, I remember an argument of Master More's, which he bringeth in a book that he made against Bilney; and here, by the way, I will tell you a merry toy. Master More was once sent in commission into Kent, to help to try out, if it might be, what was the cause of Goodwin Sands and the shelf that stopped up Sandwich Haven. Thither cometh Master More, and calleth the country afore him—such as were thought to be men of experience, and men that could, of likelihood, best certify him of the matter concerning the stopping of Sandwich Haven. Among others, came in before him an old man with a white head, and one that was thought to be little less than an hundred years old. When Master More saw this aged man, he thought it expedient to hear him say his mind in the matter; for, being so old a man, it was likely he knew most of any man in that presence and company. So Master More called this old aged man unto him and said, 'Father,' said he, 'tell me, if ye can, what is the cause of this great arising of the sands and shelves here about this haven, the which stop it up that no ships can arrive here? Ye are the eldest man that I can espy in all this company, so that if any man can tell any cause of it, ye, of likelihood, can say most in it, or, at leastwise, more than any other man here assembled.' 'Yea, forsooth, good master,' quoth this old man, 'for I am well-nigh an hundred years old, and no man here in this company any thing near unto mine age.' 'Well, then,' quoth Master More, 'how say you in this matter? What think ye to be the cause of these shelves and flats that stop up Sandwich Haven?' 'Forsooth,' quoth he, 'I am an old man; I think that Tenterden Steeple is the cause of Goodwin Sands. For I am an old man, sir,' quoth he, 'and I may remember the building of Tenterden Steeple, and I may remember when there was no steeple at all there. And before that Tenterden Steeple was in building, there was no manner of speaking of any flats or sands that stopped the haven; and, therefore, I think that Tenterden Steeple is the cause of the destroying and the decay of Sandwich Haven.' And even so, to my purpose, is preaching of God's word the cause of rebellion, as Tenterden Steeple was cause Sandwich Haven is decayed."

There is one sentence of English words uttered by this same divine, which has a deeper and more enduring interest, and that was when he and Ridley stood in their dread fellowship of martyrdom at the stake; when the fagot, kindled with fire, was brought and laid at Ridley's feet, Latimer, happy, as the martyr's crown was poised above his brow, on which four-score years had placed their crown of glory, spake in this manner: "Be of good cheer, Master Ridley, and play the man; we shall this day light such a candle, by God's grace, in England, as, I trust, shall never be put out."*

The gentle Edward's reign had too quickly given place to his sister's—that hateful reign—when the palace of England's monarchs grew dark with the power of the detested Spaniard, and the long list of martyrs fastened forever the title of "*blood*" to the sweetest of female names. Just at the close of Queen Mary's reign, English literature produced one work, showing a force of imagination which would have placed its author in the highest rank of our poets, had he not turned his genius away from poetic study to devote it, during a very long life, to the political service of his country. "The Mirror of Magistrates" is the title of a work planned by Thomas Sackville—Lord Buckhurst—and intended to comprise a series of poetic narratives of the disasters of men eminent in English story. The first of these, on the Duke of Buckingham, with the preface, or "Induction," as it is styled, was all that was accomplished; but those four hundred lines displayed an inventive energy which was a foreshadowing of the allegorical imagination which soon after rose in "The Faery Queen." Sackville's Induction stands as the chief, the only great poem between the times of Chaucer and of Spenser. Allegorical poetry presents no more vivid imagination than his personification of war, or of old age, in that single line

"His withered fist still striking at death's door."

What a gloomy conception was the plan of the poem! It has been likened to a landscape which the sun never shines on. More than that might be said, when we think

* Life of Latimer, prefixed to his Sermons, vol. i. p. clvii.

how congenial it was to the time of its composition. There hung on Sackville's genius not only a dark gloom, but it may be thought to have caught a ghastly complexion from the lurid lights of the flames of religious persecution. We may picture this thoughtful poet, turning his footsteps beyond the confines of London, on a winter's day, the dreary season described at the opening of the poem

> "Wandering till nightfall,
> The darke had dimm'd the day ere I was 'ware."

And what was the spectacle he might have encountered? The dispersing throng that had just gathered round the stake, where flames had wrapped a martyr's body, the fire not yet burnt out in the smouldering ashes; perhaps the desolate family, the outcast wife and children, lingering near the spot where a spiritual hero had sealed his faith. It was a fit season for poetry's darkest imaginings, and well might Sackville frame his gloomy personification of sorrow to guide him in fancy into the realms of death, to hear there, from the lips of the dead, the stories of their woes. Under this dreary guidance, his genius entered into the shadowy domains of imagination; but soon after he brought the powers of his mind forth into the world's political service, in which he continued during the whole of Elizabeth's reign, and part of that of her successor, when the hand of death was laid upon the veteran statesman suddenly, at the council-board of James I. It is a remarkable fact that, in actual life, he personally witnessed two reverses of fortune—political downfalls transcending any his tragic muse could have called up in his mournful poem. Sackville was one of the judicial tribunal which pronounced the doom of Mary Stuart: it was from his lips that the unhappy Queen received the message of her doom; and it was part of his stern duty to behold the last look of that royal fair one, the "long array of woes and degradations" at length closing, and to witness the blow which severed from a now wasted body the head that once had glittered with the diadems of France and of Scotland. It was also Lord Buckhurst's lot (and these were perhaps the only two calamities of his long and honourable career) to sit in judgment on the Earl of Essex, when that nobleman fell from his high place of queenly favour.

The reign of Mary was followed by a period more propitious to the national literature, in the latter part of the sixteenth century. That half century, almost entire, was the time of her sister's reign. In styling it the Elizabethan literature, there is a propriety beyond mere chronological convenience, for the influences of her reign were in manifold ways favourable to the development of the mind, to the expression of thought and feeling. The heart of the sovereign beat with the heart of the people; and chivalry mingled with loyalty to do honour to the woman-monarch. Such was the predominant feeling, passing, indeed, often into the extravagance of adulation, but outlasting all her pomp and powers; for, in the preface to our English version of the Bible she stands recorded in the glowing phrase, "that bright occidental star, Queen Elizabeth, of most happy memory." In her sway, there was a magnanimity, which she had learned not in the luxuries of regal childhood, but in the school of adversity and a doubtful destiny. History presents no finer contrast than between those two days of her life: the first, when, a culprit on suspicion of treason, she was brought in custody along the Thames, to be committed to the Tower, and perceiving that the barge was steering to the traitor's gate, she refused to enter that guilty portal, and in the utter destitution of a young and unfriended woman, called God to witness she was innocent; when the first intelligence that reached her as a prisoner was that the scaffold had already drunk the blood of a meeker victim, the Lady Jane Grey, and she knew it was thirsting for hers. After a few, though weary and dismal years, she was again an inmate of the ancient fortress of the metropolis, but it was to go forth the Queen of a rejoicing nation, surrounded by cohorts of her devoted nobles, and multitudes of a happy people; and when before the crown was set upon her brow, lifting her eyes to heaven, she poured forth her fervid thankfulness to the Almighty for his wondrous dealings, for his wondrous mercies. "Wherever she moved," says the record of this the first of her magnificent progresses, "it was to be greeted by the prayers, the shouts, the tender words, and uplifted hands of the people: to such as bade 'God save your grace,' she said again, 'God save you all;' so that on either side there was nothing but gladness, nothing but prayer, nothing but comfort."*

Such was the fit opening of a reign for which was destined the highest glory that has dwelt with the nation's language and literature. An impulse was given by the civil and ecclesiastical condition of the realm, for it abounded in all that could cheer and animate a nation's heart. There was repose from the agony of spiritual persecution, submission to Rome was at an end, and the church in England was once more standing on its ancient

---

* Hollinshed, as quoted in Miss Strickland's "Queens of England," vol. vi. chap. iv, p. 127, Am. ed.

British foundations. It mattered little what foreign danger threatened, for there was the proud sense of national independence and national power, its moral force greater even than its physical. I have spoken this evening of wars, like the wars of York and Lancaster, fraternal feuds, which waste and harden a nation's heart; but there are wars of another kind which animate that heart with a high enthusiasm, a truth well proclaimed in a strain of lyrical poetry, fitting the ebb and flow which belong to that species of song to truth's varied aspects:

> "War is passion's basest game,
> Madly played to win a name.
> * * * *
> War is mercy, glory, fame,
> Waged in freedom's holy cause,
> Freedom such as man may claim,
> Under God's restraining laws."*

The same year in which Shakspeare is supposed to have gone up from Stratford to London was a proud one in his country's annals, for it was then that stout hearts and the stormy alliance of the ocean saved the soil from the pollution of foreign invasion, and the boastful attempt of the Spaniard, whose hateful presence in the palace when he shared the throne was not forgotten, and who was coming now with the terrors of the Inquisition in his train. When the scattered remnants of the Armada were driven, not back to the ports of Spain, but as far north as the stormy latitude of the Hebrides, there must have been a high and general fervour kindling each heart; and none more so than the large heart that beat in the

* Wordsworth's Ode on the Installation of Prince Albert as Chancellor of the University of Cambridge, in 1847.

breast of William Shakspeare. An intense nationality, and a happy loyalty to the government, as represented in the sovereign—fervid as were these emotions in the days of Queen Elizabeth—could not but affect vividly the national literature, especially the dramatic literature, placed as it was in close contact with the people. This influence is manifest in Spenser, in Shakspeare, in Ben Jonson, and all the great authors of the time; and doubtless it was one of the causes that helped them to their greatness.

The English language, too, was now better fitted for all the uses of literature, more adequate to the needs of philosophic thought, and of deep and varied feeling—at once stronger, more flexible, and more copious. It was now flowing *one* mighty flood, no longer showing the separate colours of the two streams which filled its channel—colours caught from the different soils, the Saxon and the Norman, in which they had their springs. The hidden harmonies of the language were disclosed, and its power of more varied music shown. The people's speech had grown to its full stature.* The language became affluent in expressions incorporated with it from the literature of antiquity, for classical learning in its

* Dr. Johnson, in the preface to his Dictionary, a work demanding his gigantic powers and congenial to them, has admirably remarked, that "From the authors which arose in the time of Elizabeth, a speech might be formed adequate to all the purposes of use and elegance. If the language of theology were extracted from Hooker and the translation of the Bible; the terms of natural knowledge from Bacon; the phrases of policy, war, and navigation from Raleigh; the dialect of poetry and fiction from Spenser and Sydney; and the diction of common life from Shakspeare,—few ideas would be lost to mankind, for want of English words in which they might be expressed." H. R.

best forms was made, as it were, part of the mind of modern Europe; and in England, under Elizabeth, the great universities, which during the immediately previous reigns had suffered from violence that had pierced even those tranquil abodes, were gathering anew their scattered forces. The attainments of the Queen herself, gained by the superior education which Henry VIII. had the sagacity to give his daughters, (it is one of the few good things to be said of him,) created another sympathy between the sovereign and her subjects. Beside the influence of ancient literature, necessarily limited to the learned, there was the larger and more open influence of the nation's own older literature—Chaucer's poetry dear to the people, and honoured by his grateful successors—for it was to Chaucer, let it be remembered, that Spenser applies the well-known phrase, the "well of English undefiled." There was the early romance, and that strange expression of the mediæval mind, the "Mysteries" and "Moralities," "Miracle Plays"—that allegorical drama, in which abstractions were personified, and the actors were such things as "Pride," "Gluttony," "Swift-to-Sin," "Charity," and, what might perhaps be the more appropriate personifications for later times, "Learning-without-money," and "Money-without-learning," and "All-for-money." In the great controversy of the Reformation, these devices for edification were freely employed by both divisions of the church to promote their respective opinions. An act of parliament in the reign of Henry VIII., for the promotion of true religion, forbade all interludes contradictory to established doctrines. In the preparatory processes of the Elizabethan literature, there was also the early minstrelsy in all its forms, tales told by the fireside in the long English winter evenings, and songs sung, as Shakspeare speaks of, by women as they sat spinning and knitting in the sun. How deep was the influence of the popular minstrelsy, is apparent from that well-known sentence of Sir Philip Sydney: "I never heard the old song of Percie and Douglas, that I found not my heart moved more than with a trumpet; and yet it is sung but by some blinde crowder, with no rougher voice than rude style; which being so evil apparelled in the dust and cobweb of that uncivil age, what would it work, trimmed in the gorgeous eloquence of Pindar?"* Sydney's feeling becomes still more intelligible when we recall how the same strain clung to the heart of Walter Scott, (it was his favourite of the old ballads:) when visiting the ruined castle of Douglas, feeling the sure approaches of death, he repeated to Lockhart the old poem, the pathos of the last stanza having an application not to be mistaken, and leaving him in tears:

"My wound is deep—I fain would sleep—
Take thou the vanguard of the three,
And hide me beneath the bracken bush
That grows on yonder lilylee.
This deed was done at the Otterbourne,
About the dawning of the day;
Earl Douglas was buried at the bracken bush,
And the Percy led captive away."†

Thus, as I have sought to show, there were propitious influences, *from* the past and *of* the present, which gave to our language the most illustrious period of its literature—that which is usually called the "Elizabethan,"

---

* Defence of Poesy, p. 34. Oxford ed. 1829.

† Lockhart's Scott, vol. x. p. 86.

passing over into the seventeenth century. First in it, was the English version of the Bible; for, although the present standard is that of King James, published in 1611, it belongs more properly in the history of English literature to an earlier period, modelled, as the new translation was, after Archbishop Parker's, commonly called "The Bishop's Bible," of the year 1568. The first of the instructions given to the translators in King James's time, was, "The ordinary Bible read in the churches, commonly called the Bishop's Bible, to be followed, and as little altered as the original will permit." We may, therefore, associate the language of our Bibles more truly with the age of Elizabeth than with that of the first of the Stuarts. To the same period belongs the first of the great English prose-writers, Richard Hooker, the earliest of that unbroken series of authors, during the last two hundred and fifty years, who have shown the resources of our English prose; Bacon, Taylor, Milton, and Barrow, Dryden, Bolingbroke, Swift, and Burke, Johnson, Goldsmith, and Cowper, and, in our own times, Scott and Southey, Sydney Smith and Landor. Mr. Hallam, in his Constitutional History, turns aside from his subject to express his deep sense of the claims which Hooker, as the author of the "Ecclesiastical Polity," has "to be counted among the great luminaries of English literature. He not only opened the mind, but explored the depths of our native eloquence. So stately and graceful is the march of his periods, so various the fall of his musical cadences upon the ear, so rich in images, so condensed in sentences, so grave and noble his diction, so little is there of vulgarity in his racy idiom, of pedantry in his learned phrase, that I know not whether any later writer has more admirably displayed the capacities of our language, or produced passages more worthy of comparison with the splendid monuments of antiquity." *

The chief glory, however, of the Elizabethan age, is its poetry, at once the most abundant and the highest in the annals of English literature. No fewer than two hundred poets are referred to the period by a catalogue which, by good authority, is thought not to exceed the true number. But it is not number alone. There are the names of Edmund Spenser and of William Shakspeare.

When Spenser, in 1590, gave to the world the first books of "The Faery Queen," it was done in a manner worthy of the age and of his great inspiration. It was dedicated to his Queen—"The most high, mighty, and magnificent empress, renowned for piety, virtue, and all gracious government, Elizabeth, by the grace of God, Queen of England, France, and Ireland, and VIRGINIA." Yes, there stands the name of that honoured State; and, while there is many a reason for the lofty spirit of her sons, the pulse of their pride may beat higher at the sight of the record of "the ancient dominion" on the first page of the Faery Queen. The poet placed it there as a tribute to her from whom the name was taken, and also to the gallant enterprise of Raleigh and his adventurous followers.

The poem is ushered in not only by the dedication to the sovereign, but by a series of introductory verses addressed to the most illustrious statesmen and soldiers of the court, Hatton, and Burleigh, and Essex, Howard, Walsingham,

* Hallam's Constitutional History of England, vol. i. p. 291.

and Raleigh—to Buckhurst, (whose own muse was slumbering now;) and not only to these, the living men of power and place, but, with a truth of affection worthy of the poet's gentle spirit, to the mourning sister of his lost friend, Sir Philip Sydney, and closing with an address, full of the chivalry of the times, "to all the gratious and beautiful ladies in the court."

Having occasion now to hasten to a few other subjects, I propose to reserve what I wish to say of the Faery Queen, until the next lecture, when I desire to speak of Spenser as a sacred poet, in connection with some counsel on the subject of Sunday reading. At present, let me recommend that remarkable series of papers from the pen of Professor John Wilson—the Christopher North of Blackwood's Magazine—papers of the highest value as pieces of true imaginative criticism, written with such a glowing admiration of Spenser's genius, that I know of no better means than the perusal of them for extending the study of this great allegory. They are to be found in Blackwood's Magazine for 1833.

The large luminary of Spenser's imagination had scarce mounted high enough above the horizon to kindle all it touched, when there arose the still more glorious shape of Shakspeare's genius, radiant like Milton's seraph—"another morn risen on mid-noon." This was the wonderful dramatic era in English letters. Within about fifty years, beginning in the latter part of the sixteenth century, there was a concourse of dramatic authors, the like of which is seen nowhere else in literary history. The central figure is Shakspeare, towering above them all; but there were there, Ben Jonson, and Beaumont, and Fletcher, and Ford, and a multitude of whom a poet has said,

> "They stood around
> The throne of Shakspeare, sturdy, but unclean."*

Their productions were numerous: one of them, Heywood, speaks of having had a share in the authorship of two hundred and twenty plays, of which only twenty-five have been preserved. They often worked, too, in fellowship, such as linked the names of Francis Beaumont and John Fletcher forever together—a beautiful literary companionship, the secret of which seems to be lost in the more calculating selfishness of later times.

It is scarce possible, it seems to me, to mistake that this abundant development of dramatic poetry was characteristic of times distinguished by the admirable union of action and contemplation in many of the illustrious men who flourished then; for instance, Sir Philip Sydney devoting himself to the effort of raising English poetry to its true estate, kindling his heart with the old ballads, or drawing the gentle Spenser forth from the hermitage of his modesty; at the same time sharing in affairs of state, in knights' deeds of arms, and on the field of battle meeting an early death, memorable with its last deed of charity, when, putting away the cup of water from his own lips burning with the thirst of a bleeding death, he gave it to a wounded soldier with the words, "Thy necessity is yet greater than mine:" or Raleigh preserving his love of letters throughout his whole varied career, at court, in camp, or tempest-tost in his adventures on the ocean. It seems to me that an age thus characterized by the combination of thought and deed in its representative men, had its most congenial literature in the drama—that form of

* Walter Savage Landor.

poetry which Lord Bacon has described as "history made visible."

I have said little of the greatest name that adorns the literature of the age of Elizabeth and the few succeeding years, and have now left myself no space to speak of what demands such ample room as comment on Shakspeare. It is a field that has been of late very much travelled over. Its interest, if truly sought, can never be exhausted. There is a mere chance that I may be pointing your attention to what has not attracted it before, when I ask whether you have ever noticed the power of Shakspeare peculiarly as a writer of English prose. Of its kind, it is as admirable as his poetic language. It is interspersed through his plays, never introduced probably without some exquisite art in the transition from verse to prose, from metrical to unmetrical diction. Let us for a few minutes look at this subject, and I will place side by side two passages, counterpart in some measure in subject; first, of verse, that familiar passage on the music of the spheres, which Hallam's calm judgment pronounced "perhaps the most sublime in Shakspeare:"*

* Hallam's Literature of Europe, chap. iii. § 11, vol. iii. p. 147. It is difficult to refrain from quoting, hackneyed as they are, the lines which immediately precede those in the text, the playful dialogue of the Venetian lovers, ending with the solemn, reverential outburst of Lorenzo, as, turning from the bright, mortal eyes of his mistress, he looks up to the stars of heaven. There are some lines of Shelly, on Night, which do not suffer in comparison with any thing since the Merchant of Venice:

> "How beautiful this Night! the balmiest sigh
> Which vernal zephyrs breathe in morning's ear,
> Were discord to the speaking quietude

"Look, how the floor of heaven
Is thick inlaid with patines of bright gold!
There's not the smallest orb which thou behold'st
But in his motion like an angel sings,
Still quiring to the young-eyed cherubim.
Such harmony is in immortal souls:
But whilst this muddy vesture of decay
Doth grossly close it in, we cannot hear it."

Whose prose but Shakspeare's could stand by the side of such verse? I turn to an equally familiar passage in Hamlet: "I have of late (but wherefore, I know not) lost all my mirth, forgone all custom of exercise: and, indeed, it goes so heavily with my disposition, that this goodly frame, the earth, seems to me a sterile promontory: this most excellent canopy, the air, look you, this brave o'erhanging firmament, this majestical roof, fretted with golden fire, why, it appears no other thing to me than a foul and pestilent congregation of vapours. What a piece of work is a man! How noble in reason! How infinite

---

That wraps this moveless scene. Heaven's ebon arch,
Studded with stars unutterably bright,
Through which the moon's unclouded splendour rolls,
Seems like a canopy which love has spread
To curtain her sleeping world. Yon gentle hills,
Robed in a garment of untrodden snow:
Yon darksome rocks, whence icicles depend,
So stainless that their white and glittering spires
Tinge not the moon's pale beam; yon castled steep,
Whose banner hangeth o'er the time-worn tower
So idly, that wrapt fancy deemeth it
A metaphor of Peace,—all form a scene
Where musing solitude might love to lift
Her soul above this sphere of earthliness:
Where silence undisturbed might walk alone,
So cold, so bright, so still." W. B. R.

in faculties! in form and moving, how express and admirable! in action, how like an angel! in apprehension, how like a god! the beauty of the world! the paragon of animals! And yet, to me, what is this quintessence of dust? Man delights not me, nor woman neither, though, by your smiling, you seem to say so."

Now let me exemplify a quick transition from prose to verse: when Coriolanus is soliciting the plebeian votes, citizens tell him he has not loved the common people: the irony of his answer is prose:—"You should account me the more virtuous, that I have not been common in my love. I will, sir, flatter my sworn brother, the people, to earn a dearer estimation of them; 'tis a condition they account gentle; and since the wisdom of their choice is rather to have my hat than my heart, I will practise the insinuating nod, and be off to them most counterfeitly; that is, sir, I will counterfeit the bewitchment of some popular man, and give it bountifully to the desirers. Therefore, beseech you, I may be consul." The bitterness of the soliloquy that follows is verse:

"Better it is to die, better to starve,
Than crave the hire which first we do deserve.
Why in this wolvish gown should I stand here,
To beg of Hob and Dick, that do appear,
Their needless vouches? Custom calls me to't:
What custom wills, in all things should we do't,
The dust on antique time would lie unswep't,
And mountainous error be too highly heap'd
For truth to overpeer. Rather than fool it so,
Let the high office and the honour go
To one that would do thus."

The poet's power over language as an instrument is curiously apparent in this, that when he so purposes, he takes all heart out of the words, and makes them sound as if they came merely from the lips. Observe how this occurs in the speeches of Goneril and Regan as contrasted with Cordelia's words: or the contrast between the utter hollowness of the king's request to Hamlet, and the reality that there is in his mother's language. The king's is thus:

> "For your intent
> In going back to school in Wittenberg:
> It is most retrograde to our desire;
> And we beseech you, bend you to remain
> Here, in the cheer and comfort of our age,
> Our chiefest courtier, cousin, and our son."

The queen speaks to her son:

> "Let not thy mother lose her prayers, Hamlet,
> I pray thee, stay with us, go not to Wittenberg."

I propose in my next lecture to pass to the literature of the seventeenth century, and to connect with it some thoughts on the subject of Sunday reading.

LECTURE VI.

Literature of the Seventeenth Century, with incidental Suggestions on Sunday Reading.*

Hooker's Ecclesiastical Polity—Progress of English literature—Sir Walter Raleigh's History of the World—Bacon's Essays—Milton—Comus—Hymn on the Nativity—Suggestions as to Sunday reading—Sacred books—Forms of Christian faith—Evidences of religion—Butler's Analogy—Charles Lamb's Remarks on Stackhouse—History of the Bible—Jeremy Taylor—Holy Living and Dying—Life of Christ—Pulpit-oratory—Southey's Book of the Church—Thomas Fuller—Wordsworth's Ecclesiastical Sonnets—Izaak Walton's Lives—Pilgrim's Progress—The Old Man's Home—George Herbert—Henry Vaughan—Milton resumed—Paradise Lost—Criticism on it as a purely sacred poem—Shakspeare's mode of treating sacred subjects—Spenser—The Faery Queen—John Wesley—Keble's Christian Year—George Wither—Aubrey De Vere—Trench's sonnet.

In following the progress of English literature, the difficulty of considering it according to what may be regarded as the successive eras is greatly increased the farther we advance. The literature becomes more abundant in both departments, prose as well as verse, and the influences that affect it, and are affected by it, are found to be more various and complicated. English prose-writing was hardly entitled to be looked on as literature until nearly two hundred years after English poetry had disclosed many of its finest resources. It was not till about the year 1600 that Hooker, in the "Ecclesiastical Polity,"

* February 7, 1850.

accomplished for English prose what Chaucer had done for English poetry before the year 1400. Accustomed, as we now are, to the combination of prose and poetry as making up a literature—language unmetrical filling, too, a larger space than the metrical—we are apt to forget how long a period there was during which English literature may truly be said to have been without its prose. In the early literature, therefore, Chaucer may be thought of as the solitary rather than the central figure; and thus of such a period a general view may be taken, which, at the same time, may show the individual genius that belonged to it. As we move forward, however, we find a more numerous company of poets, each having claim to attention, and, along with them, an increasing concourse of the prose-writers. You can readily perceive how it becomes more and more difficult to make any such grouping of the many actors in our literature, at the several periods, as may set them before you a well-arranged company rather than a confused throng; to discover which was the great mind of the age, and yet not lose sight of others that circled round it. We trace the progress of the nation's literature more laboriously, because more and varied elements entered into it, and because more minds were contributing to it. It becomes more necessary, in a brief and outline course of lectures like this, to allude, in a very cursory manner, to authors and their productions, well deserving extended consideration under more favourable circumstances.

As I have advanced toward that period of our literature in which names illustrious, both in prose and in poetry, come crowding to our thoughts, I feel the necessity of asking you to bear in mind that this course of lectures was designed to be merely of a suggestive character, to present a general view of the progress of English literature, and its condition at successive periods, rather than a detailed examination of particular authors or books.

It is possible to arrange in our minds the literature of our language into a series of successive eras, and this may be done with somewhat more precision than would at first be anticipated; for it is not a mere arbitrary, chronological distribution, corresponding with centuries or reigns, but an arrangement according to a certain set of influences affecting the English mind and character during a given length of time, more or less definite, to be succeeded by a new set of influences, producing a new phase of the nation's literature. Such a general view of English literature is important, not only as saving one from a great deal of confusion of thought on the subject, but also as enabling us to see the great authors of different times, each in his appropriate grouping, and to carry out special courses of reading. The succession of our literary eras, with a little reflection and effort of memory, may be so familiarized as not to be forgotten. The earliest era—the age of Chaucer, as it may aptly be styled—the last half of the fourteenth century, was characterized by the various influences which marked the mediæval civilization; the closing century of which civilization, from 1400 to 1500, was, in consequence chiefly of internal commotion in England, a hundred years' sleep of the English mind, so far as literature was concerned. The first half of the sixteenth century has no more than a comparative interest, as a period in which the English mind was making its transition from mediæval to modern modes of thought and feeling, affected, too, in some degree, by the change of the nation's ecclesiastical position. The latter part of the sixteenth century and the first part of the seventeenth century—in other words, the reigns of Queen Elizabeth and of James the First—form properly one era, although it is usually styled the Elizabethan era, in consequence, perhaps, of the greater glory of that reign in other matters than letters. The latter part of the seventeenth century, after the Restoration, is the beginning of an era extending into the eighteenth century, with which, as a truer connection, I propose to consider it in the next lecture, directing my attention now to the early and middle portion of the seventeenth century.

The prose literature of the early part of the seventeenth century received its most important addition in what may be said to be the second (in time) of the great English prose-works—Sir Walter Raleigh's History of the World, the work with which he beguiled the years of his imprisonment; his mind, within the prison-walls, travelling out into the remote regions of the ancient world's story, as actively as his body, in its years of freedom, had mingled with his fellow-men, and roamed over the distant spaces of the sea.

To the same period of our prose literature belong the authorship and the philosophy of another man famous (and I had almost said infamous, too) in public life—Francis Bacon, Baron Verulam, Viscount St. Alban, and (would it had not been so) Lord High Chancellor of England. His philosophical works belong not so much to literature as to that high department of science which is meant to guide human inquiry, and mark out the boundaries of human knowledge. His volume which *does* belong to literature in the more exact sense of the term, is the small one of "Essays or Counsels, Civil and Moral;" and it does so, for a reason, which he has himself assigned, in a phrase which has become one of the familiar phrases of the language: when, after the cloud had fallen on his character, he collected these miscellanies—he said, "I do now publish my *Essays*, which of all my other works have been most current; for that, as it seems, *they come home to men's business and bosoms.*" That the Essays do so address themselves thus universally and intimately to mankind, is apparent from a mere glance at the list of titles; and that they contain a perpetual interest, is shown from the manner in which their condensed wisdom may be evolved for new applications—a condensation of wisdom which is united with much of the imaginative processes of thought, and is therefore doubly valuable as one of the books of discipline for well teaching. "Few books," says Mr. Hallam, "are more quoted, and what is not always the case with such books, we may add, that few are more generally read. In this respect they lead the van of our prose literature: for no gentleman is ashamed of owning that he has not read the Elizabethan prose-writers; but it would be somewhat derogatory to a man of the slightest claim to polite letters were he unacquainted with the Essays of Bacon. It is, indeed, little worth while to read this or any other book for reputation's sake; but very few in our language so well repay the pains or afford more nourishment to the thoughts. They might be judiciously introduced, with a small number more, into a sound method of education—one that should make wisdom, rather than mere knowledge its object, *and might become a text-book of examination in our schools.*"*

* Literature of Europe, vol. iii. chap. iv. § xxxiv. p. 342.

In that which is essentially the literature of the seventeenth century—prose as well as poetry—the name of Milton is prominent, the beginning and the end of his career approaching respectively the opening and the close of the century. I speak of this, not simply as a matter of date, but on account of the relation of that career to the age in which it was cast. The first part of Milton's literary life is full of a beautiful reflection of the age that had gone before; his genius is then glowing with tints of glory cast upon it by the Elizabethan poetry: the meridian of it is in close correspondence with the season of the power of the Parliament and the Protector, when Milton stood side by side with Cromwell; and the latter period of it (which I propose to speak of in the next lecture) was that of sublime and solitary contrast with the times of Charles the Second. The first was the genial season of youth, studious, pure, and happy; the second was of mature manhood, strenuous in civil strife, and the dubious dynasty of the Protectorate; the third was old age, darkened, disappointed, but indomitable.

Of Milton's early poems, the most beautiful is the exquisite Masque of Comus, one of the last and loveliest radiations of the dramatic spirit, which seemed almost to live its life out in about half a century of English literature, beginning in the times of Queen Elizabeth, and ending in those of Charles the First. It has been said by more than one judicious critic of another of Milton's early poems, "Lycidas," that the enjoyment of it is a good test of a real feeling for what is peculiarly called poetry. Of Comus, I think, it might be said, as truly as of any poem in the language, that it is admirably adapted to inspire a real feeling for poetry. It abounds with so much of true imagination, such attractiveness of fancy, such grace of language and of metre, and withal contains so much thought and wisdom wherewith to win a mind unused to the poetic processes, that were I asked what poem might best be chosen to awaken the imagination to a healthful activity, I would point to Milton's Comus, as better fitted than almost any other for the purpose. The poem, both in the conception and the execution, finely illustrates the power of the imagination, its moral alchemy in

> "Turning the common dust
> Of servile opportunity to gold;
> Filling the soul with sentiments august,
> The beautiful, the brave, the holy, and the just."*

For, observe on what a homely and familiar incident the poet has built up this beautiful superstructure of fancy and philosophy. When he was dwelling at his father's rural home, the Earl of Bridgewater was keeping his court not far off, at Ludlow Castle, and it happened that his two sons, and his daughter, the Lady Alice Egerton, were benighted and bewildered in Haywood Forest; where the brothers, seeking a homeward path, left the sister alone awhile in a tract of country inhabited by a boorish peasantry. Such was all the story, simpler than the ballad of the Children in the Wood; and yet it is transfigured into a poem of a thousand lines—a moral drama showing the communion of natural and supernatural life, the mysterious society of human beings, and the guardian and tempting spirits hovering round their paths: it teaches, with a poet's teaching, how the spiritual and intellectual

* Wordsworth's Desultory Stanzas. Works, p. 243.

nature may be in peril from the charms of worldly pleasures, and how the philosophic faith and the heaven-assisted virtue are seen at last to triumph. The guardianship of ministering angels—their encampment round the dwellings of the just—is finely announced in the opening lines, spoken by the attendant spirit alighting in the wood, where the human footsteps are astray:

"Before the starry threshold of Jove's court
My mansion is, where those immortal shapes
Of bright aerial spirits live insphered,
In regions mild of calm and serene air,
Above the smoke and stir of this dim spot
Which men call Earth, and with low-thoughted care,
Confin'd and pester'd in this pinfold here,
Strive to keep up a frail and feverish being,
Unmindful of the crown that virtue gives
After this mortal change to her true servants,
Amongst the enthroned gods on sainted seats.
Yet some there be that by due steps aspire
To lay their just hands on that golden key
That opes the palace of eternity;
To such my errand is; and but for such,
I would not soil these pure ambrosial weeds
With the rank vapours of this sin-worn mould."

The genuine power of invention displayed in Comus is not disparaged; nay, the beauty of it is heightened, by the lights it reflects from the elder poets, of whom Milton was deeply studious, for he knew that poetry is not inspiration alone, but art no less. There are passages which seem almost like echoes of the sweet modulations of Shakspeare's sentences—combinations of words which we should say were Shakspeare's, could we forget they are Milton's, as when the bewildered lady speaks:

"A thousand phantasies
Begin to throng into my memory,

Of calling shapes, and beck'ning shadows dire,
And airy tongues, that syllable men's names
On sands, and shores, and desert wildernesses.
These thoughts may startle well, but not astound,
The virtuous mind, that ever walks attended
By a strong-siding champion, Conscience.
Oh! welcome pure-eyed Faith, white-handed Hope,
Thou hovering angel, girt with golden wings,
And thou, unblemished form of Chastity;
I see ye visibly, and now believe
That He, the Supreme Good, to whom all things ill
Are but as slavish officers of vengeance,
Would send a glist'ring guardian, if need were,
To keep my life and honour unassailed."

Again, there are passages which blend with a music of their own the melody of both Spenser and Shakespeare—the music of their words and of their thoughts—as when the brother speaks:

"I do not think my sister so to seek
Or so unprincipled in Virtue's book,
And the sweet peace that goodness bosoms ever,
As that the single want of light and noise
(Not being in danger, as I trust she is not)
Could stir the constant mood of her calm thoughts,
And put them into misbecoming plight.
Virtue could see to do what Virtue would,
By her own radiant light, tho' sun and moon
Were in the flat sea sunk. And Wisdom's self
Oft seeks to sweet, retired solitude,
Where, with her best nurse, Contemplation,
She plumes her feathers, and lets grow her wings,
That in the various bustle of resort
Were all too ruffled, and sometimes impaired.
He that has light within his own clear breast
May sit in the centre, and enjoy bright day."

When the lady is at last rescued from the wicked magic that encircled her, the good attendant spirit, his guardianship achieved, speeds away like Ariel, set free to the elements, and leaves in poetry words of encouragement and promise to humanity:

> "Now my task is smoothly done,
> I can fly or I can run
> Quickly to the green earth's end
> Where the bow'd welkin slow doth bend,
> And from thence can soar as soon
> To the corners of the moon.
> Mortals, that would follow me,
> Love Virtue; she alone is free:
> She can teach ye how to climb
> Higher than the sphery chime,
> Or if Virtue feeble were,
> Heaven itself would stoop to her."

One cannot part with this poem, radiant as it is with what is bright and pure and lofty in poetry and philosophy, without thinking how little that high-born woman, when her heart was throbbing in the loneliness of Haywood Forest—how little could she have thought that a young poet's words were to win for her more enduring honour than wealth or heraldry could bestow.

The most distinct foreshadowing of Milton's great epic poem, and of his own independent genius, is an earlier poem—"The Hymn on the Nativity"—which gives the poet the fame of having composed almost in his youth the earliest of the great English odes, the like of which had not, I believe, been heard, since Pindar, two thousand years before, had struck the lyre for assembled Greece. It is a lyric that might have burst from that religious bard of paganism, could he have had prophetic vision of the Advent. It is a poem that revealed a new mastery of English versification, disciplined afterward to such power in the blank verse of Paradise Lost. Nothing in the way of metre can be grander than some of the transitions from the gentle music of the quiet passages to the passionate parts, and their deep reverberating lines that seem to go echoing on, spiritually sounding, long after they are heard no more. The universal peace at the time of the Nativity is told with the very music of peace:

"No war or battle's sound
Was heard the world around;
The idle spear and shield were high up hung:
The hooked chariot stood
Unstain'd with hostile blood;
The trumpet spake not to the armed throng;
And kings sat still with awful eye,
As if they surely knew their sovereign Lord was by.

But peaceful was the night
Wherein the Prince of Light
His reign of peace upon the earth began:
The winds, with wonder whist,
Smoothly the waters kist,
Whispering new joys to the mild ocean,
Who now hath quite forgot to rave,
While birds of calm sit brooding on the charmed wave."

The stanzas that tell of hopes of a golden age again are followed by that solemn one:

"But wisest Fate says no,
This must not yet be so;
The Babe lies yet in smiling infancy,
That on the bitter cross
Must redeem our loss,
So both himself and us to glorify;
Yet first to those ychained in sleep
The wakeful trump of doom must thunder through the deep."

The grandest portion of this poem is that which tells

of the flight of the false deities of heathendom, the panic of the priests, the silencing of the oracles, and the cessation of the services of superstition, when the star was seen over the infant Saviour. The profusion of mysterious epithets and the dim imagery seem to blend the magic of the dark incantations of Shakspeare's witchcraft with the splendours of Greek mythology. Paganism and superstition—Europe's, Asia's, Africa's—all, with all the host of their ministry, are vanishing like witches at the touch of music—a babe's cry heard from the manger at Bethlehem throughout the spiritual universe :

"The oracles are dumb ;
No voice or hideous hum
  Runs through the arched roof in words deceiving.
Apollo from his shrine
Can no more divine,
  With hollow shriek the steep of Delphos leaving.
No nightly trance, or breathed spell,
Inspires the pale-eyed priest from the prophetic cell.

The lonely mountains o'er,
And the resounding shore
  A voice of weeping heard and loud lament;
From haunted spring and dale,
Edged with poplar pale,
  The parting Genius is with sighing sent :
With flower-inwoven tresses torn,
The nymphs in twilight shade of tangled thickets mourn.

* * * * *

And sullen Moloch, fled,
Hath left in shadows dread
  His burning idol all of blackest hue :
In vain with cymbals' ring
They call the grisly king,
  In dismal dance about the furnace blue :

The brutish gods of Nile as fast
Isis and Orus and the dog Anubis haste.

Nor is Osiris seen,
In Memphian grove or green,
Trampling the unshower'd grass with lowings loud;
Nor can he be at rest
Within his sacred chest;
Nought but profoundest hell can be his shroud:
In vain with timbrel'd anthems dark
The sable-stoled sorcerers bear his worshipt ark.

He feels from Juda's land
The dreaded Infant's hand."

* * * *

Of Milton's various prose-writings, and of his epic poems, it would hardly be possible to say much in a general lecture on the literature of the century. What I have to say respecting the Paradise Lost, I propose to put in this course in another connection.

I have ventured to include, in the subject of this evening's lecture, some suggestions on Sunday reading; and, in turning aside to this topic, let me first explain why I have connected it with this portion of my course. The literature of the seventeenth century includes that which is most generally regarded as the great sacred poem of our language—I mean, of course, the Paradise Lost; and, again, it is the most illustrious age of English pulpit-oratory and of theological literature. Let me, in the next place, say, that I trust it will not be thought presumptuous or impertinent in me to introduce, even somewhat casually, into a course like this, the subject of Sunday reading. I am truly solicitous, on the one side, not to put my hand unduly upon sacred subjects, which are appropriate to another profession of public teachers; and, on the other, not to treat those sacred subjects, so far as I may have occasion to touch them, as ordinary topics of literature and taste. The literature which is associated with holy things must be approached with the reverential feeling with which the picture of a sacred subject should be looked on, remembering that there is due to it something deeper than unloving, technical criticism of art.

I have been attracted to this subject by the conviction that every Sunday has its unappropriated portions of time, and also that there is an abundant literature, in English words, to be used appropriately to the day, and beneficially. The week-day opportunities for reading vary very much with the business and duties of our lives; but our Sundays, with the rest they bring, put us all more on an equality. The most punctual attendance on public worship does not absorb the day; and, the day's duties discharged, the evening can have no better employment than that which is in-door and domestic. There are the contingencies, too, that compel the spending of the whole day at home; and I believe that is a sore trial to those who have no resources for the employment of it. This is a great pity, considering how large those resources are. I do not propose to speak of the study of the Bible, because I am not willing to treat that as a literary occupation. It stands on higher ground, and ground of its own.

With regard to modes of Christian faith and systems of church-government, it surely is becoming for every one, both man and woman, to have an intelligent knowledge of their belief and membership It is right to hold, with confidence and charity combined, to well-formed and precise principles, in all that we profess to give our spiritual allegiance to; to understand our own position and to feel the strength of it, instead of that careless ignorance, that latitudinarian indifference, which is seen and heard so much of—a mock liberalism, which I speak of as unreal, because, often when it is put to the test, it is found to cover either a hollow scepticism or a bitter intolerance, instead of genuine Christian charity.

In the discipline of habits of reading, it is on many accounts important to draw a line of distinction between week-day reading and Sunday reading. Independently of the propriety of making the reading subservient to the uses of the day, such appropriation is desirable as a means of securing acquaintance with a large and very valuable portion of English literature—the department of its sacred literature being very extensive both in prose and poetry; so extensive, indeed, that when this habit is well formed and cultivated, it will be found that the Sunday reading is more apt to encroach on the week-day reading than the reverse.

The choice of books must be not only reverently suited to the day, but also large in their influences. It should be no narrow choice, for such would be unworthy of the manifold power of the day. It may associate with books which are formally and directly connected with sacred subjects, and others no less sacred in their influences, because the sanctity is held more in reserve, acting, it may be, more deeply, because less avowedly.

The sacred literature of our language may be described as containing books on the evidences of religion, sermons, devotional books, church history, biographies of saintly men and women, travels in the Holy Land, sacred allegories and other prose stories, and sacred poetry. The unappropriated portions of the Sundays of a long life might find in the English books on such subjects varied and unfailing delight and spiritual health.

Of one of the classes of books named, those on the evidences, it appears to me that injudicious use is not unfrequently made. If a man is an unbeliever, these books may be good for him; or if he has to deal with unbelievers, they may be of service to him: but to a believing Christian, man or woman, many a well-intentioned work of this kind may be not only worthless, but injurious. A great work, such as Bishop Butler's, may indeed be invaluable both as a discipline of thought and as strengthening the intellectual conviction of the truth of revelation; or such works as the Bridgewater Treatises may help to deepen the sense of the power, wisdom, and goodness of the Creator, as displayed in the universe. But there is a multitude of books which, I fear, are mischievous, for they tell the believing, faithful spirit of doubts which such a spirit never would have dreamed of—doubts engendered in the hard heart of unbelief, the miserable sophistries which skepticism has spun out. Why should the happy heart of belief even look at, much less pore over, such things, studying the refutation of fallacies never else heard of? What need of the antidote, if the poison would not come nigh you? Why should believing Christian people think it worth while to waste their time and thoughts upon such things? and above all, why the fresh and docile and believing spirit of youth, manly or womanly youth—the believing children of believing parents—be trained in the knowledge of what Hume denied, and how Gibbon scoffed, and the ribald deism of Paine, for the sake of being taught how these things may be answered? A little argumentative strength of belief may be gained, (perhaps,) but there is danger in the process that the power of affectionate, instinctive belief—a thousand-fold more precious—may be at the same time wasting and worn away.

Charles Lamb's recollection from childhood of Stackhouse's History of the Bible is full of warning on this subject. "I remember," he says, "it consisted of Old Testament stories, orderly set down, with the *objection* appended to each story, and the *solution* of the objection regularly tacked to that. The objection was a summary of whatever difficulties had been opposed to the credibility of the history by the shrewdness of ancient or modern infidelity, drawn up with an almost complimentary excess of candour. The solution was brief, modest, and satisfactory. The bane and antidote were both before you. To doubts, so put, and so quashed, there seemed to be an end forever. The dragon lay dead for the foot of the veriest babe to trample on. But—like as was rather feared than realized from that slain monster in Spenser—from the womb of those crushed errors young dragonets would creep, exceeding the powers of so tender a St. George as myself to vanquish. The habit of expecting objections to a passage set me upon starting more objections, for the glory of finding a solution of my own for them. I became staggered and perplexed, a skeptic in long coats. The pretty Bible stories which I had read, or had heard read in church, lost their purity and sin cerity of impression, and were turned into so many historic or chronologic theses to be defended against whatever impugners. I was not to disbelieve them, but—the next thing to that—I was to be quite sure that some one or other would or had disbelieved them. Next to making a child an infidel, is the letting him know that there are infidels at all."*

Such an influence is not limited to childhood, but affects in like manner the spirit of belief at any age; and therefore it is safer and wiser to seek no knowledge of atheism, or deism, or skepticism, even in the refutation of them.

This also should be borne in mind, that the evidences of religion, as discussed in the last century, when they were most rife, present Christianity in a defensive apologetic attitude, which is unworthy of it. The literary leaders of the times were the infidels Bolingbroke, and Hume, and Gibbon, and others earlier and later, the British infidelity which was followed by French infidelity. The insolence of unbelief had risen high, and the tone of the faithful was depressed; a style of defence prevailed which is out of place in a better age, where no infidel author has bold prominence in literature. That subdued mode of warfare with skepticism was oddly adverted to at the time by George the Third, (who, whatever his faults were, had the merit of being the first moral man that had sat on the British throne for more than a century:†) when Bishop Watson published his "Apology for the

---

* Prose Works, vol. ii. p. 150. Essay on Witches and other Night Fears.

† In Lord Mahon's last volume of "The History of England," are two letters of George the Third to Bishop Hurd, on the death of one of his children, in 1783, which brightly illustrate the King's private and familiar character. Vol. vii. Appendix, p. 34. W. B. R.

Bible," George the Third remarked, "Apology! I did not know that the Bible needed an apology."

Turning to the sacred literature of the seventeenth century, you find in it not only greater power of argumentation, but also blended with it a fervid devotional spirit, the glow of genuine imagination, kindling narrative, reasoning, persuasion, philosophy,—all with one broad light, so that it is not the logical faculty which alone is appealed to, but the whole spiritual nature, the intellect, and the heart, the soul of man. This would be seen most clearly, perhaps, in the writings of the most imaginative, and eloquent of the great divines of that century—Bishop Jeremy Taylor: his Sermons, or his "Holy Living and Dying," the volume which may be spoken of as the most admirable manual of devotion in the language, or to that, the greatest probably of all his works, "The Life of our Saviour." Before those who are acquainted with the writings of Jeremy Taylor, I would not trust myself to speak of them, without a larger opportunity to do honour to them than time would now give me: to those who have yet in reserve the delight which such acquaintance gives, I could hardly so speak that the soberest truth should not sound like exaggeration. Every thing, almost, that is attractive in a merely literary point of view, is to be found there: a boundless variety of illustration gathered by a marvellous scholarship, the deepest and the gentlest habits of feeling, an opulence of imagination and fancy like Shakspeare's or Spenser's, and a style that is the music worthy of such a spirit. A few years ago, the writings of Jeremy Taylor existed only in the early Folios, but now they are accessible in the more convenient forms of modern editions. The Holy Living and Dying, published separately, and in many editions, is a volume not to borrow, not to take out of a library, but to own, to hold it as a possession.

Without attempting to speak of Barrow, or the other great English divines of a former age, I can only remark, that the literature is abundant in specimens of pulpit wisdom and oratory; and that in our own day, the strength and beauty of the olden time in this respect have come back again in some of the contemporary sermon literature.

The history of the Christian church is another subject on which English literature gives us reading at once most agreeable and instructive. All the charms of Southey's prose may please you in his "Book of the Church;" or turning to the old church historian, Thomas Fuller, you may find in his History of the Church in Great Britain (one of the most remarkable works in the language) the varied powers of learning, sagacity, pathos, an overflowing wit, humour, and imagination, all animating the pages of a church history. The interest in this subject may be expanded and deepened by the studious reading of that poetic commentary on church history, the series of Wordsworth's Ecclesiastical Sonnets, in which the poet-historian, with all a poet's truthfulness and feeling, has traced the course of Christian faith, from the trepidation of the Druids at the first tidings of the Gospel, onward through the various fortunes of the church, down to the consecration of the first American Bishop. This series of poems is a beautiful and salutary study in connection with English history, for there is not an important event, or period, or influence, or saintly character in the annals of the church in England, on which there is not shed the light of wise, imaginative, and feeling commentary. You have not forgotten, perhaps, the lines which in a former lecture I quoted, on the conversion of the Saxon king, and the incident that led to it.

Much appropriate Sunday reading is supplied by the biography of the good men and women of early and late times. Amid the large variety of such records, one may be named—none more modest in origin, more unambitious in plan, but none more admirable as a memorial. I refer to Izaak Walton's Lives, of which the poet has said:

> "There are no colours in the fairest sky
> So fair as these. The feather, whence the pen
> Was shaped that traced the lives of these good men
> Dropped from an angel's wing."*

Passing to the imaginative side of our literature, there is the sacred prose allegory, "The Pilgrim's Progress," a work second, I believe, only to Robinson Crusoe in the largeness of the audience it has gained in the world. Allegory has been beautifully revived in our own day in "The Old Man's Home."†

To any one who justly appreciates the moral uses of poetry as a spiritual ministry, it will be apparent that it should enter, well chosen, into our Sunday reading; and there is no more marked characteristic of English literature than the abundance and excellence of its sacred poetry. The seventeenth century contributed largely to it—beautifully so in the well-known poems of that saintly country parson, George Herbert, and in the poetry, almost un-

---

* Wordsworth, p. 306. Sonnet on Walton's Book of Lives.

† The Old Man's Home, by the Reverend William Adams, M.A., Author of "The Shadow of the Cross."

known, till its recent reproduction, fit to be associated with Herbert's—the poems of Henry Vaughan; and in later times the English muse has not been regardless of its peculiar sacred functions.

I must hasten, however, to the great sacred poems of the language, and recur first to Milton's epics. Of these poems, considered with reference to imaginative power, and all its accessories of wondrous verse, no language could express too strongly one's sense of their sublimity and beauty. Not only for poetic description of nature and regions supernatural, but also in deep human interest, the Paradise Lost stands among the world's great poems. But when we study it as a sacred poem, and ask ourselves carefully as to the religious impressions it gives, the character becomes questionable. This is chiefly in two respects: the character of Satan, and the bold handling of the Divine nature. The Miltonic Satan is undoubtedly one of the most stupendous and awful creations of poetry; one of its grandest studies, but there is a heroic grandeur in it which wins, do what you will, a human sympathy. It is impossible to look on the Apostate Angel without awe, and somewhat of admiration, rather than abhorrence; sometimes perhaps with something of pity, as in that famous passage, where, having called his followers, myriads of the fallen angels thronged around their chief, and the peerage of Pandemonium stood in mute expectation of his voice.

> "Thrice he essay'd, and thrice, in spite of scorn,
> Tears, such as angels weep, burst forth."

It was from such a representation of Satan as is given throughout the poem, that Arnold's deep religious feeling revolted, remarking, that "by giving him a human likeness, and representing him as a bad man, you necessarily get some images of what is good as well as of what is bad; for no living man is entirely evil. Even banditti have some generous qualities; whereas the representation of the devil should be purely and entirely evil, without a tinge of good, as that of God should be purely and entirely good, without a tinge of evil; and you can no more get the one than the other from any thing human. With the heathen it was different; their gods were themselves made up of good and of evil, and so might well be mixed up with human associations. The hoofs and the horns and the tail were all useful in this way, as giving you an image of something altogether disgusting. And so Mephistophiles in Faust, and the other contemptible and hateful character of the Little Master, in Sintram, are far more true than the Satan of the Paradise Lost."*

With regard to Milton's hardihood in carrying his imagination into the mysteries of the being of the Most High, and the unreserved freedom with which the Father and the Saviour are set before us in this dramatic epic, I believe that even the least sensitive reader must be conscious of an instinctive shrinking from many passages of the poem. It is in this, even more than in the character of the Arch-fiend, that the Paradise Lost—and the Paradise Regained also—may blunt the sense of adoration, and lower, instead of raising, some of the emotions which sacred poetry ought to inspire. There are passages in the poems which, perhaps, it would be better never to read a second time. I should be loth to read them aloud here, because it would be difficult to divest them of a certain air of

* Arnold's Life and Correspondence, in a note to Appendix C., p. 468.

irreverence, which was not a purposed irreverence in the pure and lofty soul of Milton, but was an unconscious manifestation of the *intellectual* pride which was part of his character, and of the *spiritual* pride which belonged to his times.

There is an impressive contrast between the spirit with which Milton and Shakspeare have treated the most sacred subjects. A reverèntial temper, less looked for in the dramatic bard, marks every passage in which allusion is made to such subjects—a feeling of profound reverential reserve; and as this may not have been generally observed, let me group some brief and characteristic passages together. There is the beautiful allusion to Christmas in Hamlet:

"Some say, that ever 'gainst that season comes
Wherein our Saviour's birth is celebrated,
This bird of dawning singeth all night long:
And then, they say, nor spirit dares stir abroad;
The nights are wholesome; then no planets strike,
No fairy takes, no witch hath power to charm,
So hallow'd and so gracious is the time."

The mention, in Henry the Fourth, of the Holy Land—

"those holy fields
Over whose acres walk'd those blessed feet,
Which, fourteen hundred years ago, were nail'd,
For our advantage, on the bitter cross."

Again, the single line in Winter's Tale, in which Polyxenes refers to Judas and the betrayal

"my name
Be yok'd with his, that did betray the *best!*"

The allusion to the scheme of Redemption and to the Lord's Prayer in Portia's plea for mercy

"Though justice be thy plea, consider this—
That in the course of justice none of us
Should see salvation; we do pray for mercy;

And that same prayer doth teach us all to render
The deeds of mercy."

And most impressive, perhaps, of all—the deep feeling in the words of the saintly Isabella:

"Alas! alas!
Why, all the souls that were, were forfeit once;
And he, that might the 'vantage best have took
Found out the remedy: How would you be
If he, which is the top of judgment, should
But judge you as you are? O think of that;
And mercy then will breathe within your lips
Like man new made."

I can do little more now than allude to a contrast still more striking between Milton's want of reverential reserve and Spenser's handling of religious truth, moving gently and with awe, as if with an ever-abiding sense that the ground he was treading on was holy ground. It was characteristic of Milton and of his times, when religion was freely talked about and rudely handled, to make his great epic avowedly a sacred poem—to put it in direct connection, if possible, with scriptural subjects. The genius of Spenser could not have ventured on what would have seemed to his gentle and reverential nature a profane handling of hallowed things and thereupon he employed, not the direct, but the veiled mode of sacred instruction. That veil interposed by his imagination was a gorgeous one, so interwoven with the richness of pagan-poetry, "barbaric gold," and of romantic Christian fancy, that the dazzled eye often fails to look through it to the scriptural truth that is steadily beaming there. Great injustice is done to Spenser, when, bewildered with the mazes of his inexhaustible creations, or by the brightness of his exuberant fancy, we see in the

Faery Queen nothing more than a wondrous fairy tale, a wild romance, or a gorgeous pageant of chivalry. Beyond all this, far within it, is an inner life; and that is breathed into it from the Bible. It is the great sacred poem of English literature. "I dare be known to think," said Milton, addressing the Parliament of England, "our sage and serious poet, Spenser, a better teacher than Scotus or Aquinas."* When John Wesley gave directions for the clerical studies of his Methodist disciples, he recommended them to combine with the study of the Hebrew Bible and the Greek Testament, the reading of the Faery Queen; and, in our own day, Mr. Keble, the poet of "The Christian Year," has described the Faery Queen as "a continual deliberate endeavour to enlist the restless intellect and chivalrous feeling of an inquiring and romantic age on the side of goodness and faith, of purity and justice."†

Spenser himself, expounding his allegory to his friend Sir Walter Raleigh, said, "The general end of all the book is to fashion a gentleman, or noble person, in virtuous and gentle discipline."‡ Christian philosopher, as well as poet, Spenser's deep conviction, manifest throughout the poem, was that the only discipline wherewith to tame the rebellious heart of man is that morality which, in one of his own sweet phrases, bears

"The lineaments of gospel-books."§

---

* Milton's Prose Works, 8vo. p. 108. On Liberty of Unlicensed Printing.

† Quarterly Review, vol. xxxii. p. 225, June, 1825. In an article on Sacred Poetry, attributed to Mr. Keble.

‡ Spenser's Letter to Sir Walter Raleigh, prefixed to Poetical Works, vol. i. p. 5.

§ An Elegie on Friend's Passion for his Astrophell. Spenser's Poetical Works, vol. v. p. 261.

The student of sacred poetry must not be startled at meeting with thoughts, or rather images, drawn from other sources than Holy Scripture. The imagination of a great poet can make the heathen world tributary to the Christian; you meet in the Faery Queen the exploded mythology of paganism, and Scripture story, so shadowed forth together that the sanctity of the latter is no wise sullied by the contact. When one of Spenser's heroes visits the realms of the lost spirits, he beholds Tantalus with the hunger and the thirst of ages on him, and the dread of centuries to come; and not far off another wretch, plunged in the infernal waters, washing his blood-stained hands—washing eternally, hopelessly, the deep damnation of Pontius Pilate; images, one caught from pagan fable, the other from Holy Writ; images, too, of unending woe, the sufferings hereafter of a wicked life.

In like manner, when Milton recounts the hosts of Pandemonium, there is that transcendent effort of the imagination by which he grasps the mythology of classical antiquity and thrusts it down into hell, ranging the gods of Greece—Olympic Jove himself—with the inferior powers of the apostate angels, Satan's followers and servants. It is a mistake, I think, to limit our notice of sacred poetry to that which has an express and direct connection with biblical topics, for it is a high prerogative of the Christian imagination to rescue from the realms of error, fictions and superstitions, and make them safely subservient to the cause of revealed truth. It is this process, admirably conceived and executed, which entitles Southey's Curse of Kehama and Thalaba to be ranked with the great sacred poems of the language.

Thus a large range may be demanded for sacred poetry;

and yet in another aspect all narrowed to the relation in which it stands to revealed teaching and Holy Writ. That remarkable poet of the seventeenth century, George Wither—whose writings, unfortunately, are so little accessible—seems to have been disposed to look more to the resources of his own thoughts than either to the profession of preaching or the increase of books: he says it was not his religion

"Up and down the land to seek,
To find those well-breath'd lecturers, that can
Preach thrice a Sabbath, and six times a week,
Yet be as fresh as when they first began."

And speaking of books, he writes:

"For many books I care not, and my store
Might now suffice me, though I had no more
Than God's two Testaments, and then withal
That mighty volume which the world we call;
For these well look'd on, well in mind preserved,
The present Age's passages observed;
My private actions seriously o'erviewed,
My thoughts recalled, and what of them ensued,
Are books, which better far instruct me can,
Than all the other paper-works of man;
And some of these I may be reading, too,
Where'er I come, or whatsoe'er I do."*

A poet, a happy-hearted poet, like Wither, whose imagination could make cheerful employment within his prison walls, might speak thus; but for our common minds the poet's help is needed: it will often help us the better to know and feel the three volumes with which the old poet was content with—the two Testaments and the mighty volume called the world; and doubtless not only

* Wither, as quoted in "Church Poetry," p. 72.

the sacred poetry, but all high and serious poetry, may be traced to some germ of revealed truth. The highest human poetry is in affinity with the divine poetry; and, however they may differ in degree, I do not believe that they are separated by characteristic difference in kind. What are the Latin hymns of the mediæval church, such as that famous one on the Day of Judgment, which clung to the dying lips of Walter Scott, murmuring snatches of it when his mind had on all else faded away,—what were those poems but human versions of inspiration?* What are the hymns of Ken and of Keble but echoes from the lyric song of the Bible? Wordsworth's sublime communings with nature do but amplify and reiterate the Psalmist's declaration of the glory of God as manifested in the universe; and when the poet shows that

"Heaven lies about us in our infancy,"†

and teaches the holiness and beauty of the innocence of childhood—a theme for sophisticated man to reflect on—what is this but an expression of the truth that is contained in the Saviour's words, "of such is the kingdom of heaven?"

Aubrey De Vere's thoughtful lines on Sorrow, are but an echo of the divine teaching:

* "We very often heard distinctly the cadence of the *Dies Iræ;* and I think the very last stanza that we could make out was the still greater favourite:

Stabat mater dolorosa,
Juxta crucem lachrymosa,
Dum pendebat filius."

Lockhart's Scott, vol. x. p. 214. As this volume is passing through the press, we have received the news of Mr. Lockhart's death at Abbotsford, in December, 1854. W. B. R.

† Wordsworth's Ode on Intimations of Immortality. Works, p. 388.

"Count each affliction, whether light or grave
God's messenger sent down to thee. Do thou
With courtesy receive him: rise and bow,
And ere his shadow pass thy threshold, crave
Permission first his heavenly feet to lave.
Then lay before him all thou hast. Allow
No cloud of passion to usurp thy brow,
Or mar thy hospitality; no wave
Of mortal tumult to obliterate
The soul's marmoreal calmness. Grief should be,
Like joy, majestic, equable, sedate,
Confirming, cleansing, raising, making free;
Strong to consume small troubles; to commend
Great thoughts, grave thoughts, thoughts lasting to the end."*

Again: another living poet does but teach how to apply a well-known text, and feel its truth the more, when he says:

"We live not in our moments or our years—
The Present we fling from us as the rind
Of some sweet Future, which we after find
Bitter to taste, or bind *that* in with fears,
And water it beforehand with our tears—
Vain tears for that which never may arrive;
Meanwhile the joy whereby we ought to live
Neglected or unheeded disappears.
Wiser it were to welcome and make ours
Whate'er of good, though small, the Present brings—
Kind greetings, sunshine, song of birds, and flowers,
With a child's pure delight in little things;
And of the griefs unborn to rest secure,
Knowing that mercy ever will endure."†

This is a poet's teaching of the cheerfulness of Christian faith and the love of Christian content and happiness;

* Aubrey De Vere's Waldenses, with other poems quoted in an Essay on De Vere's Poems, in Taylor's Notes from Books, p. 215.

† Sonnet by the Rev. R. C. Trench, quoted in Church Poetry, or Christian Thoughts in Old and Modern Verse, p. 62.

and this is but the rebuke of unchristian sullenness, and the praise of Christian thankfulness:

"Some murmur, when their sky is clear
And wholly bright to view,
If one small speck of dark appear
In their great heaven of blue.
And some with thankful love are fill'd
If but one streak of light,
One ray of God's good mercy gild
The darkness of their night.
In palaces are hearts that ask,
In discontent and pride,
Why life is such a dreary task,
And all good things denied?
And hearts in poorest huts admire,
How love has in their aid
(Love that not ever seems to tire)
Such rich provision made."*

Thus do the Poets minister in the Temple.

* Trench's Poems, p. 116.

LECTURE VII.

Literature of the Seventeenth and Eighteenth Centuries.*

Milton's old age—Donne's Sermons—No great school of poetry without love of nature—Blank in this respect between Paradise Lost and Thomson's Seasons—Court of Charles the Second—Samson Agonistes—Milton's Sonnets—Clarendon's History of the Rebellion—Pilgrim's Progress—Dryden's Odes—Absalom and Achitophel—Rhyming tragedies—Age of Queen Anne—British statesmen—Essayists—Tatler—Spectator—Sir Roger De Coverley—Pope—Lord Bolingbroke—English infidels—Johnson's Dictionary—Gray—Collins—Cowper—Goldsmith—The Vicar of Wakefield—Cowper—Elizabeth Browning.

In proceeding to the literature of the close of the seventeenth century, we approach a period which is marked by great change. Heretofore in the succession of literary eras there had been a continuity of influence, which had not only served to give new strength and develope new resources, but to preserve the power of the antecedent literature unimpaired. The present was never unnaturally or disloyally divorced from the past. The author in one generation found discipline for his genius in reverent and affectionate intercourse with great minds of other days. Such was their dutiful spirit of discipline, strengthening but not surrendering their own native power—the discipline so much wiser and so much more richly rewarded in the might it gains, than the self-sufficient discipline, which, trusting to the pride of origi-

* Thursday, February 14, 1850.

nality or the influences of the day, disclaims the ministry of time-honoured wisdom. Milton was studious of Spenser, and Spenser was grateful and reverent of Chaucer; and thus, as age after age gave birth to the great poets, they were bound "each to each in natural piety." But when we come to those who followed Milton, the golden chain is broken. The next generation of the poets abandoned the hereditary allegiance which had heretofore been cherished so dutifully, transmitted so faithfully.

It was at this time that the earlier literature began to fall into neglect, displaced with all its grandeur and varied power of truth and beauty, displaced for more than a century by an inferior literature, inferior and impurer, so that for more than a hundred years, many of the finest influences on the English mind were almost wholly withdrawn. Indeed, it is only within the present century that the restoration of those influences has been accomplished. Here we see within our own day, the revival of early English literature, bringing from dust and oblivion the old books to light and life again, to do their perpetual work upon the earth—the work that was denied to them by an age that was unworthy of them. No longer since than ten years or less, there was no good edition of the complete works of Chaucer. Ten years ago, the sermons of the greatest preacher of the times of James the First, Donne, the Dean of St. Paul's, were almost inaccessible, entirely so, I might say, to scholars in this country, in the first and very rare folio edition. Even the writings of Jeremy Taylor were a rare treasure, until about twenty-five years ago, Bishop Heber did the good service of giving ready access to them in a modern edition; and not to speak of the miscellaneous literature, over which the dust lay so thick, all the early dramatists, save Shakspeare, lay in comparative neglect till their recent restoration.

I refer to this neglect as both a symptom and a cause of the decline of English literature, which began at the close of the seventeenth century, and lasted for about a century. Genius of a higher order would never have divorced itself from such an influence. It would have strengthened itself by loyalty to it.

Besides their disloyalty to the great poets who had gone before, the poets of the new generation were guilty of another neglect, equally characteristic, and more fatal perhaps to high poetic aspirations; I refer to the neglect of the poetic vision of nature, external nature, the sights and sounds of this material world, the glory of which, proclaimed in divine inspiration, is ever associated with "the consecration and the poet's dream." Who can question, without questioning the Creator's wisdom and goodness, that the things of earth and sky have their ministry on man's spiritual nature? We may not be able to measure or define it, but it is a perpetual and universal influence, and it must be for good. Most of all is it recognised by the poet, prepared as he is

"By his intense conceptions to receive,
Deeply the lesson deep of love which he
Whom nature, by whatever means, has taught
To feel intensely, cannot but receive."*

No great poet, perhaps I may say no great writer, is without the deep sense of the beauty and glory of the

* The Excursion, book i. 397.

universe, the earth that is trod on, the heavens that are gazed at. It is an element of the poetry of the Bible. The classical poetry of antiquity shows it; it abounds, in vernal exuberance, in Chaucer; you meet with it perpetually in Spenser, and Shakspeare, and Milton, and in the prose of Bacon and Taylor. But when we come to the next generation, particularly of poets, the spiritual communion with nature was at an end. They had not vision of sunlight or starlight, but were busy within doors with things of lamp-light or candle-light. They took not heed of mountain, or seaside, or the open field, and nature's music there, but city, "the town," street and house were all in all to them:

> "The soft blue sky did never melt
> Into their hearts."*

If it can be shown, as it undoubtedly can, that thoughtful, genial communion with Nature is an accompaniment of all poetry of the highest order, in all ages, surely we may infer that a literary era which is deficient in this element is the era of a lower literature. Now, it has been ascertained, by careful examination, that, with two or three unimportant exceptions, "the poetry of the period intervening between the publication of the Paradise Lost and Thomson's Seasons (a period of about sixty years) does not contain a single new image of external nature; and scarcely presents a familiar one from which it can be inferred that the eye of the poet had been steadily fixed upon his object—much less that his feelings had urged him to work upon it in the spirit of genuine

* Peter Bell, part i. p. 163.

imagination."* Let us now rapidly consider some of the causes, or, at least, accompaniments, of the degeneracy of English literature, and particularly of its poetry, which began in the latter part of the seventeenth century. The civil war was over, and the fierce bloodshedding which marked England's civil wars, and which should be an awful warning to all who are sprung from that stock, the strong usurpation of Cromwell had passed away—each period with its evils.† The Restoration came, and what were the evils that came along with it? In the Middle Ages, the miseries that were the common train of war in Europe were pestilence and famine; but, after the domestic war in England in the seventeenth century—an ecclesiastical civil war—came debauchery, licentiousness, riot, and blasphemy. The rigour of Puritanism once removed, there came quickly in its stead a lawlessness in which the exultation of triumph mingled, and men took a party pride in immorality. All high moods of feeling were ridiculed: honour was a jest, and so were justice and dignity, and piety and domestic virtue; and conjugal faith

---

* Appendix to Wordsworth's Works. Essay, p. 490.

† "The *usurpation* of Cromwell" is a phrase about which, in our day, there may be some question, not, however, here to be discussed. There is American authority for it, which I cite, as curiously illustrative of the cavalier tendencies of "the Father of his country." In 1792, Washington sent to Sir Isaac Heard a memorandum as to his family, which begins thus:

"In the year 1657, or thereabouts, and during *the usurpation* of Oliver Cromwell, John and Lawrence Washington emigrated from the North of England and settled at Bridge's Creek, on the Potomac River, in the county of Westmoreland. But from whom they descended, the subscriber is possessed of no document to ascertain."—*Sparks' Washington*, vol. xii. p. 547. W. B. R.

was the greatest jest of all. The civil war had also demoralized the nation by breaking up the habits of domestic life: households were destroyed, and their proprietors found a shelter in taverns; and when the necessity for such disordered life had passed away, the low habits were left behind.

To a nation, thus diseased, there was perpetually passing the moral poison that issued from the avenues of the palace. From the earliest era of the history of the island, no portion had been so loathsome as the quarter of a century during which Charles Stuart, the younger, was on the throne. When the early life of Queen Elizabeth was visited with afflictions, she came forth from her trials with a spirit chastened and invigorated for a mighty reign. But upon Charles Stuart the lesson of adversity was wasted. The bloody fate of his father might well have thrown a solemn memory of the past over all his after life. When the Restoration brought him once more to the royal home of his childhood, he seems to have mounted the throne with a determination to make up the arrears of interrupted pleasure by a career of unrestrained debauchery, the like of which had not been seen in England before. The ancient palace was reeking with the filthy atmosphere of the tavern or viler haunts of iniquity. Moral opinion was scoffed at, and national honour betrayed. The monarch of that island which had more than once swayed the destinies of Europe, sold himself to a monarch as profligate, but prouder, for Charles became the mean-spirited pensioner of Louis the Fourteenth. Vice was in riotous possession of the high places of the land, and the throne was the seat of the scoffer. Looking from the throne thus occupied, and begirt with profligates and wits, Shaftesbury, and Buckingham, and Rochester, the old age of Milton is seen with heightened sublimity. There was hanging over the palace, the capital, the land, a dark atmosphere of sensuality, lurid, at times, with such cruelties as mingle with heartless frivolity; and Milton had passed into that seclusion of which it has been grandly said:

> "Milton,
> Thy soul was like a star, and dwelt apart:
> Thou hadst a voice whose sound was like the sea—
> Pure as the naked heavens, majestic, free."*

His varied career drew to a solemn ending. He who in youth and early manhood had given the freshness of poetic fervour a homage to the best of England's nobility, the Egertons and Spensers; he who roamed over the Alps and Italy, visiting Galileo, and communing with the friend of Tasso, and Italian scholars; he who had stood by the side of Cromwell and Fairfax and Vane, in their years of power,—was now a lone man in the land, all his strife for the commonwealth wasted, and left to what the world then little heeded, but which has made his name immortal. It is of this period of Milton's life, that Mr. Hallam has eloquently spoken in a passage which I desire to quote, especially for the sake of an educational suggestion which accompanies it:

"Then the remembrance of early reading came over his dark and lonely path, like the moon emerging from the clouds. Then it was that the muse was truly his; not only as she poured her creative inspiration into his mind,

---

* Wordsworth, p. 213. Am. Ed.

but as the daughter of memory, coming with fragments of ancient melodies, the voice of Euripides, and Homer, and Tasso; sounds that he had loved in youth, and treasured up for the solace of his age. They who, though not enduring the calamity of Milton, have known what it is, when afar from books, in solitude or in travelling, or in the intervals of worldly care, to feed on poetical recollections, to murmur over the beautiful lines whose cadence has long delighted their ear, to recall the sentiments and images which retain by association the charm that early years once gave them—they will feel the inestimable value of committing to the memory, in the prime of its power, what it will easily receive and indelibly retain. I know not, indeed, whether an education that deals much with poetry, such as is still usual in England, has any more solid argument among many in its favour, than that it lays the foundation of intellectual pleasures at the other extreme of life."*

Such is the opinion of one of the most judicious minds of the day—a mind trained in the most exact and laborious historic research; and I quote it because I apprehend that among us the tendency of late years has been to neglect this excellent discipline of the memory, which enabled our

* Literature of Europe, vol. 3. p. 425. The late Mr. Gallatin (at the time I refer to more than eighty years old) once told me that one of the purest pleasures and consolations of his advanced years was the recollection of his earliest studies, his Latin and Greek which he had learned at school, and passages of the ancient poets, that, without conscious effort, were constantly presenting themselves to his mind. The memories of intermediate politics, and finance, and business, active and unremitted, were fading away, but what he learned by rote when a boy came back fresh to cheer him. W. B. R.

elders to keep that possession in their minds of long passages of poetry, which astonishes their feebler descendants.

To return to Milton: he whose delight it had once been to roam through woods, and over the green fields, was now chained by blindness to the sunny porch of a suburban dwelling. He whose heart's pulse was a love of independence, was now a helpless dependent for every motion, for all communion with books; every step of him, who had walked through all the ways of life so firmly, was at the mercy of another. His spirit was darkened, too, with disappointment in his countrymen, and with bitter memories of domestic discords. As the Comus was a beautiful reflection of happy youth, the Samson Agonistes shadows forth the gloomy grandeur of the poet's old age. In some passages there is the breaking out of a bitter agony; but a stern magnanimity pervades the poem—a high-souled pathos befitting the sorrows of a vanquished, captive giant. With our thoughts of the hero of the tragedy mingle thoughts of the poet himself, for what was John Milton in the degenerate days of Charles the Second, but a blind Samson in the citadel of the Philistines? In the words the hero speaks, we seem to hear the voice of Milton's own spirit, subdued to a gentle melancholy:

> "I feel my genial spirits droop,
>
> * * * *
>
> My race of glory run, and race of shame;
> And I shall shortly be with them that rest."

Before passing from this subject, let me briefly notice the service which Milton rendered to English poetry in that short series of short poems—his English *Sonnets*, which

Doctor Johnson was disposed to dismiss with contempt.* Heretofore that form of verse had been appropriated almost exclusively to the expression of love or some tender emotion; but Milton showed that it could be made a high heroic utterance, as in that one on the massacre of the Piedmontese, which is a solemn cry to Heaven for vengeance that seems to echo over the Alps. This service in disclosing the hidden powers of the sonnet has been acknowledged by Wordsworth:

"When a damp
Fell round the path of Milton, in his hand
The Thing became a trumpet, whence he blew
Soul-animating strains—alas, too few!"†

And Landor has finely put this page of literary history into three lines, (so much can a few words do in a master's hand!) when speaking of Milton, he says,

"Few his words, but strong,
And sounding through all ages and all climes;
He caught the sonnet from the dainty hand
Of Love, who cried to lose it; and he gave the notes
To Glory."

Within the same twelve months in which Milton died, occurred the death of the Earl of Clarendon, who, like Milton in this, that in a season of political adversity he sought employment in letters, gave to English prose what may be considered the first of the great English histories—that wondrous portrait gallery, the "History of the Rebellion."

To the English prose of the same period belongs a very

---

* "They deserve not any particular criticism, for of the best it can only be said they are not bad." Life of Milton, p. 234. W. B. R.

† Wordsworth's Miscellaneous Sonnets, p. 187.

different work—associated also with the calamities of authors—the "Pilgrim's Progress," the great sacred prose fiction of our literature, which justifies the title given to John Bunyan by D'Israeli, who calls him "the Spenser of the people." It is one of the few books which, translated into the various languages of Europe, has gained an audience as large as Christendom. In his own country, he caught the ear of the people by using the people's own speech—genuine, homely, hearty English—at the time when the language was becoming vitiated, his simple rhetoric being as he describes it in rude verse:

"Thine only way,
Before them all, is to say out thy say
In thine own native language, which no man
Now useth, nor with ease dissemble can."*

But the author who is most truly to be looked on as the representative of the latter part of the seventeenth century is Dryden, the laureate of the court of Charles the Second. That degenerate era is reflected both in the character of Dryden's writings and in their quick-earned popularity. Content to write for his own age alone, rather than for all after-time, a brief popularity has been followed by the utter neglect—a wise neglect—of a very large portion of his voluminous productions. His genius did not raise itself above his times, but dwelling there, a habitation steaming with a thousand vices, his garland and singing-robes were polluted by the contagion.

For wellnigh fifty years Dryden was contemporary with Milton, living in the same city much of that time, and

* Quoted in Southey's Life of Bunyan, prefixed to his edition of the Pilgrim's Progress, p. 29.

in occasional intercourse; and I cannot but picture to myself how different might have been the career of the young poet, how much purer and nobler the issues of his imagination, how much happier and more genial his life, and how far more honoured his memory, if, instead of setting himself in sympathy with the dominant influences and fashions of the day, and serving them, he had sought communion with the solemn solitude of Milton! How noble a spectacle it would have been for after ages to contemplate the older bard, blind, poor, neglected, and with a grieved but unconquered spirit, the younger poet seated at the old man's feet, making himself a partner in his fallen fortunes, honouring and cherishing him, and at the same time fortifying his own heart, and enriching his own imagination! It would have been a filial piety, such as Milton gladly would have rendered to Spenser—homage such as Spenser would have paid to Chaucer.

But the soul of Dryden was not cast in heroic mould, nor was it susceptible of that purity, and innocence, and ardour of affection which is often associated with heroism. Dazzled by the prize of a speedy popularity, and losing sight of the poet's high spiritual ministry of "allaying the perturbations of the mind, and setting the affections in right tune," he turned to the base office of pampering the vices of an adulterate generation. Even when his youthful enthusiasm was fired with the ambition of composing an epic poem on King Arthur and the Knights of the Round Table, (the same subject which had attracted Milton's young imagination,) the high design was swept from his thoughts by the corruption of the times—sacrificed to the ignominious thraldom he was held in by patrons who, exacting unworthy service, would not suffer him to put on the incorruption of a great poet's glory.* In Walter Scott's indignant lines:

"Dryden, in immortal strain,
Had raised the table-round again,
But that a ribald king and court,
Bade him toil on, to make them sport;
Demanded for their niggard pay,
Fit for their souls, a looser lay,
Licentious satires, song and play;
The world defrauded of the high design,
Profaned the God-given strength, and marred the lofty line."†

When we look at Dryden's vigorous command of language, in prose and verse, the poetic energy in those departments in which his genius moved most freely, we may well conceive that a higher region of authorship was in his reach, had he united with intellectual cultivation that moral discipline, which no endowment can dispense with, without grievous peril to its powers. In the following passage from his Œdipus, there is a certain tone of reflection and imagery which is not without resemblance to the thought and language of Shakspeare:

---

* Dryden's intended epic was not a mere vision of youth, but, according to his best biographers, was in his mind at different periods of life, though always deferred by the low influences around him. At one time, King Arthur was the theme; at another, it was Edward the Black Prince subduing Spain. (*Mitford's Life, Aldine Poets, p.* 78.) Milton's young vision appears in his Epistle to Mansus:

"O mihi si mea sors talem concedat amicum
Phœbæos decorasse viros qui tam bene norit,
Siquando indigenas revocabo in carmina reges,
Arturumque etiam sub terris bella moventem!
Aut dicam invictæ sociali fædere mensæ
Magnanimos heroas; et O modo spiritus adsit
Frangam Saxonicas Britonum sub Marte phalanges!" W. B. R.

† Introduction to Marmion., Canto i. Poetical Works, vol. vii. p. 36.

"Ha! again that scream of woe!
Thrice have I heard, thrice since the morning dawn'd,
It hollow'd loud, as if my guardian spirit
Called from some vaulted mansion, '*Œdipus!*'
Or is it but the work of melancholy?
When the sun sets, shadows that showed at noon
But small, appear most long and terrible;
So when we think fate hovers o'er our heads,
Owls, ravens, crickets, seem the watch of death;
Nature's worst vermin scare her godlike sons.
Echoes, the very leavings of a voice,
Grow babbling ghosts, and call us to our graves:
Each mole-hill thought swells to a huge Olympus,
While we, fantastic dreamers, heave and puff,
And sweat with an imagination's weight;
As if, like Atlas, with these mortal shoulders
We could sustain the burden of the world."

That one fine stanza in the Ode for St. Cecelia's Day, shows what lyric grandeur Dryden might have attained to:

"What passion cannot Music raise and quell?
When Jubal struck the chorded shell,
His listening brethren stood around,
And wondering, on their faces fell,
To worship that celestial sound;
Less than a god they thought there could not dwell,
Within the hollow of that shell,
That spoke so sweetly and so well."

In no respect did Dryden more rashly and fatally abandon the authority of his great predecessors, than in his attempt to introduce *rhymed* tragedies. The introduction of rhyme into the dramatic poetry was a false substitute for that exquisite blank-verse which, in the hand of a great master, is at once so imaginative and natural, that it sounds like an ordinary speech idealized—the dialect of daily life in its highest perfection. But the rhymed dramatic dialect stood in no such near and truthful relation to the realities of life, as I may show, perhaps, by a reference to a variety of language occurring in Shakspeare. It will be remembered that the chief and best reputation of Dryden lies in this, that he enlarged the domain of English poetry by the production of the most nervous satire in verse that English literature had yet known. It has been said by Milton, in one of his prose works, that "a satire, as it was born out of a tragedy, so ought to resemble his parentage, to strike high, and adventure dangerously, at the most eminent vices among the greatest persons."* Dryden's satire had this merit. It struck at Buckingham. It was also employed on the unworthy versifiers and scribblers, for authorship had degenerated to a low craft, with all its worst enviousness and meanness, in dismal contrast with that frank and hearty intercourse which distinguished the companionship of authors in an earlier generation, living in genial fellowship, and weaving even their inspirations together in partnership that was a brotherhood.

A literary life like Dryden's closed with an old age without dignity and without happiness—the remnant of life, worn out in his Egyptian bondage, embittered both by neglect and the memory of talents misspent in the service of a sensual and sordid king and corrupt courtiers. There was nothing of the grandeur of Milton's lonely old age; but, in the period of Dryden's desolation, we may trace the chastening of adversity in some strains of a higher mood, as in those admirable lines in which he tells of his effort at Christian forbearance when provoked to

* Milton's Apology for Smectymnuus, § vi. Prose Works, p. 88, 8 vo.

resent and retort. This passage is worthy of all praise, especially when we remember his power of satire, his unimpaired poetic invective, now controlled by a higher principle:

> "If joys hereafter must be purchased here
> With loss of all that mortals hold so dear,
> Then welcome infamy and public shame,
> And, last, a long farewell to worldly fame!
> 'Tis said with ease; but, oh, how hardly tried
> By haughty souls to human honour tied!
> Oh, sharp, convulsive pangs of agonizing pride!
> Down then, thou rebel, never more to rise!
> And what thou didst, and dost so dearly prize,
> That fame, that darling fame, make that thy sacrifice.
> 'Tis nothing thou hast given; *then add thy tears*
> *For a long race of unrepenting years,*—
> 'Tis nothing yet, yet all thou hast to give:
> Then add those maybe years thou hast to live;
> Yet nothing still: then, poor and naked, come,
> Thy Father will receive his unthrift, home,
> And thy blest Saviour's blood discharge the mighty sin."*

The death of Dryden took place in the year 1700, and we pass into the literature of the eighteenth century, the first part of which is not unfrequently styled the Augustan age of Queen Anne. It was Augustan in that men of letters were basking in the sunshine of aristocratic patronage, and a courtly refinement succeeded to that grossness of manners and of speech which had disgraced society in the years just previous. Writers were no longer plunging in the mire of that obscenity which defiled the times of Charles the Second; but they were often walking in the dry places of an infidel philosophy. The religious agitation of the middle of the previous century had sunk

* The Hind and Panther, part iii. v. 1575.

down from the high-wrought power of fanaticism, first, into indecent profanity, and then, by degrees, into a more decorous, but cold, self-complacent skepticism. Enthusiasm of all kinds had burned out, and there was a low tone of thought and feeling in church and state—in the people, and, of consequence, in literature. There was no great British statesman—I mean no genuine, magnanimous statesman—from the time of Strafford, and Clarendon, and Falkland, and the great republican statesmen of the seventeenth century, down to a century later, when the first William Pitt, "the great Commoner," breathed a spirit of magnanimity once more into British politics.

The prose literature developed, in the reign of Queen Anne, a new agency of social improvement in the periodical literature, destined to acquire such unbounded influence in later times in the newspaper press and the leading Reviews. There is much to show that a more correct and refined tone of society was brought about by the papers which, under the title of "The Tatler," from the pen of Steele, began that series which became more famous in the "Spectator," and in connection with Addison. "It was said of Socrates," remarked Steele, "that he brought philosophy down from heaven to inhabit among men. I shall be ambitious to have it said of me that I have brought philosophy out of closets and libraries, schools, and colleges, to dwell in clubs and assemblies, at tea-tables, and in coffee-houses." Not many years ago, it was very generally the custom, I remember, for every young person, male and female, to go through a course of reading of the papers of the Spectator. This has fallen quite into disuse now-a-days, and I do not know that it is much to be regretted. The Spectator contains, undoubtedly, much sensible and sound morality; but it is not a very high order of Christian ethics. It contains much judicious criticism, but certainly not comparable to the deeper philosophy of criticism which has entered into English literature in the present century.* Those papers will always have a semi-historical interest, as picturing the habits and manners of the times—a moral value, as a kindly, good-natured censorship of those manners. In one respect, the Spectator stands unrivalled to this day: I allude to the exquisite humour in those numbers in which Sir Roger de Coverley figures. If any one desire to form a just notion of what is meant by that very inde-

* Let me, in other and better language than my own, say a word for our classic. "It seems to me," says the greatest of living writers of fiction and the manliest satirist of our times, "that when Addison looks from the world, whose weaknesses he describes so benevolently, up to the heaven which shines over us all, I can hardly fancy a human intellect thrilling with a purer love and adoration than Joseph Addison's. It seems to me his words of sacred poetry shine like stars. They shine out of a great, deep calm. When he turns to heaven, a sabbath comes over that man's mind, and his face lights up from it with a glory of thanks and prayer. His sense of religion stirs his whole being. In the fields, in the town; looking at the birds in the trees—at the children in the streets; in the morning or in the moonlight; over his books in his own room; in a happy party at a country merry-making or a town assembly, good-will and peace to God's creatures, and love and awe of Him who made them, fill his pure heart and shine from his kind face. If Swift's life was the most wretched, I think Addison's was one of the most enviable. A life prosperous and beautiful, a calm death, an immense fame and affection afterward for his happy and spotless name."—*Thackeray's Lectures on the English Humorists.* I may venture to express the hope that the habit of reading the Spectator will *not* fall into disuse. I know no finer line in any English poet than one of Addison's, when the Moon repeats her wondrous tale

"Nightly to *the listening earth.*" W. B. R.

finable quality called "humour," he cannot more agreeably inform himself than by selecting the Sir Roger de Coverley papers, and reading them in series.

While Addison was giving to English prose that refinement which was verging, perhaps, to somewhat of feebleness, the strong hand of Swift—a man with a stronger intellect and a rougher heart—was scattering that vigorous prose which touched the other extreme of coarseness; and Bolingbroke was giving, in his statelier and more elegant diction, that prose the study of which has by some of England's best orators been pronounced an orator's best training.

The chief representative name in the literature of the times of Queen Anne is that of Pope. His rank as a poet has been a subject of much dispute; but it may now, I think, be considered as the settled judgment of the most judicious critics, ardent admirers, too, of Pope's poetry, that his place is not with Chaucer, Spenser, Shakspeare, and Milton, the poets of the first order, but with Dryden, in a second rank. Shakspeare alone excepted, perhaps no English poet has furnished a greater amount of single lines for apt and happy quotation, on account either of their force or beauty. In the famous satire on the Duchess of Marlborough occurs this passage:

> "Strange! by the means defeated of the ends—
> By spirit robb'd of power—by warmth, of friends—
> By wealth, of followers! without one distress,
> *Sick of herself through very selfishness!*
> Atossa, curs'd with every granted prayer,
> Childless with all her children, wants an heir·
> To heirs unknown descends the unguarded store,
> *Or wanders, heaven-directed, to the poor.*"

This passage furnishes two most characteristic lines; the

first one of great force—a truth from the dark side of humanity, the wasting malady of selfishness:

> "Sick of herself through very selfishness."

The other, a beautiful expression of the sense of a good Providence:

> "Or wanders, heaven-directed, to the poor."

There is another description of lines in Pope, as favourite in the way of quotation as any: I mean those which express in smooth verse some truism, or commonplace sentiment, or something the very tameness of which makes it untrue. What line has been quoted so often?—you may see it even on tombstones—

> "An honest man's the noblest work of God."

Does anybody think so? Is honesty so rare? Has it so much of heroism in it, or so much of saintliness, that it is God's noblest work? Surely, the poet must have uttered it in contempt of his fellow-men—must have meant it in sarcasm.*

And here we may see what disqualified Pope from being the great moral poet he aspired to be—from being a great poet of the first rank. Whatever was his power of imagination, of fancy, his command of language, or flow of verse, his genius had not that spiritual healthfulness which is a characteristic of our greatest English poets. There is, running through all the writings of Pope, a large vein of misanthropy. It was his habit to proclaim contempt of the world, antipathy to his fellow-beings, except a few choice friends, whom he clung to most faith fully. It is not with such morbid feeling that a poet can

---

* From this criticism I venture to note an earnest dissent.
W. B. R.

either study or expound human nature. His ministry is to inspire his fellow-beings with high and happy emotions, to foster a just sense of the dignity of human nature, to make man lowly wise, to cheer him amid his frailties, not to depress him, to animate his heart with faith, and hope, and love, not to chill and harden it with discontent and hatred. Instead of aggravating all that is dark and forlorn in man's mingled nature, it belongs to the poet, of all others, to show that while the son of earth is lying on the earth, lonely, benighted, his head pillowed on a stone, thoughts of a better life, the soul's celestial aspirations, are ascending and descending over him, like angels in the patriarch's dream. For such, the poet's truest ministry, Pope's temperament was unhappily constituted. In a letter to Bishop Atterbury—a serious letter on a serious occasion—addressed to that prelate on the eve of his exile, he asks, "What is every year of a wise man's life but a censure or critic on the past? Those whose date is the shortest, live long enough to laugh at one-half of it: the boy despises the infant, the man the boy, the philosopher both, and the Christian all."* What could have been that notion of philosophy, what that notion of Christianity, which could make one of its attributes contempt, that infirmity of the morbid mind, in the eye of divine wisdom a vice! How different, too, such contempt of the past periods of one's life, from that deeper wisdom which inculcates the moral continuity of our being, showing how important it is for the growth of our spiritual nature that we should so dwell in each partition of our earthly time. that we may move on from one to the other with happy

* Letter, May 17th, 1723. Roscoe's Pope, vol. ix. p. 241.

memories of the past—with happy consciousness of its abiding influences!

> "The child is father of the man;
> And I could wish my days to be
> Bound each to each by natural piety."*

It is a characteristic view of human life which Pope gives in such a passage as this:

> "Behold the child, by nature's kindly law,
> Pleased with a rattle, tickled with a straw;
> Some livelier plaything gives his youth delight,
> A little louder, but as empty quite;
> Scarfs, garters, gold, amuse his riper age,
> And beads and prayer-books are the toys of age:
> Pleased with this bauble still, as that before,
> Till tired he sleeps, and life's poor play is o'er."

The "rattle," a "straw," "scarfs, garters, gold, beads, and prayer-books," equally toys and baubles, and ending alike in weariness, and then death or sleep. What a picture of life! what a picture for a poet, whose duty is to dignify and elevate, to draw, of the life of man, who with all his infirmities, is an immortal, gifted with a soul, precious in the sight of his Creator, and not unworthy the awful ransom of the Redeemer's blood! A great moral poet does not so teach. "Life's poor play!" Such is this didactic poet's deliberate doctrine. The image is Shakspeare's, but with a most significant difference:

> "Out, out, brief candle!
> Life's but a walking shadow; a poor player,
> That struts and frets his hour upon the stage,

---

* There may be noted a coincidence between these familiar lines of Wordsworth and those of Milton:

> "The childhood shows the man,
> As morning shows the day."
> *Paradise Regained*, B. 4, v. 220. W. B. R.

> And then is heard no more: it is a tale
> Told by an idiot, full of sound and fury,
> Signifying nothing."

But mark the dramatic truth, when you see what voice speaks thus; it is the utterance of the agony of a blood-stained conscience, whose guilt has so wasted out all its humanity, that it would fain lose all belief in life's realities.

The sophisticated state of society in which Pope lived, and the morbid excess of his critical powers, show themselves in his treatment of womanly character: it is full of querulousness, and sarcasm, perverse in sentiment and in morals. He exhorts a female friend

> "Not to quit the free innocence of life,
> For the dull glory of a virtuous wife."

What a line for a poet to utter! and what a contrast to those bright images of womanly heroism and beauty which the older poets delighted to picture in marriage! When Pope begins a healthier strain in that sweet couplet—

> "O blest with temper, whose unclouded ray
> Can make to-morrow happy as to-day"—

see what straightway it declines to,—such a tribute to womanly character as this, that a sister can be unenvious of a sister's beauty, and that a mother can hear unaggrieved the love that is given to a daughter, and that a wife's merit is to win a way for her own will by a crafty self-control and a refined dissimulation:

> "She who can love a sister's charms, or hear
> Sighs for a daughter with unwounded ear;
> She who ne'er answers till a husband cools,
> Or if she rules him, never shows she rules;

Charms by accepting, by submitting sways,
Yet has her humour most when she obeys."

When the household emotion of filial piety got the better of the worldly want of feeling and the artifices of society, Pope's heart spoke in the lines alluding to his mother, beautiful for their truth of feeling:

"Oh, friend, may each domestic bliss be thine!
Be no unpleasing melancholy mine!
Me let the tender office long engage
To rock the cradle of declining age;
With lenient arts extend a mother's breath—
Make languor smile, and smooth the bed of death,
Explore the thought, explain the asking eye,
And keep at least one parent from the sky."

There was an influence over the mind of Pope, which must be alluded to as belonging to the literary history of the times: I refer to the overshadowing and malignant influence of the friendship of Lord Bolingbroke—a man whose brilliant talents do not redeem his memory from the reproach of corrupt statesmanship, and the more enduring agency of evil which he exercised as one of the leading deistical writers of the eighteenth century. That influence often intercepted the light of revelation. You may see not unfrequently playing on the surface of Pope's fancy the shadows that were cast by the restless leaves of the poison-tree of a godless philosophy.*

* It may be hazardous, even as a matter of criticism, to express an opinion favourable to Bolingbroke, yet no one can read a page of his matchless English—any page taken at random from that greatest of political apologies, the letter to Wyndham—without enthusiastic admiration of his art of style, and without admitting it to be the perfection of written eloquence. Such is the opinion of Lord Mahon in his excellent delineation of his character. (*History of England*, vol. ii. p. 27.) Another writer of our day says justly: "The best test to use,

No company of writers has sunk into such general and merited oblivion as the British infidels, who were the precursors of the French skeptics in the last century. We look back with somewhat of wonder and dismay at the extent of the influence they exerted for a considerable time over the minds of their countrymen in an advanced stage of intellectual refinement. It had its sway over the most cultivated classes of society, the court, the men of letters, but happily had less effect on what is less heard of—the simple piety which never died out in the quiet parish churches of the land, and was cherished at many a lowly hearth. In the prouder spheres of society, and in literature, deism and all the motley mockery of unbelief had an almost unresisted power. I know of no sadder sentence in English literature, than that in which Bishop Butler, in the preface to his great defence of revealed religion, remarks, "It is come, I know not how, to be taken for granted by many persons, that Christianity is

---

before we adopt any opinion or assertion of Bolingbroke's, is to consider whether in writing it he was treating of Sir Robert Walpole or revealed religion. On other occasions he may be followed with advantage, as he always may be read with pleasure." *Creasy's Battles of the World*, vol. ii. p. 158. Surely He must always be regarded reverentially, as a master of English rhetoric, whom Burke studied, whose lost speeches the younger Pitt mourned as the greatest loss to modern letters, and of whom a writer like Chesterfield said, "Till I read Bolingbroke, I confess I did not know all the extent and power of the English language." Bad as were his religious opinions, they do not seem to have degenerated to the low atheistic level which some of his contemporaries reached. "When I took my last farewell of him," writes Lord Chesterfield, "he returned his last farewell with tenderness, and said, 'God, who placed me here, will do what he pleases with me hereafter; and he knows best what to do. May he bless you!'" W. B. R.

not so much as a subject of inquiry; but that it is now, at length, discovered to be fictitious. And accordingly they treat it as if, in the present age, this were an agreed point among all people of discernment; and nothing remained but to set it up as a principal subject of mirth and ridicule, as it were by way of reprisals, for its having so long interrupted the pleasures of the world."*

This was said in 1736, and to such a state of things no man contributed more than Henry St. John, Viscount Bolingbroke, he whom Pope, in the poem which professed to be his philosophical poem—"The Essay on Man"—has apostrophized as his "genius," "master of the poet and the song," his "guide, philosopher, and friend."

The middle of the eighteenth century presents English literature, and especially its poetry, reduced to its lowest estate. Those who followed Pope, to imitate him without his powers, rendered the poetry of that period tame, trite, mechanical, and monotonous in versification. What the middle of the last century has to be proud of is, Dr. Johnson's colossal work, the first great Dictionary of our language.

The last half of the century is an era of the revival of English poetry—a revival which began indeed somewhat earlier with Thomson, but which was carried on by Gray, and by Collins, and Goldsmith, and Cowper, and another whose peasant hand was a fit one to bring poetry back to nature again—Robert Burns, who led the muse into the open fields once more, to look on the flowers, and most of all, that one which "glinted forth" to delight his age, as it used to do Chaucer's, four hundred years before. We feel

* Advertisement to the first edition to Butler's Analogy, p. 48.

that we are getting out of a close atmosphere and an artificial light into the open air and sunshine again, when, passing from the previous versifiers, we come to Burns, and see that it was

"Mid 'lonely heights and hows'
He paid to Nature, tuneful vows;
Or wiped his honourable brows
Bedewed with toil,
While reapers strove, or busy ploughs
Upturned the soil."

Connected with one of the names I have mentioned as of the revivers of a truer spirit of English poetry, there is an incident of much interest, the memory of which was recovered a few years ago, and which serves to mark the period of a favourite poem. The incident has been introduced by Lord Mahon, in his admirable History of England, and I cannot do better than use his words. On the night of the 13th of September, 1759, the night before the battle on the Plains of Abraham was to give to Wolfe the fame of the Conqueror of Canada, the English general passed along the St. Lawrence, with a portion of his army in boats; the historian proceeds: "Swiftly, but silently, did the boats fall down with the tide, unobserved by the enemy's sentinels at their posts along the shore. Of the soldiers on board, how eagerly must every heart have throbbed at the coming conflict! how intently must every eye have contemplated the dark outline, as it lay pencilled upon the midnight sky, and as every moment it grew closer and clearer, of the hostile heights! Not a word was spoken—not a sound heard beyond the rippling of the stream. Wolfe alone—thus tradition has told us—repeated in a low voice to the other officers in his boat those beautiful stanzas with which a country church-yard inspired the muse of Gray. One noble line

'The paths of glory lead but to the grave'—

must have seemed at such a moment fraught with mournful meaning. At the close of the recitation, Wolfe added, 'Now, gentlemen, I would rather be the author of that poem than take Quebec!' "*

Of Gray, and Goldsmith, and Cowper this is also to be remembered—that they have enriched the literature with *prose* as attractive as their poetry. It would be hard to say in which respect Goldsmith is most agreeably and affectionately remembered—as the author of "*The Deserted Village*," or of "*The Vicar of Wakefield*." Besides, the letters of Gray, our epistolary literature received its largest contributions in these two collections, equally characteristic of the writers, and very different in their tone—the letters of Horace Walpole, covering more than half a century, filled with political and private gossip, and sparkling with the wit of an acute man of the world, in the midst of the world's busiest society—and the letters of Cowper, partly by virtue of his exquisite English, and partly by the purity and earnestness of his character, and his gentle humour, giving a charm that is indescribable to the simple incidents and occupations of his secluded life, and that places his letters with the most agreeable reading in English literature. The historical literature of the century I reserve for a connection in which I propose to speak of it hereafter.

In the revival of English poetry which I have been

---

* History of England, vol. iv. p. 163. One of Mr. Reed's modest literary labours was an American edition, with notes, of Lord Mahon's early volumes. The notes were illustrative, and very judicious. Had his life been spared, he would probably have completed the edition.

W. B. R.

speaking of, an auxiliary influence was exerted by the restoration of the early minstrelsy in Percy's Reliques. That popular poetry was made familiar to reading men, and its simple power helped English poetry to recover not only its natural graces, but the best freedom and variety of its music. Cowper caught the free movement of verse in his well-known comic ballad of John Gilpin, and not less in the tragic one—that simple and noble Dirge, on the remarkable casualty of the sinking of the Royal George at her moorings:

"Toll for the brave!
The brave that are no more!
All sunk beneath the wave,
Fast by their native shore!

Eight hundred of the brave,
Whose courage well was tried,
Had made the vessel keel,
And laid her on her side.

A land-breeze shook the shrouds,
And she was overset:
Down went the Royal George,
With all her crew complete.

Toll for the brave!
Brave Kempenfelt is gone;
His last sea-fight is fought,
His work of glory done.

It was not in the battle;
No tempest gave the shock;
She sprang no fatal leak;
She ran upon no rock.

His sword was in the sheath;
His fingers held the pen,
When Kempenfelt went down
With twice four hundred men.

Weigh the vessel up,
  Once dreaded by our foes!
And mingle with our cup
  The tear that England owes.

Her timbers yet are sound,
  And she may float again,
Full charged with England's thunder,
  And plough the distant main.

But Kempenfelt is gone,
  His victories are o'er;
And he, and his eight hundred,
  Shall plough the wave no more."

No poet of the last century did as much as Cowper for the restoration of the admirable music of the then neglected blank verse. When Cowper died, in the year 1800, exactly one hundred years after the death of Dryden, English poetry was again in possession of all its varied endowment of verse. In a course of lectures which I delivered here some ten years ago, I concluded a lecture on Cowper by quoting a poem then new and little known—the stanzas entitled "*Cowper's Grave*," by Elizabeth Browning, then known by her maiden name of Barrett. While I have avoided, as far as possible, repetitions from my former courses, I am tempted to repeat the stanzas now, because on the former occasion they made, as I have been informed, an impression that was not lost. The merit of the poem is not only in the happy allusions to Cowper's character and career of checkered cheerfulness and gloom, but also in its depth of passion and imagination.

COWPER'S GRAVE.

It is a place where poets crowned
  May feel the heart's decaying—
It is a place where happy saints
  May weep amid their praying—

Yet let the grief and humbleness,
  As low as silence, languish;
Earth surely now may give her calm
  To whom she gave her anguish.

O poets! from a maniac's tongue
  Was poured the deathless singing!
O Christians! at your cross of hope
  A hopeless hand was clinging!
O men! this man in brotherhood,
  Your weary paths beguiling,
Groaned inly while he taught you peace,
  And died while ye were smiling!

And now, what time ye all may read
  Through dimming tears his story—
How discord on the music fell,
  And darkness on the glory—
And how, when, one by one, sweet sounds
  And wandering lights departed,
He wore no less a loving face,
  Because so broken-hearted—

He shall be strong to sanctify
  The poet's high vocation,
And bow the meekest Christian down
  In meeker adoration:
Nor ever shall he be in praise
  By wise or good forsaken:
Named softly, as the household name
  Of one whom God hath taken.

With quiet sadness, and no gloom,
  I learn to think upon him;
With meekness that is gratefulness,
  To God whose heaven hath won him—
Who suffered once the madness-cloud,
  To his own love to blind him;
But gently led the blind along
  Where breath and bird could find him:

And wrought within his shattered brain
  Such quick poetic senses,
As hills have language for, and stars
  Harmonious influences!
The pulse of dew upon the grass
  Kept his within its number;
And silent shadows from the trees
  Refreshed him like a slumber.

Wild timid hares were drawn from woods
  To share his home caresses,
Uplooking to his human eyes
  With sylvan tendernesses:
The very world, by God's constraint,
  From falsehood's ways removing,
Its women and its men became,
  Beside him, true and loving!—

But while, in blindness he remained
  Unconscious of the guiding,
And things provided came without
  The sweet sense of providing,
He testified this solemn truth,
  Though frenzy-desolated—
Nor man nor nature satisfy,
  Whom only God created!

Like a sick child that knoweth not
  His mother while she blesses,
And drops upon his burning brow
  The coolness of her kisses;
That turns his fever'd eyes around—
  "My mother! where's my mother?"—
As if such tender words and looks
  Could come from any other!—

The fever gone, with leaps of heart
  He sees her bending o'er him;
Her face all pale from watchful love,
  The unweary love she bore him!

Thus woke the poet from the dream
  His life's long fever gave him,
Beneath those deep pathetic Eyes,
  Which closed in death to save him.

Thus! oh, not thus! no type of earth
  Could image that awaking,
Wherein he scarcely heard the chaunt
  Of seraphs round him breaking—
Or felt the new immortal throb
  Of soul from body parted;
But felt those eyes alone, and knew
  "My Saviour! not deserted!"

Deserted! who hath dreamt that when
  The cross in darkness rested
Upon the Victim's hidden face,
  No love was manifested?
What frantic hands outstretched have e'er
  The atoning drops averted—
What tears have washed them from the soul—
  That *one* should be deserted?

Deserted! God could separate
  From his own essence rather:
And Adam's sins *have* swept between
  The righteous Son and Father;
Yea! once Immanuel's orphaned cry
  His universe hath shaken—
It went up single, echoless,
  "My God, I am forsaken!"

It went up from the Holy's lips
  Amid his lost creation,
That of the lost, no son should use
  Those words of desolation;
That, earth's worst frenzies, marring hope,
  Should mar not hope's fruition;
And I, on Cowper's grave, should see
  His rapture, in a vision!

LECTURE VIII.*

Literature of the Nineteenth Century.

Literature of our own times—Influence of political and social relations—The historic relations of literature—The French Revolution, and its effects—Infidelity—Thirty years' Peace—Scientific progress coincident with letters—History—Its altered tone—Arnold—Prescott—Niebuhr—Gibbon—Hume—Robertson—Religious element in historical style—Lord Mahon—Macaulay's History—Historical romance—Waverley Novels—The pulpit—Sydney Smith—Manning—Poetry of the early part of the century—Bowles and Rogers—Campbell—Coleridge's Christabel—Lay of the Last Minstrel—Scott's poetry.

In my last lecture, I noticed the date of the death of Cowper, in the year 1800, as conveniently marking the close of the literature of the eighteenth century. The excellence of his prose, as well as of his poetry, and his share in that literary revival which began during the latter part of that century, make such a use of his name subservient, in a reasonable rather than an arbitrary manner, to the purposes of literary chronology. We pass thence into what may be entitled "The Literature of our own Times," or, having nearly completed its era of fifty years, "The Literature of the first half of the Nineteenth Century." It has its characteristics—distinctive qualities, with their origin from within, in the minds of those whose writings make the literature, and from without, in the influence exerted on those minds by the world's doings

* January 21, 1850.

and the world's condition. In the study of literature, it is needful, for our knowledge of it, to look at it in its relation to civil and political history, in order to understand how, in a greater or less degree, it takes a colour from the times. The mind of no author can dwell so aloof from his generation that his thoughts and feelings shall be above or beyond outward influences. He is more or less *what* he is, because he is *where* he is. These outward influences affect genius of the highest order, with this difference, indeed, that they do not limit or control it, but, by its own inborn power, it carries them up, idealized, into the highest truth for the perpetual good of all after time.

Looking back to the early and distant eras of English literature, it is not difficult to trace the relations between the literature and the national history—the record of words and the record of actions and events. The full and varied outburst of poetry, grave and gay, in Chaucer, becomes a more intelligible phenomenon when we think of it in association with the chivalry, the enterprise, and the cultivation of Edward the Third's long and glorious reign. The genius of Spenser and the genius of Shakspeare shine with a clearer light when our eyes look at it as issuing from the Elizabethan age—that age strenuous with thoughts and acts, chivalrous, philosophical, adventurous, of whose great men it might be said, as it was said of one of them, that they were so contemplative you could not believe them active, and so active you could not believe them contemplative. Milton's great epic seems, at first thought, strangely uncongenial to the immediate period of its appearance ; but ceases to be so when it is thought of as engendered in those years of ordeal through which Milton's mind had passed in the times of the Civil War, the Commonwealth, and the Protectorate. The age that Dryden lived in left a more unresisted impress on his genius—the stamp of a degenerate and dissolute generation; and the pages of Pope have their commentary in the reflection they give of an artificial and sophisticated state of society—an age of wits and freethinkers; so that when his genius rose to its most imaginative strain, it could not content itself with a theme less stimulant than the revolting story of Abelard and Eloisa.

When we come to the study of the literature of our own times, it is, of course, more difficult to trace the historic relation of literature, because it is the literature of our own times—times which have not yet become a part of history. We stand too near them—are, indeed, too much in them—to see them clearly, dispassionately, to measure the prevailing influences, and understand them justly. We cannot yet adventure to speak of the literature of this century as hereafter they may do who shall look back to it from a distance, when time, and the calm judgments time brings along with it, shall group the authors of these times in their true places; and when the narrowness of contemporary partiality, or, what is worse, contemporary prejudice, shall be expanded to a larger wisdom.

We cannot err in this, that the half century, now nearly completed, has been distinguished by great intellectual and imaginative activity. The revival, which began in the latter part of the last century, was, in a great measure, the reaction from the overwrought artifice and formality of thought, and feeling, and expression of the times that had gone before. The hearts of men began to assert once more their claims to what Nature could give them, and the poets, who are Nature's interpreters. Other agencies, besides the simple power of reaction, were at work on the European mind, giving it an impulse to break through old and contracted conventional restraints, calling forth freer movements of thought and feeling. I refer especially to the general agitation throughout Europe consequent on the French Revolution. Change was the condition of the closing years of the last century. Things which had endured for ages were perishing, not by slow gradations of decay, but by quick and unlooked-for violence. Time-honoured institutions were not suffered to attain the limit of their natural existence, and then to sink under the gradual accumulation of years, but were swiftly swept away by a new compulsion. The clenched hand of prescriptive tyranny was forced to loose its grasp; and if simpler generations of men, in the olden time, had held to the fond belief that

> "Not all the water in the rough, rude sea
> Can wash the balm from an anointed king,"

men of the new times were ready to shed the blood of king and queen with pitiless contempt. The people in one of the central monarchies of Europe had suddenly started up, and, casting away respect for prerogative, boldly questioned the authority of a power which so long had trampled on them. Men began to ask why the bounties of heaven should be garnered up for the bloated luxury of the few, while the many were pining, hungry and heart-stricken. The sympathies of Christendom were, for a season, enlisted; and the pulse of other nations began to beat quicker. The French Revolution began to assume the aspect of a general European revolution. Ancient opinions and rules of life were abandoned, and new modes of thought and feeling took their place. The political revolution became an intellectual and moral one; for, so entire was the subversion of old institutions, that in reconstructing society, men were led to speculate on its very elements, and on the principles and destiny of human nature—speculations which, from a revolutionary forsaking of the old paths, too often fostered a self-sufficient and faithless philosophy. It was not as in the American Revolution, in which our fathers, not clamorous for new privileges, were the defenders of old rights—rights as ancient as the Great Charter, advocates of the Constitution and the freedom it gave, the "good old cause." But in the revolutionary agitation that attended the French Revolution, new creeds of liberty were taught, new doctrines of the rights of man. Christianity, with its day of sanctity and repose, sacred from the Creation, was banished to make way for a sensual, brutalizing atheism, with its tenth-day holidays, (I cannot call them Sabbaths,) and with its idolatry of human reason. Theories of ecclesiastical, political, and social regeneration were propagated with apostolic zeal into all lands—doctrines which cast a shadow on the spire of every village-church, and which, while they gave some wild hopes to the down-trodden and the desperate, struck dismay where the domestic virtues were grouped at the once secure and happy fireside. It was a commotion of the very primal elements of society. The scene was a new one—suddenly a new one—in the drama of civilization: the power of strange rights was thrust into the hands of men; the burden of strange duties was harnessed on their backs. Ancient landmarks, covered with the moss of many years, were torn up. The guidance of principles, drawn not from any customary or conventional authority, but from the depths of human nature, was needed alike for those who hailed and those who abhorred the change. Men long accustomed to float on the placid waters of a river, within sight and reach of safe and smiling shores, found themselves suddenly driven out upon a stormy and shoreless sea; and, in their peril, some were earnestly gazing for a beacon-light from the lost coast, others were idly gazing at the flashing fires that crest the dark billows of the deep, and a few were looking upward hopefully for some star in the clouded sky. The agitation of the times carried some minds into the delusions of sophistry and irreverence, but it also led others into deeper moods of thought and larger sympathies. Superficial precepts, whether in government, philosophy, or literature, were not enough; but there was needed what should deal with human nature with a deeper and truer wisdom. This influence, either direct or indirect, extended over all departments of thought and action, and thus made its impression on European literature, on English literature, for the perturbation of the times stirred the mind of England, though it did not shake her ancient constitution.

When I speak of the agitation consequent on the French Revolution, I include all that forms the historic era, the revolution itself, the wars of the republic, and the wars of the French Empire; in short, the quarter of a century of tumult and war which closed in 1815 with the battle of Waterloo. It has been followed by the thirty years' peace, the longest period of tranquillity in modern history —perhaps I may say, in the world's history. The increased activity and independence of thought that attended the political convulsions of Europe, and even then found expression in literature, continued, and indeed expanded still further, in the more genial years of peace that followed.*

This half century, in which our lot has been cast, has been unquestionably one of great and varied intellectual activity, distinguished by achievements in the two chief departments of thought and inquiry, science and literature. Never perhaps have they been cultivated in truer proportion, and they have moved forward with harmonious progress, giving to mankind the various elements of civilization and improvement which are respectively in the gift of science and literature. In this connection, one cannot but feel how fortunate, how providential it was that the wonderful results of physical science which this century has witnessed were not accomplished in the last century, at a time when a low state of religious opinion was prevailing, when skepticism was dominant in literature; for at such a time the victories of science over the powers of the material universe, instead of raising our sense of the Creator's power, and inspiring that humility which true science ever cherishes, the more deeply at every advance it makes—instead of this, an age of unbelief, whose literature had divorced itself from revelation, would have been ready to use the results of science to decoy men into that insidious atheism which substitutes Nature for God, and would have entangled our spiritual nature in the meshes of materialism. The truest culti-

* Since these words were written, peace, European peace, is no more, and new names of bloody note are adding to the catalogue of modern battles. Alma and Inkermann are the last and bloodiest. And who, in reading these lectures on the Poetry and Literature of our language, can hesitate to give his sympathy to those who are fighting the battle of civilization? W. B. R.

vation of science and the truest cultivation of literature in our day have shown this harmony, that alike for the scientific and the literary study of man and nature—for the naturalist, for instance, and the poet—there is needed the same spirit of humble, willing, dutiful inquiry, a power of recipiency as well as of search. The man of science, and the poet equally, will miss the truth, if either the one or the other be such as has been described as the man who "grows to deal boldly with nature, instead of reverently following her guidance; who seals his heart against her secret influences; who has a theory to maintain, a solution which shall not be disturbed; and once possessed of this false cipher, he reads amiss all the golden letters round him."*

The intellectual activity of the nineteenth century has been displayed in a very extended and various literature, in prose and poetry, and in literature on each side of the Atlantic. With no disposition to magnify the present at the expense of the past, it may, I believe, be safely said, in an estimate of the literature of this century, that in some departments it has excelled that of the previous centuries. This is especially the case in historic literature, for never heretofore in English letters has there been so true a conception of an historian's duties, so deep a sense of the difficulties of his story, and at the same time such hopefulness of its powers. It is far better understood now than heretofore, that in order to reconstruct the testimonies of the past, so as to make not only a record but a picture of the men that lived in the past

* The marginal reference in pencil here is to Bishop Wilberforce, but I am unable to verify it. W. B. R.

and the events that belong to it, the historian must possess some of the knowledge of the statesman and of the powers of the poet and philosopher. In no respect has historical literature been more improved than in the thorough and laborious processes of research which are now demanded at the historian's hands. Thus various tracts in the world's history, known formerly with a sort of careless familiarity, have been admirably reclaimed by the better cultivation, which is rewarded with the recovery of abundant materials neglected by an indolent generation. It is such dutiful and laborious research, united with other high qualifications, which has placed our countryman, Mr. Prescott, among the best historians in our times.

Nor is it only by more accurate methods of research that this department of literature is now distinguished. A deeper philosophy of history has entered into it. The historic sagacity of Niebuhr may be considered as having led the way in those processes which give him almost the fame of a discoverer, and which have been followed out in the history of antiquity by English as well as French historians; so that it may be said, that within the last twenty years the whole history of Greece and Rome has been not only reconstructed, but fashioned into a more life-like reality. Hannibal's campaign in Italy, in the posthumous volume of Arnold's History of Rome, is as vivid a narrative as could be given of one of Napoleon's or Wellington's campaigns.

It is in these particulars, laborious and accurate research and use of historical materials, and in a better science of history, that the later writers have entitled themselves to a reputation so much worthier than that of the best-known historians in the last century. Of those historians, Gibbon is the only one whose history preserves to this day its authority, on the score of such extensive research and deep learning as were required by his large theme. With regard to Hume and Robertson, the two most popular historians, the labours of later students of history have demonstrated that their works are of that indolent and superficial character which destroys their authority as trustworthy chroniclers. I do not suppose that any careful and conscientious inquirer after historic truth would at the present day consider a question of history determined by a statement in the histories of either Hume or Robertson.*

Another and a very high merit may be claimed for history in the English literature of our times: I mean the religious element which has been developed in it, and most of all by Arnold. This is a noble contrast to the aggressive infidelity, and the low and false views attendant on it, which vitiates the histories of Gibbon and Hume, corrupting the learning of the former, and coupling a positive

* As this volume is passing through the press, my eye has been attracted by two contemporary criticisms, though from very different sources, on Gibbon and Hume; the one by Lord John Russell, in a recent speech at Bristol, the other by Landor in a poetical contribution to the Examiner. The first I have not space to quote or to refer to, further than to say it is precisely in accord with Mr. Reed's criticism. Of the other, I can cite but a few lines. Of Gibbon the poet well says:

"There are who blame them for too stately step,
And words resounding from inflated cheek.
Words have their proper places, just like men.
I listen to, nor venture to reprove,
Large language swelling under gilded domes—
Byzantine, Syrian, Persepolitan."

And he concludes:

"History hath beheld no pile ascend
So lofty, large, symmetrical as thine." W. B. R.

evil with the defects of the latter; so that history was made a godless, infidel study, subservient to the shallow skepticism of the eighteenth century. With minds blinded to Christian truth, and tempers alien from all Christian earnestness, they looked upon religious feeling as either fraud or superstition, and so they spoke of it in the narrative of portions of the world's history in which the Christian church was leading the nations of Europe to the truth.

It is not only in such offensive, assailant unbelief, as Gibbon's and Hume's, that history has been in fault, but there has also been the negative fault of the omission of all thought of a providential government and guidance of the nations of the earth. We are thus tempted to draw too broad a line between sacred and profane history, and to fancy that there was a providence over the one chosen people, but that all the kindred peoples of the earth were abandoned to chance, to fate, to any thing but the government of God. Now Arnold's great achievement in historical science is, that in treating the history of a pagan people, he gives to his reader a sense of a divine providence over the Roman nation, for the future service of Christian truth, at the same time that this religious element is not irreverently obtruded or mingled with incongruous subjects. When Hume, in his History, reaches the end of a splendid era in the English annals, he closes it with this meagre reflection, "that the study of the early institutions of the country is instructive as showing that a mighty fabric of government is built up by a great deal of accident, with a very little human foresight and wisdom." In our meek hours of faith we are taught that not a sparrow falls to the ground without God's providence; and then we turn to the infidel history, to be admonished that the "kingly commonwealth" of England, that has swayed the happiness of millions of human beings, and from which sprang this vast Republic of the West, was "built up by accident;" that there was a little human foresight, and all the rest was *chance.*

When Arnold was planning his history, he said, "My ighest ambition . . . is to make my history the very reverse of Gibbon in this respect, that whereas the whole spirit of his work, from its low morality, is hostile to religion, without speaking directly against it; so my greatest desire would be, in my history, by its high morals and its general tone, to be of use to the cause, without actually bringing it forward."*

Besides this high quality, another merit of recent historical literature is, that it has modified what used to be called the "dignity of history," and has blended with it more of the lively interest of biography. An excellent specimen of such historical composition, an accurate, calmly-tempered, and attractive history, will be found in Lord Mahon's History of England during an important part of the last century.†

In this department of literature the greatest power of attraction has been proved in the first volumes of Mr. Macaulay's History of England, for they have won a far larger number of readers, it is believed, than did any one of the Waverley novels in Scott's palmiest day. Such

* Life and Correspondence, p. 139, Am. ed.

† There is no work that can be more safely put in the hands of the American historical student than Lord Mahon's, not only for its tolerant and philosophic views of English affairs, but as enabling a reasonable American to feel and understand how his own history appears to a generous and friendly foreign observer. Such a process is very salutary in this self-complacent meridian. W. B. R.

rapid and wide-spread popularity is proof of power, the measure of which will be taken more accurately after the lapse of some years than now, when it is new to us. Mr. Macaulay's aim, as an historian, is to bring into history a greater number and variety of the testimonies of the life of the past than history has been in the habit of taking cognizance of. With great powers of accumulating such multifarious memorials of former times, with a dexterous skill in combining them, and with a brilliant, effective style, he has gained such applause as, perhaps, was never given to historian before. It is most attractive and exciting reading—the more delightful, if you can lull to sleep all questioning of truthfulness, and can bring your mind to a passive, submissive recipiency of Mr. Macaulay's absolute and contemptuous condemnation of characters you might otherwise have been inclined to honour or respect. There are few writers who exact from the reader such unquestioning obedience—obedience, too, to sarcasm and scorn. It has been justly said that an historian's first "great qualification is an earnest craving after truth, and utter impatience, not of falsehood merely, but of error."* I would ask any reader of this work, even with the fresh fascination on him, whether, on closing the volumes, he feels an assurance of the presence there of such an earnest craving after truth. Mr. Macaulay has another ambition, fostered, perhaps, by his habit of writing as a reviewer, and not yet duly disciplined in him—the ambition, or, as it may be more fitly called, the vanity of showy and startling display. Of the majestic beauty of quiet and simple truth he seems to have no conception. His moral and intellectual nature seem not to be justly balanced. This

* Arnold's Lectures on Modern History, p. 293.

appears in another form of intellectual pride—an absence of all genial appreciation of lofty character—heroic or saintly—an unbelief in high and earnest moods of thought and feeling, and a pride of power in despoiling men of the sentiments of reverence and admiration they had been glad to bestow. The more habitual those sentiments have been, the greater the power displayed in scattering them. If Mr. Macaulay should carry his history on to that period when it will be necessary for him to treat of what he has not as yet thought it worth while to allude to, colonial America, as part of England's history, and when he will have occasion to speak of Washington and Franklin, I venture to predict that the temptation to bid the world abate their admiration will be irresistible; and that then some of Mr. Macaulay's American admirers, who are now rather intolerant of the least dissent, will fain recall some of their present praises.

It is an easy transition from the historical literature to another department, scarce separable from it, and in which, also, this century is entitled to a pre-eminence. I refer to the "historic romance," especially as developed in the Waverley novels. Scott may be said to have created this new department of English letters. Never has the true idea of historic fiction been more happily seized—the calling up, in a living array, not merely the names, but the character, the manners, the thoughts and passions of past ages. Two of the finest historical minds of our times, Arnold in England and Thierry in France, have expressed their high admiration of Scott's remarkable historic sagacity. With studious and laborious habits of research, he had large-hearted sympathies, an acute instinct of historic truth, and, above all, the truthful creative power of imagination; which powers combined, enabled him to achieve in prose literature what Shakspeare, with like originality, had accomplished in historical poetry, by his chronicle plays and the tragedies of Greek and Roman story.

Apart from their historical value, the Waverley Series raised a far higher and truer standard of novel writing than had been known before; giving, instead of the vapid sentimentalism and the romantic extravagance and folly which had been in fashion, good sense and genuine feeling, humanity's true character, with its passions, its weaknesses, its virtues, and its heroism, and a company of life-like impersonations of womanly character, from the throne to the cottage. The services Scott did would be better appreciated by comparison with the common run of novels in vogue some forty or fifty years ago, which Charles Lamb has described as "those scanty intellectual viands of the whole female reading public, till a happier genius arose and expelled forever the innutritious phantoms in which the brain was 'betossed,' the memory puzzled, the sense of when and where confounded among the improbable events, the incoherent incidents, the inconsistent characters, or no characters, of some third-rate love intrigue; . . . persons neither of this world nor of any other conceivable one; an endless string of activities without purpose, of purposes destitute of motive."*

This description of novels ceased to be tolerable to the improved taste which Scott created, and the effect of which was immediate and manifest. There is perhaps reason to apprehend that the good influence has begun to wear away, and that another revolution in novel

* Essay on the Sanity of True Genius. Prose Works, vol. iii. p. 81.

literature is going on—an appetite for more stimulant fiction being fostered, partly by corrupt foreign influences, and also by the craving for something more exciting than a just and pure imagination gives.

The literature of our times has been very abundant and often excellent in a variety of miscellaneous prose literature. In pulpit oratory, voices have been heard that bring back the sound of the sacred eloquence of England in the age of her great divines.

Looking to our English prose as an instrument of expression, it may be said to have been brought in our times to a high state of excellence, for in our contemporary literature it is possible to find passages—characteristic passages—which bear comparison with the best English prose of any former period, combining indeed with the merits of the earlier prose new powers suited to the new uses that the progress of a people's mind demands. A high order of excellence of English prose, both as to the choice of words, the structure and the rhythm of the sentences, is a much rarer attainment than people are apt to suppose. It is of such high excellence that I speak, when I say that in our contemporary literature it is to be found in the prose of Arnold, of Southey, of Sydney Smith, and of Byron, and Landor, and in the sermons of Manning. A high authority in English philology places the prose of Landor as first among living authors;—the prose in the "Imaginary Conversations," a work of great but very unequal merit, and also in some smaller productions.

The poetic literature of this half century has displayed an abundance that proves an imaginative activity equal to the intellectual activity of our times. We are apt sometimes to yield to the notion that our modern days are unpoetic, and that the sphere of imagination has been contracted by the influences of later times. But when this half century shall be looked back to from a distance, the judgment of posterity cannot but be that it was distinguished by great poetic fertility and power—a period that has produced many elaborate poems of a high order, and a large amount of such minor poetry, as may be seen, when such poetry is good, shining in modest beauty in the same sky with the larger luminaries. Considering the number of poets who have been successful in their appropriate spheres, the amount, the variety, and the merit of the poetry which the nineteenth century has already given to English literature, it may be more fitly compared with the Elizabethan age, rich as it was in the company of poets, than with any other period of our language. Indeed it may be added, that one cause of literary power in our times is to be discovered in this, that never before has there been such dutiful zeal for the revival and restoration of the elder literature; never before has that literature been so carefully and reverently studied. The best criticism on Shakspeare, on Spenser, on Milton, is that which this century has produced; and within the same time has there been the most earnest desire to promote the study of Bacon and the great divines.

In attempting to group, with reference to time, the poets of the present century—the poets of our own times—some curious considerations at once present themselves. It is now more than a quarter of a century since the death of Byron and of Shelley, both poets of a younger generation than Wordsworth; and we begin to think of them as belonging to past times, while the elder poet survives, now in his eightieth year. But what is more remarkable, there are living two poets, who were known as poets when Wordsworth was a youth—Bowles and Rogers, each on the verge of fourscore and ten. It seems scarcely credible that there should be living now a poet (I refer to Mr. Rogers) whose first poem was published sixty-four years ago, in 1786, fourteen years before the death of Cowper, (whom he has survived half a century,) and within a twelvemonth after the publication of the Task.* A subsequent poem of Rogers, "The Pleasures of Memory," a subject of universal interest agreeably presented, established his reputation, and was no doubt the prompting of Campbell's poem on "Hope." Rogers' higher poetic power is, however, to be found in a later work, which, appearing at a time when new poets had gained the public ear, never attained the same popularity as his earlier poem, which was more fortunate in its time. From the poem—I allude to the "Italy"—I am tempted to cite one passage for the sake of the fine picture it gives of an occurence of which I made a passing mention in a former lecture—the interview of Galileo and Milton:

"Nearer we hail
Thy sunny slope, Arcetri, sung of old
For its green vine, dearer to me, to most,
As dwelt on by that great astronomer,
Seven years a prisoner at the city-gate;
Let in but in his grave-clothes. Sacred be
His cottage, (justly was it called the Jewel,)
Sacred the vineyard, where while yet his sight
Glimmer'd, at blush of dawn, he dress'd his vines,
Chaunting aloud in gayety of heart

* This was written in 1850, and now, in 1855, this aged poet still lives, the survivor of him who thus spoke of him. W. B. R.

Some verse of Ariosto. There, unseen,
In manly beauty, Milton stood before him,
Gazing with reverent awe, Milton his guest,
Just then come forth, all life and enterprise;
He in his old age and extremity,
Blind, at noonday exploring with his staff,
His eyes upturned as to the golden sun,
His eyeballs idly rolling. Little then
Did Galileo think whom he bade welcome,
That in his hand he held the hand of one
Who could requite him, who would spread his name
O'er lands and seas; great as himself, nay greater:
Milton, as little, that in him he saw,
As in a glass, what he himself should be;
Destined so soon to fall on evil days
And evil tongues; so soon, alas! to live
In darkness, and with dangers compassed round,
And solitude."*

Of the other aged poet, William Lisle Bowles, who has survived so many of his brother bards, I can only remark, in so cursory a survey of the contemporary literature as this must be, that Coleridge acknowledged a deep obligation to his poems—a tribute which in itself is proof of some beauty and power in them.

The most decided and marked influence of a contemporary production is that which is known to have been exerted by Coleridge's Christabel—an influence that may be traced on the genius of Scott, Shelley, and Byron. It was an influence that Scott acknowledged with all his characteristic frankness, and Byron too, though with more reserve, for it was not his habit to acknowledge or perhaps to recognise such influences. "Christabel" was circulated in manuscript many years before it was pub-

* Italy, p. 115.

lished; and, recited among the poets, it made, especially on their minds, an impression that proved an agency of poetic inspiration to them. Mr. Lockhart tells us that the casual recitation of "Christabel" in Scott's presence so "fixed the music of that noble fragment in his memory," that it prompted the production of the "Lay of the Last Minstrel."* It was a great lesson to the poets, in that it disclosed an unknown, or at least forgotten, freedom and power in English versification—a music the echoes of which are to be heard in the poems both of Scott and Byron. The grandeur of its imagery, too, moved the poets to whom it was made known, as in that sublime and familiar passage on a broken friendship:

"They stood aloof, the scars remaining,
Like cliffs which had been rent asunder;
A dreary sea now flows between;
But neither heat, nor frost, nor thunder,
Shall wholly do away, I ween,
The marks of that which once hath been."

"Christabel" proved its influence over the poetry that followed, by the power with which both the natural and the supernatural were imaged in it; in the latter respect, particularly, Scott felt the power of the poem. There is probably nothing finer of its kind in poetry than those passages which tell of the wicked might of witchcraft in the eye of the witch, who has assumed a beautiful human form: it is first felt as Christabel passes with her by the nearly extinct embers on the hall-hearth:

"They passed the hall that echoes still,
Pass as lightly as you will!
The brands were flat, the brands were dying,
Amid their own white ashes lying;

* Lockhart's Scott, vol. ii. p. 210.

But when the lady passed, there came
A tongue of light, a fit of flame;
And Christabel saw the lady's eye,
And nothing else saw she thereby,
Save the boss of the shield of Sir Leoline tall,
Which hung in a murky old niche in the wall."

And in that other passage, which shows the magic might of witchcraft in the witch's eye as she fascinates her mute victim with it, the shrinking up of the eye, the sudden dilation again when the look of innocence is counterfeited once more, and Christabel's unconscious imitation of the serpent-look that fascinated and appalled her:

"A snake's small eye blinks dull and shy,
And the lady's eyes they shrunk in her head—
Each shrunk up to a serpent's eye;
And with somewhat of malice, and more of dread,
At Christabel she looked askance!
One moment—and the sight was fled!
But Christabel in dizzy trance,
Stumbling on the unsteady ground;
Shuddered aloud, with a hissing sound.
And Geraldine again turned round;
And like a thing that sought relief,
Full of wonder and full of grief,
She rolled her large bright eyes divine
Wildly on Sir Leoline.

The maid, alas! her thoughts are gone;
She nothing sees—no sight but one!
The maid devoid of guile and sin,
I know not how, in fearful wise,
So deeply had she drunken in
That look, those shrunken serpent eyes,
That all her features were resigned
To this sole image in her mind;
And passively did imitate
That look of dull and treacherous hate!

And thus she stood, in dizzy trance,
Still picturing that look askance
With forced, unconscious sympathy,
Full before her father's view,
As far as such a look could be
In eyes so innocent and blue!
And when the trance was o'er, the maid
Paused awhile, and inly prayed:
Then falling at the Baron's feet,
'By my Mother's soul do I entreat
That thou this woman send away!'
She said: and more she could not say;
For what she knew she could not tell,
O'ermastered by the magic spell."

It is that description of the serpent-look of the witch's eyes that, being read in a company at Lord Byron's, so affected Shelley's sensitive fancy that he fainted.*

Along with the influence of this poem on the imagination of Walter Scott, there was blended the influence of his long-cherished and studious culture of the early minstrelsy, for which he laboured with patriotic as well as poetic zeal. The genius of Scott, thus wrought on, produced that series of poems which fills a large space in the poetic literature of the early part of this century. With much of Homeric animation, and with the pathos of Greek and British minstrel combined, he sung of the chivalry and the rude heroism of the olden time; and to those heroic lays there was given a popularity which was dimmed only by the sudden splendour of the speedy and

* In Moore's Life of Byron, vol. iv. p. 147, is the anecdote which I presume is referred to. Lord Byron was most earnest in his admiration of Christabel. His correspondence is full of it. "I won't have any one," he writes to Mr. Murray in 1816, "sneer at Christabel; it is a fine, wild poem." W. B. R.

more fervid popularity which was won by the genius of Byron.

There is nothing in literary biography finer than the composure, the magnanimity (rather let me call it) with which Scott, making up his mind that he was about to be supplanted in popular favour by a greater poet, tranquilly turned his genius to a new department of invention, in which, as it proved, no rival was to reach him. There is truth, too, in what Scott's biographer has said of this part of his career, that, "Appreciating, as a man of his talents could hardly fail to do, the splendidly original glow and depth of Childe Harold, Scott always appeared to me quite blind to the fact, that in the Giaour, in the Bride of Abydos, in Parisina, and, indeed, in all his early serious narratives, Byron owed at least half his success to clever, though perhaps unconscious, imitation of Scott, and no trivial share of the rest to the lavish use of materials which Scott never employed, only because his genius was, from the beginning to the end of his career, under the guidance of high and chivalrous feelings of moral rectitude."*

This last remark recalls the account given of a conversation of Scott, toward the close of his life, which may be mentioned before I pass to the name of Byron. Not long before Sir Walter's death, a friend remarked to him that he must derive consolation from the reflection that his popularity was not owing to works which, in his latter moments, he might wish recalled. Scott remained silent for a moment, with his eyes fixed on the ground. "When he raised them," says the narrator, "as he shook me by

* Lockhart's Scott, vol. v. p. 31.

the hand, I perceived the light-blue eye sparkling with unusual moisture; he added, 'I am drawing near the close of my career. I have been, perhaps, the most voluminous author of the day, and it *is* a comfort to me to think that I have tried to unsettle no man's faith, to corrupt no man's principle, and that I have written nothing which, on my death-bed, I should wish blotted."* In this utterance of dignified self-complacency, he stands justified by the story of his wondrous authorship. With regard to Scott's poetry, there are indications that, in the calmer judgment of posterity, the world is willing to restore a part, at least, of the fame it too quickly took away. It is only the other day that Landor, ranking Scott's poems with the *classics*, has said,

"The trumpet-blast of Marmion never shook
The walls of God-built Ilion; yet what shout
Of the Achaians swells the heart so high!"

In the concluding lecture I propose to proceed with the general considerations of the literature of this century—its chief productions and influences; among which I desire to speak of the character and influence of Lord Byron's poetry, the prose and poetry of Southey, the poetry of Wordsworth, the influence of Mr. Carlyle's writings, and also of some of the women who, both in prose and poetry, have adorned the literature of our times.

* Lockhart's Scott, vol. x. p. 196.

LECTURE IX.

Contemporary Literature.*

Lord Byron—His popularity and its decline—His power of simple, vigorous language—Childe Harold—The Dying Gladiator—The Isles of Greece—Contrast of Byron's and Shakspeare's creations—Miss Barrett—Miss Kemble's sonnet—Byron as a poet of nature—His antagonism to Divine Truth—The Dream, the most faultless of his poems—Don Juan—Shelley—Leigh Hunt's remarks on—Carlyle—His earnestness—Southey—His historical works—Thalaba—Wordsworth—His characteristics—Female authors—Joanna Baillie—Miss Edgeworth—Mrs. Kemble—Mrs. Norton—Miss Barrett—Cry of the children, &c.

In bringing this course of lectures toward a conclusion, I shall resume the cursory view of the contemporary English literature which I began in the last lecture. When the literary history of this period shall hereafter come to be written, a voluminous chapter will be needed for what the English language has given expression to within it. During the first quarter of this century, the writings of Lord Byron had the most high-wrought and wide-spread celebrity. His was the commanding name of the day for some ten or twelve years in the first quarter of this century. Scott, as a poet, calmly withdrew at the approach of the new influence. He had probably exhausted that fine, but not very deep, vein of poetry, which gained him a quick popularity and a permanent place among English poets; he withdrew from the region

* Thursday, February 28, 1850.

of verse to pass into those unexplored spaces of the imagination in which he was to establish his chief fame as the great writer of historical romance.

The popularity of Byron, take it for all in all, was probably the most splendid that ever poet was applauded and flattered with. His song had larger audience over the earth, and on that audience it exerted an unwonted fascination, swaying the feelings of multitudes, and making its words and its music familiar on their lips. It was popularity too quick grown to last without a large diminution; the love of his poetry was too passionate to stand the test of time. It is not worth while now to measure the extraneous causes which helped that popularity: his rank, his beauty, his audacity, the exposure of his domestic discord, his foreign adventures, half wanderer, half exile—all were elements in that fascination, wherewith all the world watched him and welcomed his words. Without meaning, in a lecture in which I have so much to dispose of, to dwell on the personal history of Lord Byron, let me only remark, in passing, how striking is the contrast between the husband's sentimental soliciting of the world's sympathies, along with a sensual defiance of all that is most sacred by the laws of God and of man; and, on the other hand, the heroic silence and self-control of the wife, and, along with it, a life of devoted and toilsome charity, in which she has sought the reparation of her hopes and happiness. Who can question which was the injured one?

The extraneous causes of Byron's popularity would be altogether inadequate to account for it. Much as they may have helped it, they alone never could have given it. Looking at it now as a matter of literary history, the true causes are to be discovered, I believe, both in the strength and in the weakness of his genius. If that strength had been less than it was, he could not have gained the influence he did over the minds of his fellow-men: if there had been less of weakness blended with his might, he would not have gained that influence so widely and so soon. Such is the paradox of poetic popularity. The same causes will explain the decline of Byron's influence. I mean the extent of that decline, furnishing a discrimination between what is permanent and what is perishable in his poetry. All that I propose to do is to notice some of the chief characteristics of his poetry, so as to judge thereby of its past popularity and the estimation it is now held in.

Lord Byron gained the public ear, in part, by his command of the simple Saxon part of the language. In his choice of words, he is one of the most idiomatic of the English poets: his genuine English is shown forth in his poetry and the vigorous prose style of his letters—the English-Latinized words being present in small proportion. This admirable command of the "best treasures" of our tongue was not, I think, accompanied with an equal power of structure and combination, in the absence of which there is betrayed the want of that studious and dutiful culture of the language and versification which the greatest of the poets recognise as part of their discipline, and to which, no doubt—the art and the inspiration combined—we owe both the exquisite graces of Shakspeare's verse and the magnificent harmonies of Spenser's and Milton's.

With such power over his language, as an organ of expression, Byron had other powers which are the poet's endowment; and the one and simple solution of his fame is his gift of imagination, accompanied with, or perhaps more truly including, fine poetic sensibilities. Now when these sensibilities were in a natural and healthy mood; when his heart was open to genuine influences, so that there was the true poetic sympathy between the inner world of spirit and the outer world of sense; when, in short, Nature had her will with this wayward child,—the utterance was a true and beautiful flow of poetic inspiration, as in that tranquil passage in Childe Harold:

"Clear, placid Leman! thy contrasted lake
With the wild world I dwelt in, is a thing
Which warns me, with its stillness, to forsake
Earth's troubled waters for a purer spring.
This quiet sail is as a noiseless wing
To waft me from distraction. Once I loved
Torn Ocean's roar, but thy soft murmuring
Sounds sweet as if a sister's voice reproved,
That I with stern delight should e'er have been so moved.

It is the hush of night, and all between
Thy margin and the mountains, dusk, yet clear,
Mellow'd and mingling, yet distinctly seen,
Save darken'd Jura, whose capt heights appear
Precipitously steep; and drawing near
There breathes a living fragrance from the shore
Of flowers yet fresh with childhood; on the ear
Drops the light drip of the suspended oar,
Or chirps the grasshopper one good-night carol more."

This is true poetic description, in which, while the poet appears only to express a docile recipiency of what Nature bestows, he gives back to be blended with it both his own emotion and the light which a poet's imagination creates.

A passage proving higher power is the well-known description of the Gladiator, in the same poem. It is a higher strain, for it is a description purely visionary—telling of no spectacle of the bodily sight—but a reality of spiritual vision. The poet stood within the vacant and silent circuit of the Coliseum, no sound touching his ear, no sight save the ruins reaching his eye, but inspired by the local association, and by the image which sculpture had made familiar, he sees and hears through centuries; and the thronged amphitheatre rises up before him with all the horrid sights and sounds of Rome's brutal sports, in his rapt vision of the dying athlete: nay more, (and this is the grandest part of the vision, full of a moral beauty,) looking to the wild region of the Danube, he beholds the distant cottage of the Gladiator, with his children in happy ignorance of the murdered father's misery; and further—such can be a poet's seeing—he beholds Alaric and his hosts coming down in vengeance on the doomed and guilty city:

"I see before me the Gladiator lie;
He leans upon his hand—his manly brow
Consents to death, but conquers agony,
And his droop'd head sinks gradually low—
And through his side the last drops, ebbing slow
From the red gash, fall heavy, one by one,
Like the first of a thunder shower;* and now

* This—"the first of a thunder shower," as applied to the heavy blood-drops from the Gladiator's wound—always seemed to me a defective figure; but where, in any poem, will any thing be found more perfect in its simple illustrative beauty than the lines of Childe Harold on the march to Waterloo?

"And Ardennes waves above them her green leaves
Dewy with Nature's tear-drops, as they pass,
Grieving, if aught inanimate e'er grieves
Over the unreturning brave." W. B. R.

The arena swims around him—he is gone
Ere ceased the inhuman shout which hailed the wretch who won.

He heard it, but he heeded not—his eyes
Were with his heart, and that was far away:
He reck'd not of the life he lost, nor prize,
But where his rude hut by the Danube lay—
There were his young barbarians all at play,
There was their Dacian mother—he, their sire,
Butcher'd to make a Roman holiday—
All this rush'd with his blood.—Shall he expire
And unavenged? Arise, ye Goths, and glut your ire!"

In this, there is genuine poetic vision, genuine feeling; in a word, true imaginative power, and wondrous words of simple English to give voice to it.

I would refer to another passage, less striking, but also characteristic of Byron's best power, and which I wish to cite, because it admirably exemplifies how simple, both in conception and in expression, is true poetic sublimity. It is the passage in which the poet, assuming the character of a Greek, utters his emotion on the plain of Marathon; and the imaginative truth and sublimity of the lines admit of a very simple analysis. There are presented two of the grandest of earth's natural objects—a range of mountains on the one side, and the sea on the other; between them a tract of ground hallowed by one of the world's greatest battles, the victory that saved Europe from Asia's conquest; and that combining power, which is one of the chief functions of the imagination—not only groups, nay, more than groups—unites these three great objects, mountain, plain, and ocean, with all their memories, but also vivifies them with the deep emotion of the solitary human being standing in the midst of them:

"The mountains look on Marathon,
And Marathon looks on the sea;
And musing there an hour alone,
I thought that Greece might still be free;
For standing on the Persian's grave,
I could not deem myself a slave.

A king sat on the rocky brow,
Which looks o'er seaborn Salamis;
And ships, by thousands, lay below,
And men in nations; all were his!
He counted them at break of day;
And when the sun set, where were they?"

Such passages illustrate the best moods of Byron's genius, and it would be agreeable to unweave more of the same description from all that is false and morbid in his poetry, but such a process would be altogether inadequate for the understanding of that poetry and the influence it exerted. When we remember how largely a weak sentimentalism entered into that popularity, there can be little doubt that it was won by the poet's weakness as well as by his power; by what was morbid as well as by what was healthful. We may form a judgment now of the character of his poetry, by looking at his dealing with what were his two chief themes, human character, and the material world—the universe of sight and sound. Now with regard to his treatment of human character, whether it be in the expression of his own thoughts and feelings, or in the invention of poetic persons, and whether these inventions be meant to be independent of himself, or to shadow forth his own nature, there is, in all, disease, deep-seated, clinging disease. You search in vain for a single healthful impersonation of humanity; all the creations are hollow images, with no life or heart in them. Turn to Shakspeare's creations, even those most removed from common life, or follow Spenser into the shadowy regions of Fairy Land, or Milton into his supernatural spaces, and so faithful are their creations to a deep science of humanity, that every human heart recognises the truth of them: they live and have a reality by virtue of their poetic truthfulness. But of Byron's heroes or of his heroines, which is a natural, truthful character, such as great poets give for the admiration or for the admonition of their fellow-beings? No pure and lofty idea of womanhood appeared in his female personages; he scarce lifts them above the sensual softness of oriental degradation, investing it in a delusive light of false and fanciful sentiment. His male personages (they are not truthful enough to be called *characters*) are strangely alike in their unreality. "But" (as has been justly remarked by the sagacious author of Philip Van Artavelde*) "there is yet a worse defect in them. Lord Byron's conception of a hero, is an evidence not only of scanty materials of knowledge from which to construct the ideal of a human being, but also of a want of perception of what is great or noble in our nature. His heroes are creatures abandoned to their passions, and essentially, therefore, weak of mind. Strip them of the veil of mystery and the trappings of poetry, resolve them into their plain realities, and they are such beings as, in the eyes of a reader of masculine judgment, would certainly excite no sentiment of admiration, even if they did not provoke contempt. When the conduct and feelings attributed to them are reduced into prose, and brought to

* Preface to Philip Van Artavelde, p. xv.

the test of a rational consideration, they must be perceived to be beings in whom there is no strength, except that of their intensely selfish passions; in whom all is vanity; their exertions being for vanity under the name of love or revenge, and their sufferings for vanity under the name of pride. If such beings as these are to be regarded as heroical, where in human nature are we to look for what is low in sentiment or infirm in character?"

How nobly opposite to Lord Byron's ideal was that conception of an heroical character which took life and immortality from the hand of Shakspeare:—

"Give me that man
That is not passion's slave, and I will wear him
In my heart's core; ay, in my heart of heart."

It was, however, with these fictions, that the popular fancy was fascinated, not only because the poet's genius gave a charm to them, but because that which addresses itself to what is false and morbid in man or woman will find a response, happily only for a time. In like manner, there was an attraction in the unreserved disclosures which the poet was all the while making of his own feelings and passions, taking the large concourse of his listeners into his confidence; and running through those feelings there was the poison of moral disease. On the pages of Byron you can scarce escape from some form or other of morbid feeling, a vicious egotism, pride, contempt, misanthropy: these are attributes not of strength, but of weakness; and knowing, as we now do, the story of his career, is it not pitiful that one so gifted should have gone whining through life, complaining of man, and rebellious of God, and all the while self-indulgent alike in sensual and sentimental voluptuousness? It is well said, that if life be "ever so unfortunate, a man's folding his hands over it in melancholy mood, and suffering himself to be made a puppet by it, is a sadly weak proceeding. Most thoughtful men have probably some dark fountains in their souls, by the side of which, if there were time, and it were decorous, they could let their thoughts sit down and wail indefinitely. That long Byron wail fascinated men for a time, because there is that in human nature."* Herein was the mischief that Byron's poetry did in its season of authority: reversing the poet's function, which is to heal what is unhealthy, to strengthen what is weak, to chasten what is corrupt, and to lift up what is sinking down: he fostered what was false, ministered to what was morbid, and, moreover, tempted them on to the willing delusion that their weakness was strength. Thus unreal and false habits of feeling were engendered, and men and women, under this delusion, grew sentimental and fantastic, and flattered themselves that there was beauty in the ugliness of pride, that there was magnanimity in the littleness of contempt, and depth of passion in the shallowness of discontent, and majesty in unmanly moodiness and misanthropy. Now all this, which came from the Byron teaching, was false both in morals and in poetry; for in this mortal life crowded with its realities for every hour of every human being's existence, all fantastic and self-occupied sadness is a folly and a sin—unmanly in man, unpoetic in the poet, well rebuked by a woman-poet's strenuous words:

"We overstate the ills of life, and take
Imagination, given us to bring down
The choirs of singing angels, overshone
By God's clear glory,—down our earth to rake

* Friends in Council, p. 198.

The dismal snows instead; flake following flake
To cover all the corn. We walk upon
The shadow of hills across a level thrown,
And pant like climbers. Near the alder-brake
We sigh so loud, the nightingale within
Refuses to sing loud, as else she would.
O brothers! let us leave the shame and sin
Of taking vainly, in a plaintive mood,
The holy name of *Grief!*—holy herein,
That by the grief of *One*, came all our good."*

I know of nothing that more betrays the moral weakness of Byron, than that he gave so much of his power to spread the contagion of a morbid melancholy, the selfish, thankless, faithless weariness of life, which another woman-poet has justly called a blasphemy:

"Blaspheme not thou thy sacred life, nor turn
O'er joys that God hath for a season lent
Perchance to try thy spirit, and its bent,
Effeminate soul and base, weakly to mourn.
There lies no desert in the land of life,
For e'en that tract that barrenest doth seem,
Laboured of thee in faith and hope, shall teem
With heavenly harvests and rich gatherings, rife.
Haply no more, music and mirth and love,
And glorious things of old and younger art,
Shall of thy days make one perpetual feast:
But when these bright companions all depart,
Lay there thy head upon the ample breast
Of Hope,—and thou shalt hear the angels sing above."†

In Lord Byron's portraiture of human character, his genius was prostituted to a worse abuse, in that it confounds and sophisticates the simplicity of conscience—breaks down the barriers between right and wrong, by abating the natural abhorrence of crime, and arraying the

* Sonnet on Exaggeration. Mrs. Browning's Poems, vol. i. p. 344.

† Poems by Frances Anne Kemble, p. 150.

guilt of even the vilest vice in a false splendour and pride. How different from Shakspeare's genuine morality, so loyal to the best moral instincts, never making vice attractive, not tempting us even to look fondly on the proud and sinful temper until it be chastened by adversity, still less holding up for admiration the moral monsters in whom one virtue is linked with a thousand crimes!

Let me next hasten to notice something of the character of the poetry of Byron, considered as a poet of nature: I mean, of the material world. In the last lecture I had occasion to remark, that it seemed to me a happy circumstance that the great results in physical science did not take place during the low state of religious belief that existed in the last century, but were reserved for a better period of opinion, which could make those results subservient to the cause of truth, instead of being perverted to the uses of materialism. I would now add that, while in our times there has been such active scientific study of nature, happily the poetic culture of nature has been no less earnest, and thus a deeper knowledge of the marvels and the glory of the universe has been promoted both by the processes of analysis and observation, and by the processes of the imagination. Let us see how Byron contributed to this, and what he has done to help his fellowmen to the poetic visions of nature. No poet ever enjoyed larger or more various opportunities of communing with earth and the elements. He was familiar with ocean and lake, with Alpine regions, and with Grecian and Italian lands and skies. He had a quick susceptibility to all that is grand and beautiful in the world of sense, as he wandered over the earth.

"The sounding cataract
Haunted (him) like a passion: the tall rock,
The mountain, and the deep and gloomy wood,
Their colours and their forms, were then to (him)
An appetite; a feeling and a love
That had no need of a remoter charm,
By thought supplied, nor any interest
Unborrowed from the eye."*

But his love of nature was not only passionate; it was thoughtful and imaginative. He knew that true poetic description must go beyond the rapture which mere bodily sight can give, and deal with all of which this material world is symbolical. His strong poetic instincts, when they chanced to be associated with true and healthy feeling, gave forth often grand or beautiful description; he aspired to the highest reach of poetic description of nature, for of himself he said,

"With the stars
And the quick spirit of the universe
He held his dialogues; and they did teach
To him the magic of their mysteries.
To him the book of night was open'd wide,
And the voices from the deep abyss reveal'd
A marvel and a secret."†

But these aspirations were frustrated, for a moral weakness perverted and lowered them, causing an inequality in his poetry which it is lamentable to look at. At one moment we believe that we are about to behold him

"Springing from crystal step to crystal step,
In the bright air, where none can follow him;"‡

but straightway we see the winged energy dragged down

* Wordsworth's Lines written above Tintern Abbey. Works, p. 159.
† The Dream, stanza viii.
‡ Landor, Imaginary Conversation, vol. iii. p. 363.

to earth, soiled with earthy things, and stumbling in the darkness and the mire of low and turbid passions. Aspiring to commune with the infinite, the poet's heart, and therefore his genius too, were cramped within the narrow confines of petty pride and weak hatred. The blindness of idolatry came over him. The world of sight and sound became a divinity to him. That which was meant for only a means to higher ends was made all in all to him. The material world, framed as it so wondrously is, to minister not only to our bodily wants, but to the imaginative appetites which feed on the grand and the beautiful, hemmed his faithless spirit in; and the genius of Byron had not power enough to extricate him from the shallow sophistries of materialism. His strong passion for nature, divorcing itself from the vision of faith, began to spread itself in misty rhapsodies, meaningless of every thing but the old errors of sensuous systems of unbelief. When Byron's poetry began to utter materialism, it began to utter folly, and then it ceases to be poetry, for poetry is allied to wisdom, and not to madness. He talked of loving earth only for its earthly sake, "becoming a portion of that around him;" of high mountains being a feeling to him; and

"That he could see
Nothing to loathe in nature, save to be
A link reluctant in that fleshly chain,
Classed among creatures, when the soul can flee,
And with the sky, the peak, the heaving plain
Of ocean, and the stars mingle, and not in vain:

* * * * *

And when at length the mind shall be all free
From what it hates in this degraded form,
Reft of its carnal life, save what shall be,
Existent happier in the fly and worm:

Where elements to elements conform,
And dust is as it should be, shall I not
Feel all I see, less dazzling, but more warm?
The bodiless thought? The spirit of each spot,
Of which, even now, I share at times, the immortal lot."*

Now strip this, and the multitude of passages like it, of all that is fantastic; measure it, as you please, either by the practical rules of common sense, or, by what is more appropriate, the standard of imaginative truth and wisdom, and what is it but the perplexity and the folly of materialism? What natural instinct, let me ask, is so strong in the human heart as that which recoils from the dread anticipation that this living flesh of ours, or the cherished features of those that are dear to us, will be fed upon by the worms in the grave?—a thought that would crush us down in desperate abasement, but for the one bright hope beyond, and then, to think of a poet exulting in the prospect of that remnant of his carnal life "existent happier in the worm!" When Byron is honoured as a great poet of nature, it is well to understand where he will lead his disciple, and where he will desert him. The material world has high and appropriate uses in the building up of our moral being: the study of it, in a right and believing spirit, is full of instruction; but it is worthless and perilous if we lose sight of the great truth of the soul's spiritual supremacy over it; that there is implanted in each human being an undying particle, destined to outlive not this earth alone, but the universe. This poet, "sick of himself for very selfishness," his heart aching with its hollowness, sent his materialized imagination to roam over the world of sense, ocean and mountain, seeking what the world could not

* Childe Harold, canto iii, 72, 74.

give. "Where shall wisdom be found? and where is the place of understanding? The depth saith, It is not in me, and the sea saith, It is not with me."*

Now, if we seek a solution of the strange inequality of Byron's poetic power, and the perversion and imperfection of his descriptions of nature, it is in this happy truth that the cultivation of the imagination is dependent on the moral feelings; and all

> "Outward forms, the loftiest, still receive
> Their finer influences from the life within."

Coleridge, in his Ode on Dejection, tells us that the poetic vision of nature is sealed even to that uncongenial mood—

> "The wan and heartless mood—
> A grief without a pang, void, dark, and drear;
> A stifled, drowsy, unimpassioned grief,
> Which finds no natural outlet—no relief
> In word, or sigh, or tear.
> * * * * *
> My genial spirits fail,
> And what can these avail
> To lift the smothering weight from off my breast?
> It were a vain endeavour,
> Though I should gaze forever
> On that green light that lingers in the West:
> I may not hope, from outward forms, to win
> The passion and the life, whose fountains are within.
> * * * * *
> —— From the soul itself must issue forth
> A light, a glory, a fair luminous cloud,
> Enveloping the earth;
> And from the soul itself must there be sent
> A sweet and potent voice, of its own birth—
> Of all sweet sounds the life and element!"

---

* Job xxviii. 12, 14.

But if the fountain of the life within be not only darkened with dejection, but turbid with evil passions—if the soul itself be distempered—it cannot send forth "the beautiful and beauty-making power," but, in its stead, such perplexed and lurid flashes as burst from the genius of Byron.

That wise expounder of poetic power and of nature, the author of "The Modern Painters," has justly said that "all egotism and selfish care or regard are, in proportion to their constancy, destructive of imagination, whose play and power depend altogether on our being able to forget ourselves, and enter, like possessing spirits, into the bodies of things about us."* Now there is deep instruction in this—that, whenever Byron's imagination rose above that selfishness which was his clinging vice, his greatest power was displayed; and it is woful to see how often this leprosy is breaking out on the poet's brow as he stands by the incense-altar.

There is this further admonition in all that Byron failed in—an admonition plain and irresistible—that just so far as poet or philosopher places himself in antagonism to Divine Truth, so far must he fail in all that he adventures in the deep things of nature, of man, of his own soul. "Science," it has been justly said, "in the hands of infidelity, degenerates into crumbling materialism: it is blind to the beauty, deaf to the harmony of the universe; as its objects rise, it sinks; when it comes to treat of human nature, its views are base and degrading; its morality is a matter of barter, or a wary drifting along before the animal impulses. And what can the poetry

* Ruskin's Modern Painters, vol. ii. p. 180.

of infidelity be, except a deifying of the senses and the passions, while the consciousness of higher cravings and aspirations, which cannot be wholly extinguished, vents itself in bursts of self-mockery, or in the cold sneer of derision and contempt for all mankind?"* The highest truth and grandeur that pagan poetry attained, what were they but aspirations for the coming Christian truth? And when, in Christian times, the poet rejects that truth, refusing its light, he takes up his abode in darkness deeper than the heathen's, and it is impossible for him to comprehend, much less expound, nature, himself, or his fellow-men; for nowhere can the unaided, solitary mind of man travel, whether it be into his own moral and spiritual nature, with the mysterious tribunal of conscience, so weak and so strong, or into the hearts of mankind, or to the mute creation, or into the spaces of the universe, to the blade of grass at our feet, or the most distant star in the firmament,—nowhere can it travel, but it shall find itself baffled by mystery—mystery, the burden of which grows heavier and heavier the farther it is removed from the only truth that can solve it:

"For the soul,
At every step when she around her cell,
Sees, yet adores not the Adorable.
More faint and faint the gleams which with Him dwell,
Break out on her; more feebly His dear voice,
That which alone bids nature to rejoice,
More faint and faint she hears; till all alone,
From scene to scene of doubt, she wanders on

* The Mission of the Comforter, by Julius Charles Hare, vol. i. p. 200.

Along a dreary waste, starless and long,
Starless and sad, a dreary waste along,
Uncheer'd, unsatisfied, for evermore
Companionless, and fatherless, and poor."*

With a mind too vigorous for inaction, and a temper too proud and wilful for either the moral or intellectual discipline which the greatest writers recognise as a duty they ask no exemption from, Lord Byron, amid the large variety of his productions, has left no one elaborate, well-sustained poem; and the evidence of his genius is to be found in passages or in the short poems, such as the "*Prisoner of Chillon*," or, what is perhaps the first and most faultless of his poems, (which I should be glad to pause on,) "*The Dream*."

If a fitful irregularity was characteristic of this splendid career of authorship, no less so was the close of it. All restraint growing more vexatious and burdensome to him, whether the discipline of his art, the discipline of society, or the discipline of conscience, he fashioned that ribald poem, Don Juan, to let his fancy riot in. It was an ignominious retreat for genius, the last act of self-degradation. I cite one stanza from it, to show, by a contrast that shall follow, to what base uses a poet can bring his talent. He looks at the metropolis of England, with the dome of St. Paul's, sublime in magnitude, and venerable by the devotions of many generations—the dead and the living—and thus he images it:

"A mighty mass of brick, and smoke, and shipping,
Dirty and dusky, but as wide as eye
Could reach, with here and there a sail just skipping
In sight—then lost amidst a forestry

* The Christian Scholar, by the author of The Cathedral, p. 255.

Of masts;—a wilderness of steeples peeping
On tiptoe through their sea-coal canopy;
A huge, dim cupola, like a foolscap crown
On a fool's head—and this is London-town!"*

I do not pause to say what pitiable prostitution this is of the poetic talent, corrupting the fancy with such a mean association of poor and heartless wit; but, in the contrast, let me sweep the scoff from out your thoughts by a short sentence, not clothed in verse, but overflowing with poetry, not graced with metrical music, but glowing with the purity and the grandeur of imaginative truth: "It was only the other morning," says the living writer from whom I quote, "as I was crossing one of the bridges which bear us from our mighty metropolis, that paramount city of the earth, that I was struck, for the thousandth time it may be, by the majesty with which the dome dedicated to the apostle of the Gentiles rises out of the surrounding sea of houses; and I could not but feel what a noble type it is of the city set upon a hill; I could not but acknowledge that thus it behooves the church to rise out of the world, with her feet amid the world, with her head girt only by the sky."†

Byron's career of authorship and life brought him, it might be said almost without exaggeration, *superannuated* at the age of thirty-seven, to the grave. There is a passage in "Manfred" which has, I think, a fearful significancy as an image of that proud defiance with which Byron thrust away what alone could have restored a heart wasted with self-indulgence, wounded with self-torment. The lines tell of the death of Otho:

* Don Juan, canto x. v. 82.

† Archdeacon Hare's charge at Lewes, in 1840, p. 6.

"When Rome's sixth emperor was near his last,
The victim of a self-inflicted wound,
To shun the torments of a public death
From senates once his slaves, a certain soldier,
With show of loyal pity, would have stanched
The gushing throat with his officious robe;
The dying Roman thrust him back, and said—
Some empire still in his expiring glance,—
'It is too late.'"

While the influence of Lord Byron's poetry has declined, (how rarely now is it quoted!) the estimation of Shelley's genius has risen. With fine poetic endowment, both of imagination and feeling, and with a willing spirit of poetic discipline by the study of his art, his mind, unhappily, was bewildered in the mazes and the misery of a speculative skepticism, which possibly a nature generous, sincere, and enthusiastic as his, might have outgrown in a longer life. There was an earnestness in his character that elevates his memory above that of Byron, but the cloud of unbelief brought kindred confusion over his vision, as when he speaks of life and death:

"In this life
Of error, ignorance, and strife,
Where nothing is, but all things seem,
And we the shadows of a dream,
It is a modest creed, and yet
Pleasant, if one considers it,
To own that death itself must be
Like all the rest, a mockery."*

In the beautiful lines written among the Euganean Hills, you cannot but see how Shelley's profound sense of the beauty of earth is imbittered by the gloom of infidelity:

* The Sensitive Plant, Shelley's Works, vol. iii. p. 1.

"Many a green isle needs must be
In the deep, wide sea of misery;
Or the mariner, worn and wan,
Never thus could voyage on,
Day and night, and night and day,
Drifting on his weary way,
With the solid darkness black
Closing round his vessel's track,
While above the sunless sky,
Big with clouds, hangs heavily."

It is no untruthful tenderness that has described Shelley as "an unhappy enthusiast, who, through a calamitous combination of circumstances, galling and fretting a morbidly sensitive temperament, became a fanatical hater of the perversions and distortions conjured up by his own feverish imagination. . . . He was under the miserable delusion of hating, under the name of Christianity, what was not Christianity itself, but rather a medley of antichristian notions which he blindly identified with it."

Considering how pure Shelley's poetry is from all such sensual depravity as vitiates the pages of Byron, and how earnest he was in speculations he believed to be for the good of his fellow-men, one would fain look with pity on his errors as well as on his tragic death. It is with an honest power of friendship that Leigh Hunt says of Shelley, that "Whether interrogating nature in the icy solitudes of Chamouny, or thrilling with the lark in the sunshine, or shedding indignant tears with sorrow and poverty, or pulling flowers like a child in the field, or pitching himself back into the depths of time and space, and discoursing with the first forms and gigantic shadows of creation, he is alike in earnest and at home."* A more

* Book of Gems, vol. i. p. 40.

sober judgment, well describing a great deal of Shelley's poetry, is given by Mr. Henry Taylor, in the preface to Philip Van Artavelde: "Much beauty, exceeding splendour of diction and imagery, cannot but be perceived in his poetry, as well as exquisite charms of versification; and a reader of an apprehensive fancy will doubtless be entranced while he reads; but when he shall have closed the volume, and considered within himself what it has added to his stock of permanent impressions, of recurring thoughts, of pregnant recollections, he will probably find his stores in this kind no more enriched by having read Mr. Shelley's poems, than by having gazed on so many gorgeously coloured clouds in an evening sky: surpassingly beautiful they were while before his eyes; but forasmuch as they had no relevancy to his life, past or future, the impression upon the memory barely survived that upon the senses."

In even the most cursory survey of the literature of our times, it becomes a part of its history that one of the prose-writers, who has made a strong and peculiar impression on many thoughtful intellects, is Thomas Carlyle. Converting simple English speech into a strange Teutonic dialect, he uses a style which, while it is odious and repulsive to some, seems, by a sort of fascination, to compel the attention of others; and yet this uncouth style, so alien from what the use of centuries has proved to be genuine English, that it almost sounds like the making strange noises to gain and force a hearing, is so redeemed by the author's vigour, and is in such affinity with the strangeness of imagery and illustration with which he utters his strong thinking and hearty feeling, that one is willing to look on it, not as affectation, but as the natural expression of such a mind—a fashion of speech for himself alone. The impression Mr. Carlyle has made is owing, no doubt, chiefly to his intense earnestness; and he has done good service in teaching men the worthlessness of all formality from which the truth has died out, and by exposing unreality, mockery—the forms of untruthfulness and counterfeit, described by the emphatic, homely term, "sham." The time has not yet come for a full estimate of Mr. Carlyle's genius; for there is not assurance enough whither he may lead his disciples. A deep sense of earnestness does not give all the moral security that is needed; for vice has its earnestness, far less real indeed, as well as virtue; and thus the mere sense of earnestness, though for the most part giving good guidance, may betray, if it be not held in just subordination to the supremacy of the sense of truth. The admiration of power, as in Carlyle's just tribute to all the robust reality of Dr. Johnson's character, may be appropriate and wise; but, gazing too much at mere power, it may disparage the sense of right, or rather confound might with right. The readers of Mr. Carlyle's writings therefore, while they may draw moral good and wisdom from them, must needs follow him with some caution, for he may lead them into strange places. When I consider what the English language, in all its natural simplicity, and beauty, and majesty, has been in the hands of the great masters of it, whether in prose or verse, I cannot divest myself of a misgiving that such strange and self-willed use as Mr. Carlyle makes of his mother-tongue is a symptom of something unsound in the constitution of his mind.

I pass, by an association of contrast, to Southey, whose

use of the language shows that natural and scholarlike beauty which is an element of his reputation, both as a prose-writer and a poet. His career of authorship, in both departments, has been most remarkable: in prose, embracing, with much miscellaneous essay-writing of a high order, one of the most popular biographies in our literature, the Life of Nelson, and a learned and elaborate historical work, such as his History of Brazil; and in poetry the political odes, resembling Milton's political poems in power, a great variety of minor pieces, and such extended productions as the heroic narrative poem of Roderic, and those highest efforts of his genius, the poems in which he brought Asiatic forms into the service of Christian poetry and truth, spiritualizing those forms of error as Spenser hallowed and purified chivalry and its customs. The most attractive of these poems is Thalaba—the finest achievement, perhaps, of what has been well styled Southey's judicious daring in supernatural poetry. It shadows forth, as its pervading but not obtruded moral, the war and victory of faith, a spiritual triumph over the world and evil powers, and thus is one of the great *sacred* poems in our literature. I should have been glad of an opportunity to show more fully the high imaginative character of this poem, and how much interest may be found in the study of it. I can now do little more than remark that the poet has taken not so much Mohammedanism, (certainly not at all in its impurity,) but "a system of belief and worship developed under the covenant with Ishmael," a remnant of patriarchal faith traditional among the pure and the believing in Arabia; and upon it he has brought the light of Christian imagination to shine, as the angel's face beamed on the fugitive bondwoman when he bade her turn her wandering footsteps home again, and opened for her outcast and fainting child a fountain in the desert. "Thalaba" is a poetic story of faith—its spiritual birth, its might, its trials, and its victory—such a story as none but a Christian poet could have told. As you follow the hero along his wondrous career to its sublime and pathetic close, the feeling which the rapt imagination retains is a deep sense of the majestic strength given to the soul of man when God breathes into it the spirit of faith. It has been truly remarked of Shakspeare's dramas, that the opening scene always bears an impress characteristic of the sequel; and never was the same principle of art more finely proved than in the beautiful opening stanzas of Thalaba—not least admirable in this, the reverential reserve with which they breathe of Scripture truth and story:

"How beautiful is night!
A dewy freshness fills the silent air;
No mist obscures, nor cloud, nor speck, nor stain
Breaks the serene of heaven;
In full orbed glory yonder moon divine
Rolls through the dark blue depths.
Beneath her steady ray
The desert circle spreads,
Like the round ocean, girdled with the sky.
How beautiful is night!

Who, at this untimely hour,
Wanders o'er the desert sands?
No station is in view,
Nor palm-grove, islanded amid the waste.
The mother and her child,
The widowed mother, and the fatherless boy,—
They at this untimely hour
Wander o'er the desert sands.

Alas! the setting sun
Saw Zeinab in her bliss,
Hodeirah's wife beloved:
Alas! the wife beloved,
The fruitful mother late,
Whom, when the daughters of Arabia named,
They wished their lot like hers,—
She wanders o'er the desert-sands
A wretched widow now;
The fruitful mother of so fair a race,
With only one preserved,
She wanders o'er the wilderness.
No tear relieved the burthen of her heart;
Stunned with the heavy woe, she felt like one
Half-wakened from a midnight dream of blood:
But sometimes when the boy
Would wet her hand with tears,
And, looking up to her fixed countenance,
Sob out the name of *mother!* then she groaned.
At length, collecting, Zeinab turn'd her eyes
To heaven, and praised the Lord;
'He gave—he takes away!'
The pious sufferer cried:
'The Lord our God is good!'

* * * *

She cast her eyes around:
Alas! no tents were there
Beside the bending sands;
No palm-tree rose to spot the wilderness;
The dark blue sky closed round,
And rested like a dome
Upon the circling waste—
She cast her eyes around,
Famine and thirst were there;
And then the wretched mother bowed her head
And wept upon her child."

During nearly the first forty years of this century did Southey devote himself, as long as his powers lasted, to an honourable activity in his country's literature, associating, like Scott, in genial companionship with all the good and great in the same cause: the record of his life, (his son is now giving it to the world,) like the inimitable biography of Scott, is not only a personal narrative, but a history of the literature of our times. I know not where you could look for that history so agreeably told as in these two biographies.*

* My brother was an earnest admirer of Southey, not only of his prose and verse, but of his personal character as revealed in his writings; and I well remember the triumphant pleasure he felt and expressed to me when the fact was revealed, a few years ago, that Southey was not responsible for the ancient acrimony of the Quarterly Review toward America. He seemed to exult that his favourite had not maligned his country. While he was in England last summer, he visited Miss Southey at Keswick; and I am tempted to make an extract from one of his letters home, if only to illustrate the gentle habit of his mind and current of his thoughts: "As we parted," he says, "Katharine Southey said she supposed I wished to see the church. I said we were on our way there, and she at once offered herself and the children for an escort through the fields. The children, Edith, and Bertha, and Robert, were sweet, loving, little bodies, who kept close to us during the whole visit. A short walk along the hedges —it was a beautiful day—brought us to the churchyard, and opposite the gate. Miss Southey said she would wait for us and the children. They had a winning, affectionate way, that would have charmed you, of taking us by the hand and leading the way. We went into the church, and saw the very impressive recumbent statue of Southey; these recumbent monumental figures are always imposing and solemn, this one peculiarly so. The children then took us to Southey's grave. While there, the little boy, putting his hands on the tomb, said to his sister, 'Edy, who in here?' and she told him, 'Grandfather.' This did not seem to satisfy him, for, coming back, he renewed his question, 'Edy, who in here?' and then she varied her young rhetoric, and said, 'Aunt Katy's father and mother.' One spoils, I fear, this prattle in repeating it, but on the spot, and with all the asoociations, it was delightful." *MS. Letter*, 19 *June*, 1854. About the time this letter

In this rapid and very inadequate view of contemporary literature, I have reserved little space for an influence which is felt most amply and gratefully where it is felt at all, and which, in my belief, will prove the most

---

was written, or not long after, Southey's second wife, better known as Caroline Bowles, died in a distant part of England; and since her death some very interesting though painful letters from her, descriptive of Southey's latter days of fading or faded intellect, have found their way into the newspapers. I am tempted to make short extracts from two of these, dated in 1840, which seem to me very touching: . . . . "Nothing gratifying, nothing hopeful, have I now to tell, though there is still great cause for thankfulness in continued exemption from all acute pain and bodily suffering; but I think there is increased feebleness; and certainly, from week to week, the mental failure progresses. Spark after spark goes out of the little light now left. Yet a capacity for enjoyment remains; and, God be thanked! and in his way, he still lives in his books, taking, to all appearance, as much delight in them as ever. I have no doubt, however, that there is at times a painful consciousness of his condition." . . . . "Of late my dear husband has been less restless in the day-time, sitting quietly on the sofa, turning over his leaves for an hour or two at a time, so that I have been able to occupy myself a little, as of old, with my pencil; . . . . and now my latest and perhaps last attempt satisfies even me, for I have somehow made out an excellent likeness of that dear husband, of whom there has never yet been a resembling portrait. . . . . Here is a chapter of egotism, but never was Raphael so contented with the most glorious of his works as I with this, my poor defective drawing. 'Yes, this me,' was the remark of my dear husband when I showed it to him."

I cannot refrain from still farther extending this note by a poem commemorative of Southey by Landor, which I find in the Annual Register for 1853—a book, by-the-by, let me say, where year after year, when there is any current poetry, beautiful selections are always to be found. It is quoted from "The Last Fruits of an Old Tree:"

"It was a dream, (ah! what is not a dream?)
In which I wandered through a boundless space
Peopled by those that peopled earth erewhile.

permanent poetic influence of these times: I refer, I need hardly add, to the poetry of Wordsworth, of which, it might have been expected, I should have made room to speak more at large. I should certainly have rejoiced in

---

But who conducted me? That gentle Power,
Gentle as Death, Death's brother. On his brow
Some have seen poppies; and perhaps among
The many flowers about his wavy curls
Poppies there might be; roses I am sure
I saw, and dimmer amaranths between.
Lightly I thought I lept across a grave
Smelling of cool fresh turf, and sweet it smelt.
I would, but must not linger; I must on,
To tell my dream before forgetfulness
Sweeps it away, or breaks or changes it.
I was among the Shades, (if Shades they were,)
And lookt around me for some friendly hand
To guide me on my way, and tell me all
That compast me around. I wisht to find
One no less firm or ready than the guide
Of Alighieri, trustier far than he,
Higher in intellect, more conversant
With earth and heaven, and what so lies between.
He stood before me — Southey. 'Thou art he,'
Said I, 'whom I was wishing.' 'That I know,'
Replied the genial voice and radiant eye.
'We may be questioned, question we may not;
For that might cause to bubble forth again
Some bitter spring which crost the pleasantest
And shadiest of our paths.' 'I do not ask,'
Said I, 'about your happiness; I see
The same serenity as when we walkt
Along the downs of Clifton. Fifty years
Have rolled behind us since that summer-tide,
Nor thirty fewer since along the lake
Of Lario, to Bellagio villa-crowned,
Thro' the crisp waves I urged my sideling bark,

the opportunity of deepening the sense of thoughtful admiration and gratitude to Wordsworth's genius in any mind that has already possessed itself of the treasures of such emotions, and possibly of persuading some so to approach that poetry as to find in it, what it can surely give to all who are willing as well as worthy to find it—a ministry of wisdom and happiness, both in the homely realities of daily life, and in the deepest spiritual recesses of our being. But such a theme transcends the limits now left for me; and I propose therefore only to notice two or three points having a connection with subjects I have already had occasion to speak of. With regard to language, an English editor of Wordsworth has said, "By no great poet, besides Shakspeare, has the English tongue been used with equal purity, and yet such flexible command of its resources. Spenser gives us too many obsolete forms, Milton too much un-English syntax, to make either of them available for the purpose of train-

---

Amid sweet salutation off the shore
From lordly Milan's proudly courteous dames.'
'Landor! I well remember it,' said he.
'I had just lost my first-born, only boy,
And then the heart is tender; lightest things
Sink into it, and dwell there evermore.'
The words were not yet spoken when the air
Blew balmier; and around the parent's neck
An angel threw his arms: it was that son.
'Father! I felt you wisht me,' said the boy.
'Behold me here!'
Gentle the sire's embrace,
Gentle his tone. 'See here your father's friend!'
He gazed into my face, then meekly said,
'He whom my father loves hath his reward
On earth; a richer one awaits him here.'" W. B. R.

ing the young men of our country in the laws, and leading them to apprehend and revere the principles of their magnificent language. But in Wordsworth . . . . is the English tongue seen almost in its perfection; its powers of delicate expression, its flexible idioms, its vast compass, the rich variety of its rhythms, being all displayed in the attractive garb of verse, and yet with a most rigorous conformity to the laws of its own syntax."* This high tribute will bear the test of close study; and, let me add, that this admirable command of the language is the reward of that dutiful culture which is a characteristic of the poet.

In the early part of this lecture, I had occasion to speak of those miserable poetic sophistries which tempted men and women to think that there is magnanimity in the littlenesses of a morbid pride, and poetic beauty in dreary moodiness. It was Wordsworth's function, with his manly wisdom, with the true feeling of his full-beating heart, and with the further-reaching vision of his imagination, to sweep these heresies away, showing by his own example that

> "A cheerful life is what the Muses love,
> A soaring spirit is their prime delight,"†

and teaching that lesson, which poetry and morals alike should give:

> "If thou be one whose heart the holy forms
> Of young imagination have kept pure,
> ———Henceforth be warned; and know that Pride,
> Howe'er disguised in its own majesty,
> Is littleness; that he who feels contempt

* The advertisement to "Select Pieces from Wordsworth," p. 4.

† Lines left upon a Seat in a Yew Tree. Works, p. 338.

For any living thing, hath faculties
Which he has never used; that thought with him
Is in its infancy. The man whose eye
Is ever on himself doth look on one,
The least of Nature's works—one who might move
The wise man to that scorn which wisdom holds
Unlawful ever. Oh be wiser, thou;
Instructed that true knowledge leads to love,
True dignity abides with him alone
Who, in the silent hour of inward thought,
Can still suspect, and still revere himself,
In lowliness of heart."

I have also had occasion to show how morbid and dangerous the love of innocent, inanimate nature may become when it is linked with infidelity—how it will sink down into a vile and weak materialism. By no poet that ever lived has the face of nature, the world of sight and sound, from the planetary motions in the heavens down to the restless shadow of the smallest flower, been so sedulously studied during a long life, and all the utterance his poetry gives of that study is meant to inspire

"The glorious habit by which sense is made
Subservient still to moral purposes,
Auxiliar to divine."*

Never, as in the sensuous and irreligious poets, is the material world suffered to encroach upon the spiritual, still less to get dominion over it. So far from any such delusion, observe how, in that well-known passage in *The Excursion*, the sublimity of which is sometimes overlooked in the beauty of the illustration, he proclaims this truth—that the universe, this material universe, is a shell, from which the ear of Faith can hear mysterious murmurings of the Deity.

* Excursion, book iv. p. 432.

"I have seen
A curious child, who dwelt upon a tract
Of inland ground, applying to his ear
The convolutions of a smooth-lipped shell:
To which, in silence hushed, his very soul
Listened intensely;—and his countenance soon
Brightened with joy; for murmurings from within
Were heard, sonorous cadences! whereby,
To his belief, the monitor expressed
Mysterious union with its native sea.
Even such a shell the universe itself
Is to the ear of Faith."*

The love of nature thus taught, associated with holy thoughts and reverent emotions, is made perpetual enjoyment, open, too, to every human being: and he who receives the poet's teaching may make the poet's words his own:

"Beauty—a living presence of the earth,
Surpassing the most fair ideal forms
Which craft of delicate spirits hath composed
From earth's materials—waits upon my steps;
Pitches her tents before me as I move,
An hourly neighbour. Paradise, and groves
Elysian, Fortunate Fields—like those of old
Sought in the Atlantic main—why should they be
A history only of departed things,
Or a mere fiction of what never was?
For the discerning intellect of man,
When wedded to this goodly universe
In love and holy passion, should find these
A simple produce of the common day."†

I had reserved for the conclusion of this lecture some notice of the female authors of this century. Ungracious as it will be for such a subject, I feel that I must give it a brevity considerate of your patience. It is a fine cha-

* Excursion, book iv. p. 432.

† Preface to the Excursion, p. 394.

racteristic of the literature of our times, that the genius of woman has shared largely and honourably in it. It has been so, from the share which Joanna Baillie had in the restoration of a more truthful tone of poetic feeling, and the delightful fictions with which Maria Edgeworth used to charm our childhood, down to the later company of women who still adorn both prose and poetic literature. There have been instances of female authorship in such modest retirement that the world has not known them well enough. There is much that illustrates the gracefulness and delicacy of the womanly mind, but over and above all this, and combined with it, the literature of our times has developed an energy which womanly authorship had not shown before: I do not mean a masculine energy, but a genuine womanly power. Those writers who are, I think, chiefly distinguished for such power, as well as beauty of genius, are Mrs. Jameson, as a prose-writer, and especially in her admirable criticisms both on art and literature; Mrs. Kemble, Mrs. Norton, and Mrs. Browning, formerly Miss Barrett. Indulge me with a few minutes more for an illustration or two of the poetic power I speak of. Every person, probably, after youth is passed, is conscious at some time of a deep craving for repose, for a tranquillity inward and outward: this universal feeling is thus expressed in these lines:

> "But to be still! oh, but to cease a while
> The panting breath and hurrying steps of life,
> The sights, the sounds, the struggle, and the strife,
> Of hourly being; the sharp biting file
> Of action fretting on the tightened chain
> Of rough existence; all that is not pain,
> But utter weariness! oh! to be free,
> But for a while, from conscious entity!

To shut the banging doors and windows wide
Of restless sense, and let the soul abide,
Darkly and stilly, for a little space,
Gathering its strength up to pursue the race;
Oh, heavens! to rest a moment, but to rest,
From this quick, gasping life, were to be blest!"*

It is an honourable and characteristic distinction of the female authorship of the day that it has devoted itself, in several forms, to the cause of suffering humanity.

"Some there are whose names will live
Not in the memories, but the hearts of men,
Because those hearts they comforted and raised;
And where they saw God's images cast down,
Lifted them up again, and blew the dust
From the worn features and disfigured limb."†

Would you know what might there is in the voice that speaks from a woman-poet's full heart, what power of imagination no less than of sympathy and pity, find that earnest plea which Elizabeth Barrett uttered against the horrid sacrifice to Mammon, which was once the shame of Britain's factories. It is entitled "*The Cry of the Children.*" I quote only the opening and closing stanzas:

"Do ye hear the children weeping, O my brothers,
Ere the sorrow comes with years?
They are leaning their young heads against their mothers,
And *that* cannot stop their tears.
The young lambs are bleating in the meadows,
The young birds are chirping in the nest,
The young fawns are playing with the shadows,
The young flowers are blowing toward the West;

---

* Poems by Frances Anne Kemble, p. 151.

† Landor's Lines to "The Author of Mary Barton," in the Examiner, March 17, 1849.

But the young, young children, O my brothers,
They are weeping bitterly;
They are weeping in the playtime of the others,
In the country of the free.
* * * * * *
They look up with their pale and sunken faces,
And their look is dread to see,
For you think you see their angels in their places,
With eyes meant for Deity;
'How long,' they say, 'how long, O cruel nation,
Will you stand, to move the world, on a child's heart,
Stifle down with a mailed heel its palpitation,
And tread onward to your throne amid the mart?
Our blood splashes upward, O our tyrants,
And your purple shows your path:
But the child's sob curseth deeper in the silence
Than the strong man in his wrath!'"

I am loth to leave so stern a strain of impassioned verse the last in your minds: she speaks with as genuine, but a gentler, voice of poetic power in the lines entitled "Patience Taught by Nature:"

"'O dreary life!' we cry, 'O dreary life!'
And still the generations of the birds
Sing through our sighing, and the flocks and herds
Serenely live, while we are keeping strife,
With heaven's true purpose in us, as a knife
Against which we may struggle. Ocean girds,
Unslackened, the dry land: savannah swards
Unweary sweep: hills watch unworn; and rife,
Meek leaves drop yearly from the forest trees,
To show, above, the unwasted stars that pass
In their old glory. O thou God of old!
Grant me some smaller grace than comes to these;
But so much patience, as a blade of grass
Grows by, contented through the heat and cold."*

* Mrs. E. Barrett Browning's Poems, vol. i. p. 342.

LECTURE X.

Tragic and Elegiac Poetry.*

Contrast of subjects, serious and gay—Tragic poetry—Illustrated in history—Death of the first-born—Clarendon's raising the standard at Nottingham—Moral use of tragic poetry—Allston's criticism—Elegiac poetry—Its power not mere sentimentalism—Gray's Elegy, an universal poem—Philip Van Artevelde—Caroline Bowles—"Pauper's Death Bed"—Wordsworth's Elegies—Milton's Lycidas—Adonais—In Memoriam—Shelley's Poem on Death of Keats—Tennyson—In Memoriam reviewed.

THE two lectures I am about to deliver relate to subjects aside from the continuous course just completed. They are, however, illustrative of it, though not part of it; and therefore, I hope, not inappropriate or unwelcome. The first lecture relates to the literature of tragedy and sorrow, the second to the literature of wit and humour; whether I shall add another to this brief supplementary course will depend on personal considerations which I need not now refer to. It is not necessary, I hope, for me to disclaim, in this arrangement of two of these lectures, all attempts at the mere effect of contrast, for it is no ambi-

* The course of lectures delivered in 1850 terminated with the Ninth, on Contemporary Literature. Those that follow, together with one on Wordsworth's Prelude, were prepared in March, 1851. I have thought it best to add them to this course, as, in a certain degree, illustrative of the general subject of English Literature. The one on the Prelude was rather the introduction of a new poem to those who had never read it, than a criticism on one that was familiar. It mainly consisted of extracts, with brief comment. On this account I do not think it worth while now to reproduce it. W. B. R.

tion of mine to catch the attention of my hearers by any such artifice, or to startle them with an antithesis of subjects. My purpose in placing, immediately after the serious subjects of the first lecture, the literature of Wit and Humour, was rather to show that the transition need not be a violent one; that there may be found in literature a response to the sad and solemn feelings of our nature, and also for its happy and joyous emotions; and that over both these departments of letters there may be seen shining the same moral light. I have set these subjects, apparently so different, in close continuity, in the hope of thus proving the completeness of such companionship as books can add to that between living human beings—a companionship for life, in shadow or in sunshine; in the hope of showing that there is a wisdom in books which holds genial and restorative communion with tears and a sorrowing spirit, and no less genial and salutary with that other attribute of humanity, smiles and a cheerful heart. Thus there may be a discipline for faculties and powers too often fitfully or unequally indulged or cultivated—a discipline of the thoughts and feelings which are associated with the sorrows of life, and no less of those which have fellowship with its joys and merriment: for those who are docile to receive, or sedulous to seek them, there are lessons which teach a sanity of sadness and also a sanity of gladness. It is, too, a ministry of human sympathy; for as it explores the sources of genuine grief and joy, it not only helps us the better to know our own hearts, but to enter into the feelings that are in the hearts of our fellow-beings, and thus to "rejoice with them that do rejoice, and weep with them that weep."

Tragic poetry has been well described as "poetry in

its deepest earnest." The upper air of poetry is the atmosphere of sorrow. This is a truth attested by every department of art, the poetry of words, of music, of the canvas, and of marble. It is so, because poetry is a reflection of life; and when a man weeps, the passions that are stirring within him are mightier than the feelings which prompt to cheerfulness or merriment. The smile plays on the countenance: the laugh is a momentary and noisy impulse; but the tear rises slowly and silently from the deep places of the heart. It is at once the symbol and the relief of an o'ermastering grief, it is the language of emotions to which words cannot give utterance: passions, whose very might and depth give them a sanctity, we instinctively recognise by veiling them from the common gaze. In childhood, indeed, when its little griefs and joys are blended with that absence of self-consciousness, which is both the bliss and the beauty of its innocence, tears are shed without restraint or disguise: but when the self-consciousness of manhood has taught us that tears are the expression of emotions too sacred for exposure, the heart will often break rather than violate this instinct of our nature. Tragic poetry, in dramatic, or epic, or what form soever, has its original, its archetype in the sorrows, which float like clouds over the days of human existence. Afflictions travel across the earth on errands mysterious, but merciful, could we but understand them: and the poet, fashioning the likeness of them in some sad story, teaches the imaginative lesson of their influences upon the heart.

In history, what is there so impressive as when the historic muse, speaking with the voice of the tragic muse, tells of terror and of woe? If science teaches that this earth of ours is a shining planet, the records of history as surely teach that it rolls through the spaces of the firmament, stained with blood and tears. So has it ever been. In the annals of the ancient dynasty of Egypt, what is there like that tragic midnight, when the first-born of the land were smitten, "from the first-born of Pharaoh that sat on the throne, unto the first-born of the captive that was in the dungeon:" what in the chronicles of Babylon, like that tragic hour, when there came forth the fingers of a man's hand, and wrote upon the palace wall an empire's doom? In classic story, what rises up to the memory more readily than the heroic sacrifice in the tragic pass of Thermopylæ? What pages in the annals of our fatherland have a deeper interest than when the career of King Charles turned to tragedy, when gloom was gathering over his fortunes, from the day when the royal standard was raised at Nottingham, and ominously cast down in a stormy and unruly night, onward to the bloody atonement on the scaffold.* In the history of

* Clarendon's celebrated description of the raising of the standard of Charles the First, at Nottingham, cannot be too often quoted. It is very grand and very sad.

"According to the proclamation," says the historian, "upon the twenty-fifth day of August (1642) the standard was erected about six of the clock of the evening of a very stormy and tempestuous day. The king himself, with a small train, rode to the top of the castle hill; Varney, the knight-marshal, who was standard-bearer, carrying the standard, which was then erected in that place, with little other ceremony than the sound of drums and trumpets: melancholy men discerned many ill presages about that time. There was not one regiment of foot yet levied and brought thither; so that the trained bands which the sheriff had drawn together was all the strength the king had for his person or the guard of the standard. There appeared no conflux of men in obedience to the proclamation: the arms and ammu-

France, what passage is there so impressive—as gathering into one awful moment a consummation of a long antiquity, and casting a dark shadow over the future—as that which tells of the descendant of sixty kings, laid bound, hand and foot, beneath the glittering axe? And in our own history, what is there so sublime, as when the young nation was baptized in blood on its first battle-field?

What has been finely called "the power and divinity of suffering" is shown also in the moral interest which clings to spots sacred by the memory of affliction—an interest which prosperous grandeur cannot boast of. A thoughtful traveller has thus expressed the feeling on visiting the palace of the Doges at Venice: "It is a strange building with its multitudinous little marble columns and grotesque windows, and the giant staircase all glorious of the purest Carrara marble, carved and chiselled into ornaments of the most beautiful minuteness. A splendid palace indeed it is: yet, while my eye wandered in a few minutes over the gorgeous part of the structure, it was long riveted with undiminished interest upon the little round holes close to the level of the sullen canal beneath the Bridge of Sighs—holes which marked the passages to the dungeons beneath the level of the canal, where, for years, the victims of that wicked merchant-republic were confined.

---

nition were not yet come from York, and a general sadness covered the whole town, and the king himself appeared more melancholic than he used to be. The standard itself was blown down the same night it had been set up, by a very strong and unruly wind, and could not be fixed again in a day or two, till the tempest was allayed. This was the melancholy state of the king's affairs when the standard was set up." *History of the Rebellion*, book v. p. 308. W. B. R.

"And why is it that suffering should have a spell to fix the eye above the power of beauty or of greatness? Is it because the cross is a religion of suffering, a faith of suffering, a privilege of suffering, a perfection arrived at by and through suffering only? Half an hour was enough for the ducal palace. I could gaze for hours upon those dungeon-holes, gaze and read there, as in an exhaustless volume, histories of silent, weary suffering, as it filed the soft heart of man away, attenuated his reason into a dull instinct, or cracked the stout heart as you would shiver a flint.

"There is seldom a line of glory written upon the earth's face, but a line of suffering runs parallel with it; and they that read the lustrous syllables of the one, and stoop not to decypher the spotted and worn inscription of the other, get the least half of the lesson earth has to give."*

Lord Bacon, in one of those essays in which he has so sententiously compacted his deep thoughts, said, "Prosperity is the blessing of the Old Testament; adversity is the blessing of the New, which carrieth the greater benediction and the clearer revelation of God's favour. Yet even in the Old Testament, if you listen to David's harp, you shall hear as many hearse-like airs as carols: and the pencils of the Holy Ghost have laboured more in describing the afflictions of Job than the felicities of Solomon."†

The moral use of tragic poetry consists then in such employment of poetic truth that the poet's sad imaginings shall serve to chasten, to elevate, and to strengthen the

* Sights and Thoughts in Foreign Churches and among Foreign Peoples; by Frederick William Faber, M. A. p. 285, 288.

† Essay on Adversity.

soul—a moral ministry which justified as sage and solemn a spirit as Milton's in speaking of "the lofty, grave tragedians," and styling them "teachers best of moral prudence, high actions and high passions best describing."* And the great critic of antiquity, with all the sublime solemnities of his country's tragic drama in his thoughts, in the presence, as it were of that spectral mystery of fate, which overshadowed the Athenian stage, has told us that "Tragic poetry is the imitation of serious action, employing pity and terror for the purpose of chastening the passions."

This discipline, however, it must be borne in mind, can have no practical influence on character, if it accomplish nothing more than the production of emotions, instead of being carried on into action; for it is a great law of our moral being that feelings, no matter how amiable and virtuous, will surely perish, if they be not converted into *active* principles; nay, they may coexist with conduct the most selfish and unfeeling; there may be a worthless sentimentalism utterly delusive and negative, and this, by due transition, may pass into odious self-indulgence, or still more odious inhumanity. In the worst days of the French Revolution, the very men who in the theatres applauded the heroic sentiments in the tragedies of Corneille, and were melted even to tears by the pathos of Racine, rose upon the morrow's morn to join in the ferocious cries for blood that echoed in the streets of Paris.

And further, if this example shows how worthless and wicked mere sentimentalism may be, self-indulgent in the luxury of ideal woe, it also shows that the sight of actual

* Paradise Regained, book iv. v. 261.

suffering may obliterate all sympathy, and harden the heart by familiarity with human distress or agony looked on as a spectacle. Now it is the function of art, through whatever medium it addresses the heart, so to transfigure the tragic realities of life, as to make the contemplation of them endurable and salutary, which otherwise would be appalling, repulsive, and, if repeated, destructive of true sensibility. That wise artist, the late Washington Allston, speaking with the truest philosophy of his art and of human nature, said it is "through the transforming atmosphere of the imagination (that) alone the saddest notes of woe, even the appalling shriek of despair, are softened, as it were, by the tempering dews of this visionary region, ere they fall upon the heart. Else how could we stand the smothered moan of Desdemona, or the fiendish adjuration of Lady Macbeth, more frightful even than the after-deed of her husband, or look upon the agony of the wretched Judas, in the terrible picture of Rembrandt, when he returns the purchase of blood to the impenetrable Sanhedrim? Ay, how could we ever stand these but for that ideal panoply through which we feel only their modified vibrations? Let the imitation be so close as to trench on deception, the effect will be far different. I remember," adds Mr. Allston, "a striking instance of this in a celebrated actress, whose copies of actual suffering were so painfully accurate, that I was forced to turn away from the scene, unable to endure it; her scream of agony in Belvidera seemed to ring in my ears for hours after. Not so was it with the great Mrs. Siddons, who moved not a step but in a poetic atmosphere, through which the fiercer passions seemed rather to loom like distant mountains when first descried at sea, massive and solid, yet resting on air."*

I pass from these brief hints, scarcely worthy of a place in a lecture on tragic poetry, to that kindred species which is found in the literatures of all nations, and which is entitled Elegiac Poetry. Serving, as all true poetry does, for a ministry and discipline of feeling, it could not neglect that one form of affliction which sooner or later comes to every human being—sorrow for the dead. The phases of this emotion are as various as the heart or the countenance. With some it is impetuous and turbulent, stormy as a cloud, but it pours down its shower, and then its form changes and it melts away, no one can tell whither. The passion sometimes is proud and self-willed and rebellious: or it is moody and sinks into sullenness. Again, it is gentle and resigned, and easy to be entreated. Sometimes it is social, and delights in the relief of utterance and sympathy. With others it holds no communion with speech or tears, but dwells in the depths of the silent heart. The poet, as an interpreter and guide of humanity, and especially as always raising the mind of man above the pressure of tangible and temporal things into the region of the spiritual and the immortal, finds one of his worthiest duties in training this species of sorrow into the paths of wisdom. In the small space now at my command, I can attempt to notice only a few of the truths that the poets in their elegies have taught. Let me first say, that there is a spurious form of elegiac poetry, which might be dismissed with a word of pity rather than of con-

* I am unable to verify this citation from Allston. W. B. R.

demnation, was it not a counterfeit of that genuine grief which is wronged by the imitation. I refer to that form which is the expression of unreal and subtly selfish sentimentalism, which is not too strongly condemned when it is spoken of as "a base lust of the mind, which indulges in the excitement of contemplating its own emotion, or that of others, for the excitement's sake."* Such sentiment is often ostentatious, obtrusive, and factitious; and real grief recoils from it into a deeper seclusion. But where the feelings are truthful, and poetry gives them worthy form, their truth is proved by the prompt and the universal response. What else can explain the large acceptation which a poem like Gray's Elegy in a Country Churchyard found at once, and finds to this day, not only wherever English words are known, but by translation into more languages than any English poem has ever been turned into. Indeed, throughout our thoughtful English poetry, the duty has ever been worthily recognised of upholding the communion between the living and the dead, and of so disciplining sorrow that it shall not be a dreary, self-indulgent, self-consuming sentiment, but a moral power, diffusing purity and wisdom, and dwelling in the high places of humanity. English poetry often speaks in the spirit of the elegy, though it may not assume the form of it. In that grand historical poem, "*Philip Van Artavelde*," when the hero, alluding to a stirring and disturbed condition of society, says,

"Lightly is life laid down amongst us now,
And lightly is death mourned—
We have not time to mourn;"

* North British Review, vol. xiii. p. 551.

his old preceptor, Friar John, makes answer in words that contain the whole philosophy of elegiac poetry:

"The worse for us!
He that lacks time to mourn, lacks time to mend.
Eternity mourns that. 'Tis an ill cure
For life's worst ills, to have no time to feel them.
Where sorrow's held intrusive and turned out,
There wisdom will not enter, nor true power,
Nor aught that dignifies humanity.
Yet such the barrenness of busy life!"

It is the theme of the elegiac poet to show these virtues of sorrow, its power to strengthen, to purify, to elevate, and to give moral freedom—its strength to consume the small troubles which so often waste and weaken our best powers. For this the poet needs the genius to look into the deepest and most mysterious parts of the human soul, to sympathize with its most acute sensibilities, and to illustrate all the consolatory agencies which are vouchsafed to man. In the first place, the poetic power may do a salutary work, by restoring a just sense of the awfulness of death—a sense so apt to grow callous, especially in large cities, where the solemnities of the grave are a trivial spectacle.* The heart loses some of its most natural and purest sensibilities when it becomes indifferent to the aspect of any of the circumstances or forms of death. An elegy on a pauper's death-bed was made to express these truths:

"Tread softly—bow the head,
In reverent silence bow—
No passing bell doth toll;
Yet an immortal soul
Is passing now.

* History tells, on more occasions than one, that one of the moral evils which follow in the path of pestilence, is that men are brutalized by the common sight of the dead and the dying. H. R.

Stranger! however great,
With lowly reverence bow:
There's one in that poor shed,
One by that paltry bed,
Greater than thou.

Beneath that beggar's roof,
Lo! Death doth keep his state:
Enter—no crowds attend—
Enter—no guards defend
This palace-gate.

That pavement damp and cold
No smiling courtiers tread;
One silent woman stands,
Lifting with meagre hands
A dying head.

No mingling voices sound—
An infant wail alone;
A sob suppressed—again
That short, deep gasp, and then
The parting groan.

Oh! change—oh! wondrous change—
Burst are the prison bars—
This moment *there*, so low
So agonized, and now
Beyond the stars!

Oh! change—stupendous change!
There lies the soulless clod:
The sun eternal breaks,
The new immortal wakes—
Wakes with his God."*

There might be gathered from English poetry large and wise discipline of all the emotions with which the living render homage unto the dead; and the thoughtful student would find his recompense in it. The laments of Spen-

* The Birth-day, and other Poems, by Caroline Bowles, p. 227.

ser are full of the tender sensitiveness of that gentle bard: the class of poems which Wordsworth has left under the title of Elegies abound in the "true poetic teaching of wise, strong-hearted Christian sorrow." I must, however, confine myself to three elegiac poems, the most remarkable in our language: Milton's "Lycidas," Shelley's "Adonais," and Mr. Tennyson's "In Memoriam." These poems may well be grouped together from the similarity of the occasions, and for the high, the varied imaginative power displayed in them. Each is a lament over the death of a friend of high intellectual and moral promise, called away in early manhood. The "Lycidas" is fashioned in a great degree by the spirit of classical elegy; the element of Christian belief present, however, in it. In Shelley's poem on the death of Keats the classical form is yet more manifest in purposed imitations of the Greek elegies.* That unhappy enthusiast, Shelley, with all his purity of character and loftiness of genius, could couple with classical imagery only the reveries of a bewildered unbelief. There is, in reading his poem, a feeling of deeper sorrow for the poet that wrote than for him that was lamented. The highest consolation, his fine imagination

---

* My attention has been specially called to the extent of these imitations, by a list of parallel passages in the Greek elegies, prepared by two of my former pupils, who have preserved their zeal for literature, ancient and modern, amid their professional studies. H. R.

The accomplished scholars to whom my brother refers, are William Arthur Jackson and G. Hermann Robinett. Mr. Jackson has kindly placed at my disposal his notes on these parallelisms, and I regret that I have not room to print them here. Let me add, for I shall have no other chance of noting it, that my brother felt very high pride in the scholars of the University, who, having been reared by him, had not forgotten his precepts or their early studies. W. B. R.

can reach to, is that his dead friend lives as a portion of the universe:

"He is made one with nature: there is heard
His voice in all her music, from the moan
Of thunder, to the song of night's sweet bird;
He is a presence to be felt and known
In darkness and in light, from herb and stone,
Spreading itself where'er that power may move,
Which has withdrawn his being to its own;
Which wields the world with never-wearied love,
Sustains it from beneath, and kindles it above.
He is a portion of the loveliness
Which once he made more lovely."

These are at best but dreary speculations; and when the poet, in spite of himself, is carried out of them by an instinctive belief in individual life beyond the grave, instead of that absorption into nature which would be annihilation, he rises into that grand strain on the unfulfilled promise of the genius of Keats:

"The inheritors of unfulfilled renown
Rose from their thrones, built beyond mortal thought,
Far in the unapparent. Chatterton
Rose pale, his solemn agony had not
Yet faded from him; Sidney as he fought,
And as he fell, and as he lived, and loved,
Sublimely mild, a spirit without spot,
Arose; and Lucan, by his death approved:
Oblivion, as they rose, shrank like a thing reproved.

And many more whose names on earth are dark,
But whose transmitted effluence cannot die
So long as fire outlives the parent spark,
Rose, robed in dazzling immortality.
'Thou art become as one of us,' they cry,
'It was for thee yon kingless sphere has long
Swung blind in unascended majesty,
Silent, alone, amid a heaven of song:
Assume thy winged throne, thou vesper of our throng!'"

The gloom which envelopes this poem is deepened by the impressive anticipation of Shelley's own death, one of the most remarkable coincidences to be found in literature. It will be remembered that he set sail in his small boat from the coast of Genoa, was overtaken at some distance from shore by a Mediterranean thunder-storm, and ingulfed in the deep waters: they who had watched the little skiff from the shore, saw it disappear in the darkness of the storm that struck it, and when the storm cleared away, it was seen no more. The lament over Keats—"Adonais" as Shelley styled him—written about two years before, ended with this stanza—

"The breath whose might I have invoked in song,
Descends on me; my spirit's bark is driven
Far from the shore, far from the trembling throng,
Whose sails were never to the tempest given;
The massy earth and sphered skies are riven!
I am borne darkly, fearfully, afar;
While burning through the inmost veil of heaven,
The soul of Adonais, like a star,
Beacons from the abode where the Eternal are."

The poem, or rather series of poems, of Mr. Tennyson is, however, in all respects the most important contribution which has yet been given to this department of poetry; and I regret that I have left me but a very little space for a few words on the character of the book. It is no prompt and passionate poetic utterance of grief; but has a higher authority on account of the reserve of near twenty years which distinguishes it. Young Hallam, the son of the historian, to whose memory the work is a tribute, died in 1833, at a distance from home—(in the poet's own words:)

"In Vienna's fatal walls
God's finger touched him, and he slept;"

and it was not until 1850 that the poet made the world a sharer in these imaginings, composed at various intervals, and expressive of a profound and thoughtful sorrow, modified by seasons and by time. The volume must be a sealed book to all who allow themselves to think of poetry as words to be lightly or indolently read, or as a mere effusion of effeminate sentimentalism: it demands not only study, but reflection on the reader's own inmost being. To such, and to repeated reading, the wisdom and beauty of the work disclose themselves; and in this lies one of the proofs of genius in it, for the poet is treating none of the merely superficial sentiments, but the more profound emotions and the most mysterious meditations, with which the soul of man strives to preserve communion with those who have passed behind the veil that hides the dead from the living. It is an effort made in no vain curiosity; there is no irrational and immoral dallying with grief, no wandering away from the light of divine truth, in chase of the false fires of human speculations. The poet clings to the memory of his dead friend, with a high-souled loyalty, holding it as an ever-present possession of good:

> "This truth came borne with bier and pall,
> I felt it when I sorrowed most,
> 'Tis better to have loved and lost
> Than never to have loved at all."

It is grief cherished, not for grief's sake—that were unmanly, irrational, weak, and wicked—but for its highest moral uses, a spiritual companionship that lifts him who is true to it above all ignoble thoughts and passions, and makes him truer to himself and to his God, by deepening and expanding his sense of immortal life. Here is a ministry of good for every human being who knows a single grave that holds the earthly part of one that ever was dear to his eyes; and thus the poet expounds the chastening power of sorrow:

"How pure at heart, and sound in head,
With what divine affections bold,
Should be the man whose thought would hold
An hour's communion with the dead!

In vain shalt thou, or any, call
The spirits from their golden day,
Except, like them, thou too canst say,
My spirit is at peace with all.

They haunt the silence of the breast,
Imaginations calm and fair,
The memory, like a cloudless air,
The conscience as a sea at rest.

But when the heart is full of din,
And doubt beside the portal waits,
They can but listen at the gates,
And hear the household jar within."

It was said by Jeremy Taylor of one of the early fathers, that there were some passages in his writings which a lamb might ford, and others which an elephant could not swim. In this volume of poems there are pieces which are the lucid expression of thought or feeling, common to many a mind, but uncommon in the exquisite utterance: there are other passages dim and even dark, for they tell of a great poetic imagination looking into very deep places. Nowhere is this more so, than in that series of stanzas in which he describes the homeward voyage of the ship from the Danube to the Severn freighted with his friend's lifeless remains.

How wonderfully expressive are they of that complex

and confused state of thought and feeling toward the dead while they are yet within the reach of a tender care and of a sacred duty! The first of this series speaks of the dead as of the sleeping, and tenderly solicits the quiet guardianship of the ship, and the ocean, sky, and elements:

"Fair ship, that from the Italian shore
Sailest the placid ocean-plains
With my lost Arthur's loved remains,
Spread thy full wings, and waft him o'er.
* * * * *
Sphere all your lights around, above;
Sleep, gentle heavens, before the prow;
Sleep, gentle winds, as he sleeps now,
My friend, the brother of my love."
* * * * *

The voyage brings to the poet's earnest imagination the dread of dismal burial in the sea, what he elsewhere speaks of in allusion to the sailor's funeral in that remarkable line,

"His heavy-shotted hammock shroud
Drops in his *vast and wandering grave.*"

The "vast and wandering grave" seems more fearful than the "narrow house" that moves only with the earth's motion, and is quiet in the churchyard or in the chancel.*

"I hear the noise about thy keel;
I hear the bell struck in the night;
I see the cabin-window bright;
I see the sailor at the wheel.

Thou bringest the sailor to his wife,
And travelled men from foreign lands;
And letters unto trembling hands;
And thy dark freight, a vanished life.

---

* And he who thus wrote, "the friend, the brother of my love," found his "vast and wandering grave" in the Atlantic. W. B. R.

So bring him: we have idle dreams;
This look of quiet flatters thus
Our home-bred fancies: oh, to us,
The fools of habit, sweeter seems

To rest beneath the clover sod,
That takes the sunshine and the rains,
Or where the kneeling hamlet drains
The chalice of the grapes of God;

Than if with thee the roaring wells
Should gulf him fathom deep in brine;
And hands so often clasped in mine,
Should toss with tangle and with shells."

When the ship has given up her trust, the poet's last thought of her follows her with thankfulness and benediction:

"Henceforth, wherever thou mayst roam,
My blessing, like a line of light,
Is on the waters day and night,
And like a beacon, guards thee home.

So may whatever tempest mars
Mid ocean, spare thee, sacred bark;
And balmy drops in summer dark
Slide from the bosom of the stars;

So kind an office hath been done,
Such precious relics brought by thee;
The dust of him I shall not see
Till all my widowed race be run."

After the unconscious and sacred freight is placed upon the land again—the devouring ocean having done gentle service of restoration—the poet's heart is almost exultant:

"'Tis well, 'tis something, we may stand
Where he in English earth is laid,
And from his ashes may be made
The violet of his native land.

'Tis little; but it looks in truth
  As if the quiet bones were blest
  Among familiar names to rest,
And in the places of his youth.

Come then, pure hands, and bear the head
  That sleeps, or wears the mask of sleep,
  And come, whatever loves to weep,
And hear the ritual of the dead."

In this instance, the first period of grief was, by the peculiar circumstances, protracted much beyond the common duration; and thus there was delayed for a while that second period—which lasts through the mourner's life—when the separation is consummated by the grave. The sharp agony or the dull anguish which follows, is coupled perhaps, first, with the memories that are prompted by *local* association, the familiar places that are darkened by the shadow. These feelings have their record in the volume, but perhaps even more expressively in some stanzas not contained in it, and different in metre, but obviously belonging to the same subject, written perhaps on the heights of the Bristol Channel:

"Break, break, break
  On thy cold gray stones, O sea!
And I would that my tongue could utter
  The thoughts that arise in me.

Oh well for the fisherman's boy,
  That he shouts with his sister at play!
Oh well for the sailor lad,
  That he sings in his boat on the bay!

And the stately ships go on
  To their haven under the hill;
But oh for the touch of a vanish'd hand,
  And the sound of a voice that is still!

Break, break, break
  At the foot of thy crags, O sea!
But the tender grace of a day that is dead
  Will never come back to me."

If local association can thus quicken the pangs of sorrow there is also a ministry of nature soothing them, a salutary influence working either in sympathy or in consolation, so that the heart takes strength from either the tumult or the tranquillity of earth and sky. These are processes of which it belongs especially to the poet, as moralist and philosopher, to give the exposition. This poem shows the mind in its various moods in unison with the various moods of nature, calm and stormy; but throughout all such changes, the deep, unalterable sorrow is asserted when it is asked—

"What words are these have fallen from me?
  Can calm despair and wild unrest
  Be tenants of a single breast,
Or sorrow such a changeling be?

Or doth she only seem to take
  The touch of change in calm or storm;
  But knows no more of transient form
In her deep self, than some dead lake

That holds the shadow of a lark
  Hung in the shadow of a heaven?"
* * * *

This action and reaction between nature and the heart, as influenced through the imagination, is shown (to take an illustration from another poet) in those stanzas of Wordsworth, composed during an evening walk after a stormy day, when the public mind was agitated by the news of the approaching death of a favourite statesman:

"Loud is the vale! the voice is up
With which she speaks when storms are gone,
A mighty unison of streams,
Of all her voices, one!

Loud is the vale; this inland depth
In peace is roaring like the sea;
Yon star upon the mountain-top
Is listening quietly.

Sad was I, even to pain deprest,
Importunate and heavy load!
The comforter hath found me here,
Upon this lonely road."

Thus did the tranquillity of the star shining in the peaceful heavens sink down into the human heart.

To return to Mr. Tennyson's volume, let me advert to its truthfulness in another respect. There is a trial to which Christian sorrow is subjected from which, I believe, the heathen heart in ancient times must have been in some measure free. The pagan faith could at best teach only the immortality of the *soul*, but it made no attractions for the place of repose of the lifeless body; and all the skill and pains bestowed by Egyptian art, or in the Roman sarcophagus, seem to be no more than a blind obedience to some natural instincts. But one great truth of the Christian creed, lifting the mind above mere instincts to an assured ground of belief, teaches that the *body* too shall have its portion in the hereafter. Pagan belief, simpler in its error, could follow, obscurely indeed, the disembodied spirit; while the Christian mind, happier in its truth, is often perplexed between thoughts that travel to the *body's* home, and thoughts that would fain soar to the *spirit's* home.

It would, I believe, be asserting not too much to say,

that the mind of the author of "In Memoriam" must have passed through a perturbed spiritual condition, passed through it thoughtfully and triumphantly, to give to other minds guidance through the same perplexity. One of the most pitiable conditions to which that perplexity sometimes leads, is the morbid and materialized state of mind which clings in all its thoughts to the visible burial-place. You remember that deplorable example of the Spanish princess, the daughter of Ferdinand and Isabella, the mother of Charles the Fifth, the half-crazed Joanna, and the frenzied infatuation with which she clung for years to the mouldering remains of her husband. It is as one of the morbid moods of a perturbed soul that Shakspeare represents Hamlet questioning the grave-digger's technical knowledge, and handling the skull of Yorick. On the other hand, it was a genuine and wise and dutiful feeling which was expressed by Lady Russel, the widow of him who had died cruelly on the scaffold. "When," said she, "I have done (my) duty to my best friend, and (to my children,) how gladly would I lie down by that beloved dust I lately went to visit, (that is, the case that holds it.) It is a satisfaction to me you did not disapprove of what I did, as some do, that it seems have heard of it, though I never mentioned it to any beside yourself. I had considered I went not to seek the living among the dead; I knew I should not see him any more wherever I went, and had made a covenant with myself not to break out in unreasonable, fruitless passion, but quicken my contemplation whither the nobler part was fled, to a country afar off, where no earthly power bears any sway, nor can put an end to a happy society."

One expression of this noble-minded lady shows an

assumption very common in deciding that it is to "a country afar off" that the spirit has departed. As a mode of expressing the sense of separation it is natural, but in other respects it is without authority, and too often tends to a thought of utter annihilation in death. One of the great English divines says, "Little know we, how little away a soul hath to go to heaven, when it departs from the body; whether it must pass locally through moon, sun, and firmament, (and, if all that must be done, it may be done in less time than I have proposed the doubt in,) or whether that soul find new light in the same room, and be not carried into any other, but that the glory of heaven be diffused over all, I know not, I dispute not, I inquire not."* It is a belief which imaginative wisdom asserts in poetry, that after the material presence has passed away from sight and hearing, there may be a spiritual presence nearer, closer, and more real. The popular and vulgar belief in the gross fictions of ghosts and phantoms is perhaps an attestation of truth distorted.† Southey, in one of his prose works, said that the most entire constancy to the memory of the dead can be found only where there is the union of a strong imagination and a strong heart, and in his ode to the memory of Bishop Heber—

"Heber, thou art not dead, thou canst not die!
Nor can I think of thee as lost.

---

* Donne's Sermons, vol. ii. p. 400.

† It is a pity, it seems to me, that the word "*ghost*" has become so perverted and debased from its high and pure spiritual meaning, for in common speech it signifies the fantastic notion of an immaterialism something sensualized, for if impalpable yet visible, too refined for one sense, but gross enough for another, and therefore belonging to sense, and not to spirit. Thus it is that truth first is materialized and abused, and then wholly denied. H. R.

A little portion of this little isle
At first divided us; then half the globe:
The same earth held us still; but when,
O Reginald, wert thou so near as now;
'Tis but the falling of a withered leaf,
The breaking of a shell,
The rending of a veil!"

And Wordsworth, in one of his elegies, boldly proclaims:

"Thou takest not away, O Death!
Thou strikest, absence perisheth,
Indifference is no more;
The future brightens on our sight;
For on the past hath fallen a light,
That tempts us to adore."

I have apparently stepped aside from my subject in citing these authorities, but the truth they sanction is set forth in this poem in the manifold forms into which the poet's genius has fashioned it, showing how that spiritual presence has been a reality to him, helping him onward in the destiny of life. The manly loyalty of his sorrow never fails him, but, conscious of the wisdom which sorrow brings, he clings to it with gratitude.

The deep mystery that wraps the whole subject of the relation between the living and the dead is in most minds barren of all belief; and, often worse than mere negative unbelief, it boldly denies that which lies much farther beyond the reach of denial than of assertion: that any influence of the spirits of the departed upon the spirits of the living is possible, and so covenant with the dead is boldly broken. One of the most learned and logical theologians among English laymen, in the present century, the late Alexander Knox, said that there was no opinion on which his mind rested with stronger assurance than that the spirits of the departed have a larger knowledge of transactions on earth than they had in life; and that having lost his father at twelve years of age, he felt, after the lapse of half a century, that all his days had been overshadowed by paternal solicitude. These opinions occur in an argument to prove the concern felt by departed spirits for those left behind, and I refer to it because it shows one of the prime truths of this poem reached by another path, the process of strict argumentation.*

The study of "In Memoriam" will also show how it vindicates other truths affecting the life and destiny of man—elemental truths which have been assailed by some of the philosophical heresies of the day; and, indeed, there is to my mind something sublime in the poet's strong affection to his friend, passed from mortal sight, having power to sweep these heresies away. The notion, coupled perhaps with pantheism, which would deny individuality of existence in the hereafter, is dissipated by the assurance which affection gives—the feeling that it

> "Is faith as vague as all unsweet:
> Eternal form shall still divide
> The eternal soul from all beside,
> And I shall know him when we meet."

Sombre as the poem at first appears, it works its way on to happy hopes—the confidence of future recognitions, and a cheerful faith.

The poet's voice is heard, too, against another error of the times—that which would give intellect supremacy over the higher powers which are in the soul, confounding knowledge with wisdom, or even making wisdom the sub-

* Alexander Knox's Remains, vol. ii.

ordinate. The better truth comes from the memory and imaginative contemplation of the character of his friend, when, speaking of knowledge falsely elevated, he says—

"Half grown as yet, a child and vain,—
She cannot fight the fear of death:
What is she, cut from love and faith,
But some wild Pallas from the brain

Of demons? fiery-hot to burst
All barriers in her onward race
For power. Let her know her place;
She is the second, not the first.

A higher hand must make her mild,
If all be not in vain; and guide
Her footsteps, moving side by side
With wisdom, like the younger child:

For she is earthly of the mind,
But wisdom heavenly of the soul.
O friend, who camest to thy goal
So early, leaving me behind,

I would the great world grew like thee,
Who grewest not alone in power
And knowledge, but from hour to hour
In reverence and in charity."

The effect of a sorrow not weakly indulged, but at once faithfully cherished and wisely disciplined, is perhaps most comprehensively shown in those stanzas which affirm the need, for the highest purposes of sorrow, of health and strength, in all that makes up our moral being.

In concluding this lecture, let me say that I have made no attempt to make choice among the poems with a view to present effect, but rather, in this desultory way, to illustrate the general purpose and character of the work, and some of the principles involved in it. I have thus passed in silence by many of the most admirable pieces in the volume, and have not stopped to speak of the superior metrical art which pervades the verse. Indeed, I am well aware, that in many respects this is rude handling of a poem which peculiarly demands the meditative study of silent reading. It is then that you may hear and see this stream of song and of sorrow—at first flowing deeply but darkly, contending alike against its own force and against resistance, light from the sky breaking only fitfully through the gloom: you may follow it after a while, gathering its strength into a more placid channel, and you will behold it at the last flowing as deeply as at first, but calmly, and in the light of peaceful memories and tranquil hopes, and bearing in the bosom of its own deep tranquillity the reflection of the deep tranquillity of the heavens.

LECTURE XI.

Literature of Wit and Humour.*

Subtilty of these emotions—Sydney Smith and Leigh Hunt—Dullness of jest-books—Hudibras a tedious book—Sydney Smith's idea of the study of wit—Charles Lamb—Incapacity for a jest—German note on Knickerbocker—Stoicism and Puritanism—Guesses at Truth—Cheerful literature needed for thoughtful minds—Recreative power of books—Different modes of mental relaxation—Napoleon—Shelley—Cowper—Southey's merriness—Doctor Arnold—Shakspeare and Scott's humour—The Antiquary—Burke—Barrow's definition of wit—Hobbes—Forms of Humour—Doctor Johnson's grotesque definitions—Collins, the landscape painter—Examples of grotesque style—Irish Bulls—Rip Van Winkle—Sydney Smith and Doctor Parr—Humour in old tragedies—Lear and the fool—Hamlet and the grave-digger—Irony—Macbeth and the doctor—Anne Boleyn—Bishop Latimer—Fuller—Dean Swift and Arbuthnot—Gulliver—Sir Roger De Coverley—Charles Lamb—Swift and Byron's humour—Prostitution of wit—Sir Robert Walpole—Lord Melbourne—Hogarth—Danger of power of humour illustrated—Ruskin's criticism.

In my last lecture I was engaged in the consideration of some very serious subjects, the gravest that belong to literature. In passing from them at once to the Literature of Wit and Humour, I have less apprehension of the transition being felt as a violent one than that there will be found in this lecture more of seriousness than the chief title of it might lead one to expect. The movements of the mind which are connected with the faculties styled "Wit" and "Humour," are among the most subtile of

* University of Pennsylvania, March 13, 1851.

which the mind is capable, are, for the most part, difficult of description, and demand an acute and delicate analysis. In contrast with my last lecture, I am anxious at the outset to give you the assurance of a promise that I shall this evening make a more reasonable demand upon your time and thoughts, for the light artillery which I have now to do with can be more expeditiously manœuvred than the heavy ordnance to which I had to stand on the former occasion.

It is well that it should be understood between us that the subject of Wit and Humour does not at all imply that the treatment of it should be identical with the effects of those powers; on the contrary, by raising such expectation and not fulfilling it, the subject may, in reality, prove more serious than even a grave subject, wherewith such anticipations could not be associated. Though I am usually averse to adverting in any way to the difficulty of any subject on which I have undertaken to lecture, indulge me in saying that the subject of the literature of Wit and Humour is one for which there is peculiarly demanded, not only a genial and cultivated capacity to enjoy such literature, but a skill and tact in the handling of it; the importance of which I am so well aware of, that it is with no small misgiving that I have ventured upon the subject. When the late Sydney Smith, the most distinguished wit of contemporary literature, in a course of lectures on Moral Philosophy, discussed these faculties of Wit and Humour, the subject, though manifestly not an uncongenial one to him, becomes even in his hands, a somewhat sedate disquisition. When Leigh Hunt wrote his volume on "The Poetry of Wit and Humour," vivacious and pleasant and facetious as he has often shown himself in other productions, in this we find less of that sprightliness which once made sunshine for him within prison walls.

But when one comes to reflect upon it, it is not surprising that a subject of this kind should assume what appears to be an unwonted and inapposite seriousness, when it is taken out of its life of activity, and made a matter of speculation. Everybody knows what a dull process it is to explain a piece of wit.

> "A jest's prosperity lies in the ear
> Of him that hears it, never in the tongue
> Of him that makes it;"*

and much graver than explanation is the work of analysis. It is a cruel business to anatomize the creatures of wit or humour, to place them on the metaphysical dissecting-table, and there to lay bare the hidden places of their power; and it demands, too, for this serious service the most acute intellectual scalpel which the metaphysician can handle.

This also is to be considered, that not only does a jest's prosperity lie in the ear of him that hears it, but it has its life in an atmosphere of its own; it springs up from a soil of its own; and there are few plants so tender in the transplanting. A happy, well-timed, well-applied piece of wit, which would electrify a House of Commons, becomes tame and vapid when removed by repetition out of its own sustaining atmosphere: one proof of this may be observed in the fact that there are few duller books than what are called "jest-books," whether the collection be made by Hierocles or by Joe Miller, (who is, I believe, not an apocryphal person,) or by the capacious intellect

* Love's Labour's Lost.

of Lord Bacon. They are not only very lifeless reading, but are regarded with a degree of contempt, which almost denies them admission into a nation's literature, even with the authority of the name of the philosophic Lord Chancellor pleading for entrance.* The same cause makes it, to a certain degree, a difficult and delicate task to present illustrations of this subject, for even without subjecting them to the torture of analysis, they must, although synthetically considered, be detached from their context, separated from all that was preparatory of their reception, and upon which their welcome is so dependent. The magic of wit and humour will be found very often to be so intimately connected with other intellectual action and other states of feeling, that all effect is destroyed by the attempt to separate it; a dull, heavy residuum is left, and all the delicate, volatile spirit is evaporated away. It will be one of my purposes in this lecture, to show the harmonious connection of the faculties of wit and humour with states of mind and of feeling with which we do not ordinarily associate them.

Assuming, as we are entitled to do, that that alone is genuine literature which contributes in some way to fashion the reader's character, to give both strength and guidance to his thoughts and feelings, books which abound

* There are, I believe, few more tedious books in the language than Butler's Hudibras; the perpetual and sustained effort at wit becomes oppressive, and it can be read only, I am disposed to think, in small quantities. It has been not unfrequently said, in Shakspearian criticism, that the gayest and one of the bitterest characters, Mercutio, is put out of the way in the third act, not because the poet's fund of inventive wit was exhausted, (that could not be with him who carried Falstaff through three dramas,) but the continuance of Mercutio's vivacity would have been inapposite. H. R.

with wit or humour are entitled to take a place in a nation's literature, only so far as they subserve the same ends. As in one of my lectures I spoke of the error of attempting to draw too precise a boundary line around sacred literature, making it too much a thing standing apart, so, in regard to the literature of wit and humour. I shall be sorry if such a title, which I have been obliged to use, led any one to think of it as of a more distinctive existence than is the case, instead of regarding those faculties as pervading the literature in various degrees, and thus forming some of the elements of its life. I shall have occasion to trace these elements in close contact with elements of tragedy, and to show how the processes which we generalize under the names of wit and humour are kindred with the most intense passion and with the deepest feeling. Our English literature shows, I think most conclusively, in ways that are respectively example and warning, that these faculties are strongest and healthiest when they exist and are cultivated in just proportion with other faculties and feelings, without gaining a predominance or pre-eminence, which makes them perilous to him in whom they thus get the mastery, and formidable to others. The best books in the language prove the power and the beauty of this harmony and proportion of the faculties; the literature should serve as an agency of discipline to produce in readers a like well-balanced, well-proportioned condition of the mind, and in the literature of wit and humour we are to find help for the cultivation of those powers.

Sydney Smith said, "It is imagined that wit is a sort of inexplicable visitation, that it comes and goes with the rapidity of lightning, and that it is quite as unattainable as beauty or just proportion. I am so much of a contrary way of thinking, that I am convinced a man might sit down as systematically and as successfully to the study of wit as he might to the study of mathematics; and I would answer for it, that, by giving up only six hours a day to being witty, he should come on prodigiously before Midsummer, so that his friends should hardly know him again. For what is there to hinder the mind from gradually acquiring a habit of attending to the lighter relations of ideas in which wit consists?"* Now this is obviously the exaggeration of one who, in the triumphant consciousness of his own endowment, pictures the perplexity of a student of wit coming to his task as he would to the differential calculus, giving only six hours a day to it, and astonishing his friends by Midsummer with his progress. But if this is witty exaggeration, so far as creative power is concerned, it covers a truth with respect to the culture of a susceptibility to the productions of wit and humour; and that susceptibility may fairly be considered as a constituent of every vigorous and well-cultivated mind—undoubtedly so, when the full extent of the operations of wit and humour is justly appreciated.

In such culture, whether by literature or otherwise, there will of course be found the same disparity of natural endowment of those as of other faculties. As there are unimaginative intellects to which all poetry is a sealed mystery, so are there others which are impenetrable to all the influences of wit and humour, and this is owing not so much to any exclusive predominance of seriousness as to that of dulness. It was in this respect that Charles Lamb, in his Essay on "Imperfect Sympathies," com-

* Sketches on Moral Philosophy, Lecture x. p. 125, Am. edition.

plained of his inability to like a certain description of Scotchmen—that dry, literal phase of intellect, which is so alien to all poetic or humorous liberty of language. "I was present," writes Lamb, "not long since, at a party of North Britons, where a son of Burns was expected; and happened to drop a silly expression (in my South British way) that I wished it were the father instead of the son, when four of them started up at once to inform me that 'that was impossible, because he was dead.' An impracticable wish, it seems, was more than they could conceive." This character of mind (so different, I may remark from the genial Scotch humour of Burns, or Walter Scott, or John Wilson) is not peculiar to Scotland, but every one can probably find specimens of it in the range of his own acquaintance.

The most remarkable instance of obtuseness to light letters that I ever met with occurred in another region. Goeller, a German editor of Thucydides, in annotating a passage of the Greek historian, describing the violence of the Athenian factions, gives two modern illustrations: one of the Guelf and Ghibelline parties in Italy; the other—he cites Washington Irving and his book very gravely in Latin—the factions of long pipes and short pipes in New York, under the administration of Peter Stuyvesant. Imagine this erudite and ponderous German poring over Knickerbocker as seriously as over Guicciardini's History of the Italian Republics!*

* This instance of simplicity has a most grotesque effect in the original, printed at Leipsic in 1836. It literally reads thus: "Addo locum Washingtonis Irwingii, Hist. Novi Eboraci. lib. vii. cap. v."—"The old factions of Long Pipes and Short Pipes, strangled by the Herculean grasp of P. Stuyvesant." W. B. R.

But the genial mind is accessible, at least, to some one or other of the manifold influences which are very inadequately expressed by these two general names, "Wit" and "Humour." They do but describe an inventive energy of genius, which assumes a vast variety of expression, ranging from the most acute intellectual wit, through the many forms of humour, down to frolic drollery and mere fun and the broadest buffoonery. If it be asked what claim to culture this class of faculties has, the first and simplest answer is, that they are among the talents with which man is gifted—the gift bringing along with it the necessity and the duty of culture: they are powers which will run riot and run to mischief, unless guided and disciplined. They cannot be destroyed by being disowned. It was a wretched delusion when Stoicism strove to stiffen humanity into stone: and so, in later days, there was like wrong when Puritanism looked black upon natural, innocent, healthful cheerfulness, frighting the joyous temper of a people with a frown, which I believe to this day haunts the race both in Britain and in America, to an extent which is irrational, unchristian, and of course injurious, by abandoning what is festive to the world's keeping, instead of retaining them under better and safer influences. It was Wesley, I believe, who said he had no idea of allowing the devil to monopolize all the good tunes; and it is certain that that same personage (I don't mean Wesley) will be ready enough to furnish to the needs of men holydays of his contriving, if no other provision be made for what is a natural and lawful craving of toiling humanity. There will be, too, a literature of wicked wit to fascinate and poison men, unless that of a truthful and healthful kind be cultivated. It is, I believe, not an uncommon inclination, to disown and to disparage that literature which is an agency of pleasant thoughts; and in opposing to such an opinion a few serious authorities, I hope you will not apprehend an inappropriate relapse into the grave subjects of my last lecture. A great divine, preaching at a time when Puritan rigour was beginning to make itself felt, said, "Fear not thou, that a cheerfulness and alacrity in using God's blessings—fear not thou, that a moderate delight in music, in conversation, in recreations, shall be imputed to thee for a fault, for it is conceived by the Holy Ghost, and is the offspring of a peaceful conscience:"* and another who lived to see and to suffer by the new severity, Jeremy Taylor, said, "It is certain that all that which can innocently make a man cheerful, does also make him charitable, for grief, and age, and sickness, and weariness, these are peevish and troublesome; but mirth and cheerfulness are content, and civil, and compliant, and communicative, and love to do good, and to swell up to felicity only upon the wings of charity. . . . . If a facete discourse, and an amicable, friendly mirth can refresh the spirit, and take it off from the vile temptation of peevish, despairing, uncomplying melancholy, it must needs be innocent and commendable. And we may as well be refreshed by a clean and brisk discourse, as by the air of Campanian wines; and our faces and our heads may as well be anointed and look pleasant with wit and friendly intercourse, as with the fat of the balsam-tree." A living divine, speaking not professionally, but in that agreeable work, the "Guesses at Truth," has said: What a dull, plodding, tramping, clanking would

* Donne's Works, vol. ii. p. 103.

the ordinary intercourse of society be, without wit, to enliven and brighten it! When two men meet, they seem to be, as it were, kept at bay through the estranging effects of absence, until some sportive sally opens their hearts to each other. Nor does any thing spread cheerfulness so rapidly over a whole party, or an assembly of people, however large. Reason expands the soul of the philosopher. Imagination glorifies the poet, and breathes a breath of spring through the young and genial: but if we take into account the numberless glances and gleams whereby wit lightens our every-day life, I hardly know what power ministers so bountifully to the innocent pleasures of mankind."*

Another thoughtful essayist of our day has said, "If ever a people required to be amused, it is we sad-hearted Anglo-Saxons:" (the phrase includes us ever-working Americans.) "Heavy eaters," (rapidity must be substituted for weight for the Anglo-Saxon on this side the ocean,) "hard thinkers, often given up to a peculiar melancholy of our own, with a climate that for months together would frown away mirth if it could, many of us with very gloomy thoughts about our hereafter,—if ever there were a people who should avoid increasing their dulness by all work and no play, we are that people. 'They took their pleasures sadly,' says Froissart, 'after their fashion.' We need not ask of what nation Froissart was speaking."† But let me add, that the blood and temperament of race are not safeguards of contentment, for it is with the most vivacious people, Froissart's countrymen, that the perpetration of suicide is most common.

* Archdeacon Hare's Guesses at Truth, first series, p. 316.

† Friends in Council, part i. p. 56.

It is for thoughtful minds that the agency of a cheerful literature is most needed, for remember that it is such minds that are most exposed to morbid moods, to despondency, to discontent, to some dull depression, more fatal to the energies of the mind, than danger or earnest labour, which nerve the spirit to encounter them. These are intellectual and moral evils, which must be met and mastered by thoughtful self-discipline, and in that discipline, the service of literature may be found, if properly sought for, providing as it does, in such varied form, so much of restorative influence. The good will be gained, not so much by seeking it in books especially meant for amusement, as in the culture of a capacity to relish wit and humour, as they are blended with other influences also intended to give strength and health to the mind. The recreative power of literature will of course be relative to the character and habits of the reader, and happily it is as largely varied as they are, thus suiting their various needs. It is stated by Lord Holland in his "Foreign Reminiscences," that Napoleon, when he had an hour for diversion, not unfrequently employed it in looking over a book of logarithms, which he said was at all seasons of his life a recreation to him.* It would be curious, and

---

* Lord Holland's Foreign Reminiscences, p. 174, Am. ed. I am rather sorry to see this volume quoted as authority for any thing; but as it is not matter of defamation, it may be credible. I know nothing more painful in political literature than these posthumous effusions of Lord Holland, who was known on this side the Atlantic, thanks very much to one of Mr. Macaulay's reviews, as a good-humoured, liberal nobleman, in the sunshine of whose hospitality literary men of England were wont to congregate—who was a scholar and a *gentle*man. These books, published since his death, as well those relating to foreign as domestic politics, show him to have been the studious recorder of

perhaps not unprofitable, to speculate on such a process of recreation, and trace its relation to the active life which was refreshed by it. The poet Shelley is said to have been extremely fond of mathematics, and every hard, dry science; and I can well conceive that such fondness may be traced to the relief and repose which such subjects brought to one whose imagination soared amid the clouds, and whose moral creed was filled with wild and wondering speculations. Another poet, whose genius had wiser mastery over his imagination, Wordsworth, in the poetic history of his mind, speaking of geometric truths, has said,

> "Mighty is the charm
> Of those abstractions to a mind beset
> With images and haunted by herself;
> And specially delightful unto me
> Was that clear synthesis built up aloft
> So gracefully :"*

and the same poet, after describing the agitation of his mind in sharing the excitement and depression of a tumultuous condition of the world, says that he

> "Turned to abstract science, and there sought
> Work for the reasoning faculty enthroned,
> Where the disturbances of space and time,
> Whether in matters various, properties
> Inherent, or from human will and power
> Derived, find no admission."

---

malignant gossip of all sorts of people. Credulity, the wicked credulity that inclines to believe evil of one's kind, is hardly a sufficient apology for such a record. For its publication there is none. His enthusiasm (if such it is) for one so selfish and defamatory as Napoleon, is, in my poor judgment, eminently characteristic. Let me here record my wonder how any American man, fond of the institutions, and proud of the traditions of his country, can have sympathy with any European Bonaparte. W. B. R.

* The Prelude, book vi. p. 503, and book xi. p. 536. Am. ed.

And, in like manner, we may suppose that it was recreation for Napoleon to turn away from a world in which men by thousands and tens of thousands moved for life and death, by his controlling will, and kingdoms shifted about "like clouds obedient to his breath"—to turn away from such life, and find a brief and happy seclusion in the tranquil and enduring truths of abstract science. It may be, too, that the book of logarithms brought with it memories of early days, before he began to bear the giant burden of Europe's fortunes, and thus carried him away to breathe in spirit the clear atmosphere of studious boyhood.

I have spoken of this case to show how various and relative a thing is recreation, as the game of chess is amusement to some minds, while others shrink from it, as Sir Walter Scott says he did, as from a toil and a waste of brains.* Charles Lamb describes the old lady who went so earnestly to her game of whist, that "she could not bear to have her noble occupation, to which she wound up her faculties, considered in the light of unbending the mind after serious studies in recreation. . . . She unbent her mind afterwards, over a book."* In like manner, with regard to books, their recreative character is greatly modified by the disposition of the recipient. Mr. Dickens has somewhere a story of a sombre-spirited sentimentalist, who pronounced Milton's "L'Allegro" his worst performance, and complained of Gray's Elegy as too light and frivolous.

If the case of Napoleon shows a peculiar recreation congenial to a spirit of the most intense energy, literary history tells of such a case as that of Cowper, where the

---

* *Lockhart's Scott*, vol. i. p. 174.

† Mrs. Battle's Opinions of Whist. Lamb's Prose Works, vol. ii. p. 74.

hauntings of melancholy were allayed by sportive invention. His biographer tells us, that "For a while Lady Austen's conversation had as happy an effect upon the melancholy spirit of Cowper as the harp of David upon Saul. Whenever the cloud seemed to be coming over him, her sprightly powers were exerted to dispel it. One afternoon, when he appeared more than usually depressed, she told him the story of John Gilpin, which had been told to her in her childhood, and which, in her relation tickled his fancy as much as it has that of thousands and tens of thousands since in his. The next morning, he said to her that he had been kept awake during the greater part of the night by thinking of the story and laughing at it, and that he had turned it into a ballad. The ballad was sent to Mr. Unwin, who said in reply that it had made him laugh tears. Cowper himself said in one of his letters: 'If I trifle, and merely trifle, it is because I am reduced to it by necessity; a melancholy, that nothing else so effectually disperses, engages me sometimes in the arduous task of being merry by force. And, strange as it may seem, the most ludicrous lines I ever wrote have been written in the saddest mood, and but for that saddest mood, perhaps, had never been written at all.'"*

But it is not only for their recreative agency that the faculties of wit and humour are to be considered; they are also to be regarded as elements of genius, as entering into the constitution of the highest order of the human mind. I do not, of course, mean that every man eminent in the world of letters or of action is a wit or a humourist; but

* Southey's Cowper, vol. ii. p. 74.

that there is abundant proof, either in acts or written words, of the presence of these faculties, made more or less manifest, according to the tenor of the life or the subject of the writings, and not unfrequently breaking forth through adverse circumstances of life or unpropitious topics of books. When Dr. Arnold is describing the great Carthaginian hero putting on a variety of disguises to baffle the attempts of assassins, he says: Hannibal "wore false hair, appearing sometimes as a man of mature years, and sometimes with the grey hair of old age; and if he *had that taste for humour which great men are seldom without*, and which some anecdotes of him imply, he must have been often amused by the mistakes thus occasioned, and have derived entertainment from that which policy or necessity dictated."* A thoughtful and eloquent defender of Luther, in excusing the plainness, and even coarseness, of expression for which he has been reproached, says, "he could not mince his words, or take thought about suiting them to fastidious ears, even if there had been such to suit them to; and the humour with which he was so richly gifted, and which is the natural associate of an intense love of truth, if it be not rather a particular form and manifestation of that love, led him to strip off the artificial drapery and conventional formalities of life, and to look straight at the realities hidden beneath them in their naked contrasts and contradictions." I quote the passage simply as an authority for considering humour as a "natural associate of an intense love of truth, perhaps rather a particular form and manifestation of that love," and thus explaining, at least in part, how it enters into the

* History of Rome, vol. iii. p. 102.

constitution of genius. Observe, too, that it is the strongest and most capacious mind which will perceive most keenly and feel most deeply the manifold and perpetually occurring contradictions, and incongruities, and inconsistencies of life, the slight steppings down from the sublime to the ridiculous, the quaint contact of the comic and the solemn, provoking the laugh at the wrong time or in the wrong place, and all the strange combinations which grow out of man's mingled nature of strength and weakness, which a thoughtful mind observes in others, and is yet more deeply conscious of it in itself. These things are the themes of wit and humour. There is another order of minds, narrower in its range of observation, and less reflective on its own being, which, dwelling within the covert of some hypothesis of its own, shapes the world to its own standard, and neither sees nor feels the incongruities of humanity. Such is not genius—but a dry, hard, and mechanical sort of intellect, and wit and humour are all mystery to it.

The authors who deal most largely with human nature are those in whom the elements of wit and humour will be most displayed—in connection, however, with serious elements. This will be seen especially in those writers whose imaginations have produced the greatest number of creations—I mean of invented characters—representative of humanity. In English literature, the three who may, I think, be regarded as pre-eminent for the number and life-like reality of their creations, are Chaucer, Shakspeare, and Scott; and in their writings may be found the finest specimens of genuine humour, coupled, too, with tragic power equally admirable. It is remarkable, too, to observe how, in an early age, the large imagination of Chaucer blended with the tenderest pathos a humour coarse at times, but again as delicate as any of an age of refinement—such as his description of the "Sergeant of the Law," which is like a smile of kindly-natured humour, rather than a stroke or a sneer of satire:

> "Discreet he was, and of great reverence
> He seemed such, his words were so wise:
> * * * * *
> Nowhere so busy a man as he there n'as,
> And yet he seemed busier than he was."

Examples without number of Sir Walter Scott's genial humour, as displayed in the personages of his novels, will rise up to the thoughts of any one. How beautifully is it interwoven with the serious passages in the Antiquary! How it gleams through the clouds of civil war and the gloom of Puritan severity in Old Mortality! and what a fine relief does it not give to the deeper tragedy of the Bride of Lammermoor! In Shakspeare, the whole subject might be studied and illustrated through a boundless variety of character, from the malevolent and wicked wit of Iago, with its serpent-like venom, the inexhaustible resources of Falstaff, the morbid humour of Jaques, or the healthy humour of Falconbridge, and the many other phases of these faculties in his men and women.

These powers may be discovered also in other great poets of our language, the subjects or forms of whose poems were less favourable to their appearance. The pensive atmosphere with which the sage and solemn spirit of Spenser has enveloped the region of his Faery Land, admits, at times, some rays of a quaint humour. In Milton, the powers assume so stern an aspect, that one hesitates in associating them with wit and humour, and yet, assuredly, such are the faculties, in their most repulsive shape, both in his prose writings and his poems, betraying how a grand and noble spirit was imbittered by the adverse circumstances of both public and private life. It was eminently characteristic for him to speak of "anger and laughter," as "those two most rational faculties of human intellect," and to boast of that "vein of laughing," which "hath ofttimes a strong and sinewy force in teaching and confuting."*

The presence of these faculties in the greatest English prose writers is also susceptible of proof. In the most illustrious of the old divines, they appear in a way that is not permitted to later theologians—I refer not only to such instances as the works of the church historian, Thomas Fuller, or the sermons of "the witty Dr. South," but also to the humour which is blended with the reasonings of Barrow and the poetic eloquence of Jeremy Taylor. The wit of Swift is universally recognised as his most effective weapon: and in another masculine mind, also distempered by disease as Swift's was, there was a sort of rough humour, in Dr. Johnson's. The high-toned eloquence of Burke, though far from sparkling with wit like Sheridan's, was not without its humour: observe it, too, in his chief political treatise—the quiet humour for example, in the well-known comparison of the noisy, factious pamphleteers with solid unloquacious English sobriety· "Because half-a-dozen grasshoppers under a fern make the field ring with their importunate chirp, while thousands of great cattle reposing beneath the shadow of the British oak, chew the cud and are silent,

* Milton's Prose Works. Preface to Animadversions upon the Remonstrants' Defence against Smectymnuus, p. 55.

pray do not imagine that those who make the noise are the only inhabitants of the field; that, of course, they are many in number; or that, after all, they are other than the little shrivelled, meagre, hopping, though loud and troublesome, insects of the hour."

It is to one of the great divines of the seventeenth cenury that we owe the most famous description (it attempts not definition) of Wit: I refer, of course, to that passage so often, and yet never too often, quoted in Barrow's sermon "against foolish talking and jesting." It was composed at a time when the word "*Wit*" was beginning to change its original meaning of mental power for the more limited sense of later times, and when the faculty itself, having the special favour of the "merry monarch" was in unwonted, and, it may be added, wanton activity. Dr. Barrow said, "To the question what the thing we speak of is, or what this facetiousness doth import? I might reply as Democritus did to him that asked the definition of a man, 'Tis that which we all see and know: any one better apprehends what it is by acquaintance than I can inform him by description. It is, indeed, a thing so versatile and multiform, appearing in so many shapes, so many postures, so many garbs, so variously apprehended by several eyes and judgments, that it seemeth no less hard to settle a clear and certain notion thereof, than to make a portrait of Proteus, or to define the figure of a fleeting air. Sometimes it lieth in a pat allusion to a known story, or in seasonable application of a trivial saying, or in forging an apposite tale: sometimes it playeth in words and phrases, taking advantage from the ambiguity of their sense or the affinity of their sound: sometimes it is wrapped in a dress of humorous expression.

sometimes it lurketh under an odd similitude: sometimes it is lodged in a sly question, in a smart answer, in a quirkish reason, in a shrewd intimation, in cunningly diverting or cleverly retorting an objection: sometimes it is couched in a bold scheme of speech, in a tart irony, in a lusty hyperbole, in a startling metaphor, in a plausible reconciling of contradictions, or in acute nonsense: sometimes a scenical representation of persons or things, a counterfeit speech, a mimical look or gesture, passeth for it: sometimes an affected simplicity, sometimes a presumptuous boldness, giveth it being; sometimes it riseth from a lucky hitting upon what is strange, sometimes from a crafty wresting obvious matter to the purpose; often it consisteth in one knows not what, and springeth up one can hardly tell how. Its ways are unaccountable and inexplicable, being answerable to the numberless rovings of fancy and windings of language. It is, in short, a manner of speaking out of the simple and plain way, (such as reasoning teacheth and proveth things by,) which, by a pretty surprising uncouthness in conceit or expression, doth affect and amuse the fancy, stirring it to some wonder and breeding some delight thereto."

One cannot read this large induction and analytical description of the forms of wit, from the higher inventions down to "acute nonsense," without thinking how thoughtfully this great and learned divine must have observed the wits of the times of Charles the Second, and how genially he must have received what he so wisely expounded! Nor can I discover that the metaphysicians have been able to advance beyond this description to the more precise ground of definition. The most acute of the Greek philosophers, Aristotle, gave what is at best a negative definition of the laughable, when he said it depended on what is out of its proper time and place, yet without danger or pain. That remarkable but wrong-headed English philosopher, Hobbes, who thought that war was man's natural state, defined laughter to be "a sudden glory arising from a sudden conception of some eminency in ourselves, by comparison with infirmity of others or our own infirmity." The definitions given by Locke and by the Scotch rhetoricians, and the analysis made by Coleridge and by Sydney Smith, have done little more than trace the effect of wit or humour to an agreeable surprise occasioned by an unusual connection of thoughts. Still more difficult would it be to trace the subtle relations between wit and humour, and to analyze that higher form in which both are combined, but for which language helps us with no name. Wit may, I think, be regarded as a purely intellectual process, while humour is a sense of the ridiculous controlled by feeling, and coexistent often with the gentlest and deepest pathos, visible, it may be, even in those smiles which have been finely described, as "a sad heart's sunshine."

Often the simple sense of incongruity produces the effect of the laughable—the unfitness of the means to the end, as in some of Dr. Johnson's definitions, where his Latinized dialect makes him like the interpreter in Sheridan's farce, the harder to be understood of the two—his definition of "Network—any thing reticulated or decussated at equal distances, with interstices between the intersections," or when, in the preface to his Dictionary, in explanation of the difficulty of ranging the meanings of a word in order, he asks: "When the radical idea branches out into parallel ramifications, how can a consecutive series be formed of senses in their nature collateral?"

Again, when Johnson defines "Excise," to be "a hateful tax levied upon commodities, and adjudged, not by the common judges of property, but wretches hired by those to whom excise is paid:" and Pension, to be "an allowance made to any one without an equivalent. In England it is generally understood to mean pay given to a state-hireling for treason to his country"—a comic effect is produced by the unexpected encounter with such a fervid temper among the dispassionate definitions of a dictionary, almost as if one should meet with a spiteful demonstration in geometry.* To an ear accustomed to simple English, simple in the choice and in the arrangement of the words, the highly Latinized and stately sentences of Dr. Johnson now make an impression bordering sometimes on the ludicrous—owing, I think, to the unnatural disparity between his style and the ordinary colloquial use of language: this was curiously shown by a practical joke that was practised on that worthy and simple-mannered man, the late Sir David Wilkie, by a fellow-painter and his brother, and described in the Memoir of Collins, the landscape-painter: "Mr. Collins's brother Francis possessed a remarkably retentive memory, which he was accustomed to use for the amusement of himself and others in the following manner. He learnt by heart a whole number of one of Dr. Johnson's 'Ramblers,' and used to occasion considerable diversion to those in the secret, by repeating it all through to a new company, in a conversational tone, as if it was the accidental product of his own fancy,—now

* It may have been a definition like that of "*excise*," which occasioned the criticism from a Scotch peasant, whom Sir Walter Scott found reading aloud the Dictionary containing the authorities, "that they were braw stories, but unco short." H. R.

addressing his flow of moral eloquence to one astonished auditor, and now to another. One day, when the two brothers were dining at Wilkie's, it was determined to try the experiment upon their host. After dinner, accordingly, Mr. Collins paved the way for the coming speech, by leading the conversation imperceptibly to the subject of the paper in the 'Rambler.' At the right moment, Francis Collins began. As the first grand Johnsonian sentences struck upon his ear, (uttered, it should be remembered, in the most elaborately careless and conversational manner,) Wilkie started at the high tone that the conversation had suddenly assumed, and looked vainly for explanation to his friend Collins, who, on his part, sat with his eyes respectfully fixed on his brother, all wrapt attention to the eloquence that was dropping from his lips. Once or twice, with perfect mimicry of the conversational character he had assumed, Francis Collins hesitated, stammered, and paused, as if collecting his thronging ideas. At one or two of these intervals, Wilkie endeavoured to speak, to ask a moment for consideration; but the torrent of his guest's eloquence was not to be delayed . . . until at last it reached its destined close; and then Wilkie, who, as host, thought it his duty to break silence by the first compliment, exclaimed, with the most perfect unconsciousness of the trick that had been played him, 'Ay, ay, Mr. Francis; verra clever—(though I did not understand it *all*)—verra clever!' "

It not unfrequently happens, also, that a sense of the ludicrous in style may be traced in a false and florid rhetoric to the incongruous combination of literal and figurative forms of expression. Reading the Earl of Ellesmere's agreeable and usually well-written History of the Two

Sieges of Vienna, I noted this sentence: speaking of Sobieski, he says, "inspired by the memory of former victories, . . . he flung his powerful frame into the saddle, and his great soul into the cause." This is that juxtaposition of the literal and metaphorical, which is best exemplified by a well-known instance in a panegyric on the celebrated Robert Boyle, in which he was described as "father of chemistry, and brother of the Earl of Cork." Again, another form of the literary ludicrous, is in the incongruous combination of metaphors produced by the want of discipline in speech, increased, perhaps, by an excess of unguided fancy. Lord Castlereagh's parliamentary speeches are said to have been full of such confusion of language—without, however, spoiling the speaker's high bearing and elegance of manner: in one of these speeches he used that sentence in which, perhaps, there is as curious an infelicity of speech and confusion of figure as ever were crowded into as small a number of words, "And now, sir, I must *embark* into the *feature* on which this question chiefly *hinges*."*

* My impression is, that these traditions as to Lord Castlereagh are not now regarded as trustworthy. His is one of the cases (I speak of the American mind) in which a healthy revolution of opinion may be traced. Thirty—nay, twenty—years ago, when Gallican sympathies were active, and Moore's clever pasquinades in every one's mouth, Lord Castlereagh was an especial object of disparagement. Let any one study his correspondence, lately published, especially in 1814 and 1815, and it will be seen what a manly, honest-minded statesman he was. It is a matter, I believe, of well-ascertained diplomatic tradition, that such was his uniform temper and tone in all his relations to this country. The fact, too, is unquestionable, that extreme conservatives, such as Lord Castlereagh and Lord Aberdeen have always shown more consideration, and made themselves more acceptable to our representatives abroad, than others claiming to be more liberal. W. B. R.

And so in that form of error, which is regarded as belonging pre-eminently to Lord Castlereagh's countrymen, that strange mixture of error and accuracy, called an "Irish bull," the ludicrous effect is, I believe, produced by the sense working its way out through the complexity and confusion of the phrase.

Sir Walter Scott, in the account of his tour in Ireland, mentions an occurrence which illustrates this form of the laughable, for it is a sort of bull in action. "They were widening," he says, "the road near Lord Claremont's seat as we passed. A number of cars were drawn up together at a particular point, where we also halted, as we understood they were blowing a rock, and the shot was expected presently to go off. After waiting two minutes or so, a fellow called out something, and our carriage as a planet, and the cars for satellites, started all forward at once, the Irishmen whooping and the horses galloping. Unable to learn the meaning of this, I was only left to suppose that they had delayed firing the intended shot till we should pass, and that we were passing quickly to make the delay as short as possible. No such thing; by dint of making great haste, we got within ten yards of the rock just when the blast took place, throwing dust and gravel in our carriage; and had our postillion brought us a little nearer, (it was not for want of hollowing and flogging that he did not,) we should have had a still more serious share of the explosion. The explanation I received from the drivers was, that they had been told by the overseer that as the mine had been so long in going off, he dared say we would have time to pass it, so we just waited long enough to make the danger imminent. I have only to add, that two or three people got behind the carriage, just for nothing but to see how our honours got past."*

It is curious, let me remark, to observe how a form of expression which is essentially a bull, may be lifted out of the region of the ridiculous, as in that truly poetic expression of Keats:

> "So the two brothers and *their murdered man*
> Rode toward fair Florence."†

Now, if that be looked at in a prosaic point of view, it becomes a downright blunder, but, poetically, you see in it the activity of the imagination darting forward to the murder, a "ghastly foregone conclusion," as Leigh Hunt has well called it.

I have spoken of the incongruity of style: there may also be such incongruity of time as to make the anachronism laughable. Washington Irving, one of the finest of modern humorous writers, has shown this in that practical anachronism: "Rip Van Winkle." It is, I believe, Horace Walpole, who tells of one of the family pictures of the De Levis, a French family that prided itself on its great antiquity; it was a picture of an antediluvian scene, in which Noah was represented going into the ark with a bundle of the archives of the house of De Levi under his arm.‡ I have myself seen in a private library in this city an old Bible, with engravings, Dutch, I believe they were; one of which pictured an Old Testament event; in the foreground Samson slaying the lion, if I remember rightly,

* Lockhart's Scott.

† Keats's Poetical Works, p. 42. Isabella, or the Pot of Basil.

‡ This is in a note by Lord Dover. Horace Walpole's joke is rather less decorous. Collected Works. vol. ii. p. 298. W. B. R.

and in the background a man with a fowling-piece shooting snipe.

These are broad incongruities, bordering upon the farcical: there are others, either wilful or unconscious, which are more delicate in their impression. When Lady Sale made in her diary the simple entry, "Earthquakes as usual," the humour was in the coolness of the womanly courage, and the notion of the frequency coupled with one of the rarest and most appalling of earthly perils. It was not unlike the advertisement beginning, "Anybody in want of a diving-bell," as if a diving-bell was one of the common wants in society. A quaint example recurs to my mind in this connection: it is in Horrebou's History of Iceland, an old folio volume, which is divided into chapters according to various subjects: one of these is headed (chapter 47,) "Concerning Owls." I can quote the whole chapter without fatiguing you, for it is in these words: "There are in Iceland no owls of any kind whatever." Yet the historian seems to have considered himself under some obligation to that species of birds, so far as to devote a chapter to their absence.

These unexpected connections, which are produced by wit or humour, carried beyond the mere ludicrous effect, are seen also subserving argumentation, as these processes are combined by Swift in his "Drapier's Letters," and other occasional pieces; by De Foe, or in later times by Walter Scott, in his letters on the Scotch currency question; and yet more in Sydney Smith's writings, the wittiest reasoning and satire in the language. There is, perhaps no more characteristic passage than that suggested by his reflections on the learned prolixity of Dr. Parr. "There is an event," he goes on to say, "recorded in the Bible, which men who write books should keep constantly in their remembrance. It is there set forth, that many centuries ago the earth was covered with a great flood, by which the whole of the human race, with the exception of one family, were destroyed. It appears also, that from thence a great alteration was made in the longevity of mankind, who, from a range of seven hundred or eight hundred years, were confined to their present period of seventy or eighty years. This epoch in the history of man gave birth to the twofold division of the antediluvian and the postdiluvian style of writing, the latter of which naturally contracted itself into those inferior limits which were better accommodated to the abridged duration of human life and literary labour. Now to forget this event, to write without the fear of the deluge before his eyes, and to handle a subject as if mankind could lounge over a pamphlet for ten years, as before their submersion, is to be guilty of the most grievous error into which a writer can possibly fall. The author of this book should call in the aid of some brilliant pencil, and cause the distressing scenes of the deluge to be pourtrayed in the most lively colours for his use. He should gaze at Noah, and be brief. The ark should constantly remind him of the little time there is left for reading; and he should learn, as they did in the ark, to crowd a great deal of matter into a very little compass."* This was written in Sydney Smith's early reviewing days; but his wit took a more concentrated form, as when he said of Lord John Russel, "His worst failure is that he is utterly ignorant of all moral fear; there is nothing he would not undertake. I

* Edinburgh Review, 1809. Works, vol. ii. p. 208.

believe he would perform the operation for the stone, build St. Peter's, or assume (with or without ten minutes' notice) the command of the channel fleet; and no one would discover by his manner that the patient had died, the church tumbled down, and the channel fleet been knocked to atoms;" and then he adds quietly in a note, "Another peculiarity of the Russels is, that they never alter their opinions: they are an excellent race, but they must be trepanned before they can be convinced."* Nay, sometimes the subtle element is concentrated in a single word or phrase, as when he speaks of "a gentleman lately from the Pyramids or the upper cataracts, *let loose* upon the drawing-room;" or that phrase, so excellent in the satire, and admitting unfortunately of such frequent application, which mentions an orator "splashing in the froth of his own rhetoric"—a descriptive image which is worth a whole chapter of rhetorical admonition.

This combination of wit and reasoning makes also much of the virtue of that instruction which, in Fables, charms the mind of childhood, and is not cast aside by mature reason. It enters, too, into a people's instruction by proverbs, which have been happily described as "the wisdom of many and the wit of one."

One of the most remarkable uses of wit and humour, is that which combines them with tragedy, and makes them subservient to tragic effect. These combinations seem to be denied to modern art by the refinement or daintiness of later times; and by such denial, modern art loses much of the power which resulted from that natural blending of the humorous and the serious, each equally earnest,

* Second Letter to Archdeacon Singleton, Works, vol. iii. p. 193, 194.

which may be seen in the early minstrelsy, and in the highest form of genius and art in Shakspeare's deepest tragedies. The most careless reader must have noticed how profoundly the tragic pathos of King Lear is deepened by the wild wit and pathetic humour of that faithful and full-hearted follower—the fool. Remember how, in Hamlet, one of the most solemn scenes is preceded by the quaint professional witticisms of the gravedigger, so different and yet not discordant. In Macbeth the brief and awful interval between the murder of Duncan, and the disclosure of it, is filled with that rudely-comic passage of the drunken, half-sobered porter, to whose gross jocularity you pass from the high-wrought frenzy of Macbeth, reeking with his victim's blood, and from the yet more fearful atrocity of his wife, to return quickly to the tragic horror on the discovery of the murder; and in that transition, through a species of the comic, the harmony is preserved by the quaint allusions to hell and the vain equivocations to heaven.

Another kindred combination, which also shows a unity connecting the serious and the sportive, proving what Socrates is said to have asserted, that there is a common ground for tragedy and comedy, is in that contrast between the thought or feeling and its expression, which is termed "*irony*." It is the humorous wresting of language from its literal use for the expression of feeling, either happy or painful, but too vehement to be contented with that literal use. The pensive perplexity of a gentle and philosophic soul like Hamlet, bewildered and self-secluded in a wicked world, finds relief in almost every form of bitter or tranquil humour for meditations and for emotions that overmastered him. When the thoughtful spirit of Macbeth is distorted by guilt, and as the agony of that guilt grows more and more intense, the pent-up misery either flows forth in a subdued irony, or breaks out in that which is fierce and frenzied. In one very familiar passage, the beauty of the expression makes many a reader forget that it is pure and essential irony: when Macbeth puts to the Doctor the simple and literal inquiry after Lady Mabeth:

> "How does your patient, doctor?
> *Doctor.* Not so sick, my lord,
> As she is troubled with thick-coming fancies,
> That keep her from her rest."

Then comes the deep feeling, with its ironical questions, sounding more like soliloquy:

> "Cure her of that:
> Canst thou not minister to a mind diseased?
> Pluck from the memory a rooted sorrow?
> Raze out the written troubles of the brain?
> And, with some sweet, oblivious antidote,
> Cleanse the stuff'd bosom of that perilous grief
> Which weighs upon the heart?"

The literal answer—

> "Therein the patient
> Must minister to himself"—

brings him back to reality with the exclamation,

> "Throw physic to the dogs, I'll none of it!"

But, even in the irritable putting on of his armour, the bitter relief of an ironical humour comes again in another form:

> "What rhubarb, senna, or what purgative drug
> Would scour these English hence?"

If the truthfulness of such use of irony be doubted, let

it be remembered how abundantly and remarkably it pervades Holy Writ. I do not refer merely to the bitter, ironical taunts which the prophet hurled at the priests of Baal, but to the manifold use of it in the expression of thoughts and emotions affecting the spiritual intercourse of man and his Maker. Remember how something of the kind breaks out in the very midst of St. Paul's most solemn argument. Again, it is not contrary to nature—it is not a levity unworthy of man's nature—that these playful faculties make their appearance in the most awful realities of life. The gentle spirit of Anne Boleyn was pleasant with the headsman on the scaffold; and so

> "More's gay genius played
> With the inoffensive sword of native wit,
> Than the bare axe more luminous and keen."*

The power of wit to combine itself harmoniously and vigorously with sagacity and seriousness, is eminently exemplified in all the works of that remarkable author of the seventeenth century, the church historian, Thomas Fuller, whose wit, in the largeness of its circuit, the variety of its expression, its exuberance, and its admirable sanity, stands second only to that of Shakspeare. It has the indispensable merit of perfect naturalness, and the excellence of being a growth from a soil of sound wisdom. There are no large works in our language so thoroughly ingrained with wit and humour as Fuller's "Worthies of England," his Church History of Britain no less so, and the essays entitled "The Holy and Profane State"—essays which, in wit, and wisdom, and just feeling, are not unlike the Elia Essays of Charles Lamb. The genius

* Wordsworth's Ecclesiastical Sonnets, Sonnet 22.

of Fuller is, perhaps, unequalled in harmonizing a play upon words, quiet jocularity, kindly irony, with thoughtfulness and genuine earnestness, and in making the transition from quaintness to sublimity.

The great satire of the eighteenth century, "Gulliver's Travels," exemplifies another form of wit, too often repulsive, not only by indecent coarseness, but by that misanthropy which darkens the writings of Swift. His morbid contemplation of the vices and follies of his fellow-beings betrays the disease which, probably, clung to his whole life, distorting and darkening it with the dread that insanity had a lurking-place in his brain—that haunting consciousness, which once was expressed when walking with the author of the Night Thoughts, (like himself a dealer in distempered fancies and feelings,) Swift, after gazing earnestly at a noble elm which was, in its uppermost branches, withered and decayed, pointing to it, said to Dr. Young, "I shall be like that tree—I shall die at the top."* Arbuthnot, the friend of Swift and Pope, is believed to have had more learning and as much wit as either of them, and with it all a sweetness of temper and purity of character which made Swift exclaim, "Oh, if the world had but a dozen Arbuthnots in it, I would burn my Travels!" It is a sad pity that his genius was not more open to influences of such a character, or of the equally admirable and amiable nature of his other friend, Bishop Berkeley.

The best and most agreeable specimen of English humour (it is humour in contrast to wit) which belongs to that period, is Steele's invention, and Addison's use, of the

* Scott's Life of Swift, p. 291. Am. ed.

character of Sir Roger de Coverley. This will be felt by any one who will select the papers in the Spectator which are devoted to him, and read them continuously, following the good knight to his mansion, to the assizes, to the parish church, where, as soon as he wakes out of a nap during the sermon, he sends his footman to wake up any of the congregation who chance to be asleep; then onward to his death-bed, after having bequeathed (his will chanced to be written on a very cold day) a stout frieze coat to the men, and a comfortable hood to the women, in the parish. The same species of pure, genial, wise, and healthful humour has been sustained in the incomparable Vicar of Wakefield, and in the writings of our countryman, Washington Irving, who is gifted with many of the best qualities of Goldsmith's genius. Among the humorous writers belonging to the literature of our own day, (there are several whom I will not stop to name,) Charles Lamb represented a form of humour of a very high order, and peculiar to himself—a humour which has assumed a deeper interest and commands a higher admiration, now that we know the terrible memories and sorrows of his days—

"The troubles strange,
Many and strange, that hung about his life,"*

and his heroic self-devotion to his afflicted sister.

Our English literature of wit and humour gives abundant proof that these faculties may be either a precious or a perilous possession; precious, as ministering to thoughtful cheerfulness, and serving the cause of truth and gentleness; perilous, as coupled with intellectual pride and

* Wordsworth's Lines, written after the death of Charles Lamb, p. 467, Am. ed.

malevolent passions. I have spoken of the repulsive character of the wit of Dean Swift—still, if unattractive, there was something in his stern hatred of vice and folly, which commands respect; but when you turn to such as Lord Byron's, (as in Don Juan,) there is disease without a particle of the dignity of disease; there is lawless force of mind, owning no restraint of reverence for aught human or divine—sustained by no self-respect, by no confidence in virtue—womanly, even less than manly. Thus wit sinks down into barren scoffing. It is the lowest moral condition when crime clothes itself with jest. Salutary as the culture of the faculties of wit and humour may be, when justly proportioned and controlled, the indulgence of them as a habit is as injurious to him who so indulges it, as it is wearisome to all who encounter it. The habit of always looking at things on the laughable side is sure to lower the tone of thought and feeling, and at length can only content its restless craving by attributing the ridiculous to things which ought to be inviolate by such association. When the habitual joker is sometimes seized with a fit of seriousness, the change is such an incongruity, as to provoke the retaliation of unseasonable jocularity, and no one is as sensitive to ridicule as he who habitually handles it.

Another abuse which may be observed in intercourse with the world, is when jocularity is employed as subterfuge, to escape from the demands of earnestness and candour, and the jest is made a method of non-committal. It is said that Sir Robert Walpole used to divert his guests away from political conversation by a strain of ribald jesting; and a more modern prime minister, the late Lord Melbourne, is described as one whose first impulse, in ordinary conversation, was always to treat things lightly. This was an adroitness, which a higher order of statesmanship does not concern itself to use.

As a habit, wit will prove fatal to that better and wiser cheerfulness which is attendant on imaginative culture—the genuine poetic habit of beholding or discovering the beauty of truth, of moral worth, and whatever of beauty, spiritual or material, is given to man to enjoy. It is said that Hogarth lamented his talent for caricature, as the long practice of it had impaired his capacity for the enjoyment of beauty: while the best critic on his works applauded him as an artist "in whom the satirist never extinguished that love of beauty which belonged to him as a poet;" and who so used his genius as to "prevent the instructive merriment at the whims of nature, or the foibles or humours, of our fellow-men from degenerating into the heart-poison of contempt or hatred."

It is a narrowness of mind which causes the exclusion of either the poetic sense or of wit; it is partial moral culture which refuses the good that is to be gained from either. The larger mind and the well-disciplined heart find room for both powers to dwell together in harmony. Of such harmony let me give a single example in proof—a transition from a passage of well-conceived and well-expressed satire to one no less distinguished by a deep poetic sense of beauty; or rather not so much a transition as a harmonious combination. I quote two passages which occur in close connection in the work of a living author—Mr. Ruskin's Seven Lamps of Architecture.

"Another of the strange tendencies of the present day is to the decoration of the railroad station. Now if there be any place in the world in which people are deprived of that portion of temper and discretion which are necessary to the contemplation of beauty, it is there. It is the very temple of discomfort, and the only charity that the builder can extend to us is to show us, plainly as may as may be, how soonest to escape from it. The whole system of railroad travelling is addressed to people who, being in a hurry, are therefore, for the time being, miserable. No one would travel in that manner who could help it, who had time to go leisurely over hills and between hedges, instead of through tunnels and between banks; at least those who would, have no sense of beauty so acute as that we need consult it at the station. The railroad is, in all its relations, a matter of earnest business, to be got through as soon as possible. It transmutes a man from a traveller into a living parcel. For the time, he has parted with the nobler characteristics of his humanity for the sake of a planetary power of locomotion. Do not ask him to admire any thing. You might as well ask the wind. Carry him safely, dismiss him soon: he will thank you for nothing else. All attempts to please him in any other way are mere mockery, and insults to the things by which you endeavour to do so. There never was more flagrant nor impertinent folly than the smallest portion of ornament in any thing concerned with railroads or near them. Keep them out of the way, take them through the ugliest country you can find, confess them the miserable things they are, and spend nothing upon them but for safety and speed."*

Now turning from satire on ornament misplaced to the sense of beauty well-placed:

* Seven Lamps of Architecture p. 106. The Lamp of Beauty.

"The question of greatest external or internal decoration depends entirely on the condition of probable repose. It was a wise feeling which made the streets of Venice so rich in external ornament, for there is no couch of rest like the gondola. So, again, there is no subject of street ornament so wisely chosen as the fountain, where it is a fountain of use; for it is just there that perhaps the happiest pause takes place in the labour of the day, when the pitcher is rested on the edge of it, and the breath of the bearer is drawn deeply, and the hair swept from the fore head, and the uprightness of the form declined against the marble ledge, and the sound of the kind word or light laugh mixes with the trickle of the falling water, heard shriller and shriller as the pitcher fills. What pause is so sweet as that—so full of the depth of ancient days, so softened with the calm of pastoral solitude?"

LECTURE XII.

The Literature of Letter-Writing.*

Characteristics of a true letter—Historical and familiar letters—Lord Bacon—Dr. Arnold's remarks—Despatches of Marlborough—Nelson—Franklin—John Adams—Reception by George III.—Washington's correspondence—Bishop White's anecdote of Washington—American diplomatic correspondence—Lord Chatham's Letters—Duke of Wellington's—Archdeacon Hare's remarks on—General Taylor's official letters—Familiar letters—Cowley—Impropriety of publishing private correspondence—Arbuthnot and Johnson's remarks on—Burns's Letters—Tennyson—Howell's Letters—The Paston Letters—Lady Russell's—Pope's—Hartley Coleridge's remark—Chesterfield—Horace Walpole—Swift and Gray's—Cowper's—Scott's—Byron's—Southey's, and Lamb's Letters of Dedication—Lamb's to his sister.

In devoting a lecture to what I have entitled "The Literature of Letter-Writing," I had less hope of being able to make the treatment of such a subject interesting than of pointing out some of the uses of this department, and suggesting the agreeable and instructive reading which is to be found in collections of letters. It is a department which may be viewed in several aspects, either as tributary to history, political or literary, or as a form

---

* March 20, 1851. Had I no other reason for publishing this, the last of this series of lectures, I could find one in the familiarity it shows with American history and its original materials. Thoroughly imbued as was the writer with the spirit and sentiment of English literature, he was as well-informed in all that related to his own country, its men, and its republican institutions. W. B. R.

of biography—thus helping us to a knowledge of the movements of mankind, or of individual character, by its written disclosures. Our English literature is enriched with collections of remarkable and very various interest: so varied as to furnish an abundant adaptation to different tastes. In treating this subject, my aim will be to endeavour not to wander off into either history or biography, but, as far as possible, to confine my attention to the epistolary literature in itself, making some comments on the principal collections, and incidentally considering the character of a true letter. It happens not unfrequently that the form of the letter is assumed for the sake of convenience, when neither the writer nor the hearer is at all deluded in the belief that the production is what is usually understood by the term "a letter," or epistle. Essays, disquisitions, satires, wear the epistolary name and garb, fulfilling a not unreasonable fancy of the writer that such a medium interposes less of formality between him and his readers, and, indeed, brings them into closer and more life-like relations—the letter being somehow more of a reality between the writer and the recipient, than a book is between the author and the reader. The "Drapier's Letters" of Swift, Bolingbroke's Letter to Wyndham, the "Letters of Junius," Burke's "Reflections on the French Revolution," and other similar productions, of which there are many with an epistolary designation, do not belong to the proper class of "Letters;" to which class I propose to confine my attention—at the outset simply suggesting to your minds that it is a subject which does not admit of convenient illustration in a Lecture.

I have arranged this subject under the two general divisions "historical letters" and "familiar letters"—an arrangement which may be found convenient in the general consideration of it, but which makes no pretension to any thing of logical precision. Under the first head, I do not propose to limit the class to public or official correspondence, but rather to comprehend such letters, whether public or private, which subserve a knowledge of history, and are thus valuable in the study of it: while the second class, being under a more exact principle of classification, is intended to include those private letters, the nature of which is readily understood by the title "Familiar Letters;" and the true aim and character of which I will endeavour to explain, when I come to that division of my subject.

Lord Bacon, in his treatise on the Advancement of Learning—that great legacy, so rich in counsel for the guidance of inquiry in various departments of human knowledge, that treasury of sagacious sentences of advice—has specially referred to letters among what he calls the "Appendices" to history. "Letters," he says, "are according to all the variety of occasions, advertisements, advices, directions, propositions, petitions, commendatory, expostulatory, satisfactory; of compliment, of pleasure, of discourse, and all other passages of action. And such as are written from wise men are, of all the words of man, in my judgment, the best; for they are more natural than orations and public speeches, and more advised than conferences or private ones. So, again, letters of affairs from such as manage them, or are privy to them, are, of all others, the best instructions for history, and, to a diligent reader, the best histories in themselves."

Another wise counsellor, in a later day, the late Dr

Arnold, speaking words of special advice to the student of history, after noticing that "alchemy which can change apparently dull (historical) materials into bright gold," adds, "some of the great men of our age have, in all probability, left some memorials of their minds behind them—speeches, it may be, or *letters*, or a journal; or, possibly, works of a deeper character, in which they have handled, expressly and deliberately, some of the questions which most interested their generation. Now, if our former researches have enabled us to people our view of the past with many images of events, institutions, usages, titles, etc., to make up with some completeness what may be called the still life of the picture, we shall next be anxious to people it also with the images of its great individual men, to change it, as it were, from a landscape or a view of buildings, to what may truly be called an historical picture. Whoever has made himself famous by his actions, or even by his rank or position in society, so that his name is at once familiar to our ears, such a man's writings have an interest for us even before we begin to read them; the instant that he gets up, as it were, to address us, we are hushed into the deepest attention. These works give us an insight not only into the spirit of an age, as exemplified in the minds of its greatest men, but they multiply, in some sort, the number of those with whom we are personally and individually in sympathy; they enable us to recognise, amid the dimness of remote and uncongenial ages, the features of friends and of brethren."

Of the many indications of the great activity and zeal of historical research and study, which distinguishes the present times, none is more remarkable than the care which has been bestowed in collecting and publishing the letters, official and private, of men eminent in their day and in the thoughts of posterity—men illustrious in civil or military life. Within a short period this has grown to be an extensive and most valuable department of historical literature; and the light that has issued from it has not only dispelled frequently much of traditional, oft-repeated error, but given to the historian, both student and writer, larger privileges of power to gain the truth, and new duties in striving for it. It is within a few years past that English history has been illustrated by the publication of Cromwell's letters, of the letters of the Duke of Marlborough, the Stuart papers, the letters to and from the leader of that luckless family during all their years of hope and despair for the recovery of the throne of England, the correspondence of Lord Chatham, the despatches of Nelson, and all the despatches and general orders of the Duke of Wellington, beginning at a camp in India and closing after the battle of Waterloo. In American history, the contributions of epistolary materials have been no less valuable; for we have the whole series of the letters of Washington, extending through his career of military and civil services, and illustrating both his public and private life; the letters of Dr. Franklin, comprehending a scientific, as well as political, career, and the composite collection of letters from various pens, entitled "The Diplomatic Correspondence of the Revolution and of the period of the Confederation." Many other collections of letters have appeared both in England and the United States; but the most important which I have mentioned amply exemplify the extent to which history has of late received contributions of this kind

Their general historical value I need not stop to speak of; but let me remark that, as many minds are attracted by biography, and find in the deeds and words of their fellow-men individually an interest and sympathy more vivid than that which general history inspires, a collection of letters may have such completeness—may be so identified, both as to time and the participation of the writer in public events—that history may be read in the letters, and thus achieved through the medium of biography. It is a method of reading which will be found very agreeable, as well as instructive, and has a peculiar advantage, too, in giving the reader that discipline of mind which may be gained by the effort, to which he is attracted consciously, or unawares, of giving something of historical consistency to the informal and familiar narrative of events found in a series of letters; and, further, the moral discipline of freer opinion, instead of that more submissive process of always having his mind made up for him by that kind of historical dictation of which Charles Lamb complained, when he said, "The modern historian flings at once the dead weight of his own judgment into the scale, and settles the matter," when a wider and more independent sense of truth would come to a less arbitrary conclusion.

To all readers of history, whether the taste be for pure history or for biography, a letter will often give a reality to an historical occurrence, the truth of which is otherwise much less life-like. Allow me to give an illustration of this in a well-known incident in our own history. I refer to what may be considered the very last fact in the history of the war of American Independence, the shaking of hands as it were, when the fighting was done, the reception by George the Third of the first American ambassador, which consummated the treaty of peace, and the recognition by Great Britain of the United States among the nations of the earth. The pertinacity with which the British monarch had protracted the war, while it showed the unwise statesmanship of the times, illustrated two traits in the king's character—his obstinacy and his honesty. He probably thought he had no more right to consent to the partition of the British Empire than to pawn or part with the crown jewels; and thus an unwise and unnatural war was lengthened out, even after the question of independence was practically settled. The obstinacy of the sovereign had, however, an element of uprightness in it, which may be spoken of with respect, especially when one reflects on what is not so generally known, that anxiety and sleeplessness, during the American war, are believed, by those who had opportunities of judging, to have laid the foundation of that mental malady with which George the Third was afflicted during many of the latter years of his life. The first American minister to his court was, let it be remembered, John Adams, one whose name could not but have been familiar to the king as one of the earliest and most strenuous of the leaders of colonial resistance. The interview on his reception was one full of impressive recollections for both, accompanied with more than ordinary emotion, and it comes within the scope of general history to record that it was conducted in a manner honourable to each. It is, however, Mr. Adams's letter to Mr. Jay that alone produces an adequate conception of the interview. Mr. Adams mentions, that his first thought and intention was to deliver his credentials silently and retire, but being advised by several of the other foreign ministers to make a speech, he made a short address to the king, concluding with the expression of the hope of "being instrumental in restoring an entire esteem, confidence, and affection, or, in better words, the old good-nature and the old good-humour, between people who, though separated by an ocean, and under different governments, have the same language, a similar religion, and kindred blood."

This was well said—worthy of the representative of the young nation—manly thoughts and feelings, well meant and well worded. Mr. Adams, in his letter, goes on to say: "The King listened to every word I said with dignity, but with an apparent emotion. Whether it was the nature of the interview, or whether it was my visible agitation, for I felt more than I did or could express, that touched him, I cannot say; but he was much affected, and answered me with more tremor than I had spoken with, and said—

"'Sir, the circumstances of this audience are so extraordinary, the language you have now held is so extremely proper, and the feelings you have discovered so justly adapted to the occasion, that I must say that I not only receive with pleasure the assurance of the friendly dispositions of the United States, but that I am very glad the choice has fallen upon you to be their minister. I wish you, sir, to believe, and that it may be understood in America, that I have done nothing in the late contest but what I thought myself indispensably bound to do by the duty which I owed to my people. I will be very frank with you. I was the last to consent to the separation; but the separation having been made, and having become inevitable, I have always said, as I say now, that I would be the first to meet the friendship of the United States as an independent power.'" . . . Mr. Adams adds, "He (the king) was much affected, and I was not less so;" and certainly the occasion, as thus pictured in a letter was one fitted to awaken no small emotion, a conflict of many emotions, for how at that moment, must the memories of twenty years of civil strife, with all its varying fortunes and hopes, have risen up to the minds of those two men as they were thus confronted! If there had been obstinacy and wrong in the royal policy which had assented to the first restrictive measure on American trade in 1764, to the Stamp Act, to the Boston Port Bill, to the conduct of the war, at once cruel and imbecile, to that greatest and most tyrannic error, fatal of itself to reconciliation, the hiring of the Hessians—there was on the other hand good feeling and a manly frankness in the expression, at the close of twenty years from the beginning of the colonial diffiulties, of a solicitude that it might be understood in America that in all, he had done nothing but what he thought himself in duty bound to do.

Not the least interesting portion of such a letter is that which describes what passed after the formalities of the interview were over. "The King," writes Mr. Adams, "then asked me whether I came last from France, and upon my answering in the affirmative, he put on an air of familiarity, and smiling, or rather laughing, said, There is an opinion among some people that you are not the most attached of all your countrymen to the manners of France. I was surprised at this, because I thought it an indiscretion and a departure from dignity. I was a little embarrassed, but determined not to deny the truth, on the one hand, nor leave him to infer from it any attachment to England, on the other. I threw off as much of gravity as I could, and assumed an air of gayety and a tone of decision as far as was decent, and said, That opinion, sir, was not mistaken. I must avow to your majesty I have no attachment but to my own country. The king replied, as quick as lightning, An honest (man) will never have any other."

I have quoted these passages to show how a letter may place a familiar piece of history in a more vivid light of truth and reality than mere historic narration gives to it; illustrating Horace Walpole's remark that "nothing gives so just an idea of an age as genuine letters; nay, history waits for its last seal from them."

It is in another letter from John Adams to John Jay that there occurs a character of George the Third, as just, probably, as has been written. "The King, I really think," says Mr. Adams, "is the most accomplished courtier in his dominions; with all the affability of Charles the Second, he has all the domestic virtues and regularity of conduct of Charles the First. He is the greatest talker in the world, and a tenacious memory stored with resources of small talk, concerning all the little things of life, which are inexhaustible. But so much of his time is and has been consumed in this, that he is, in all the great affairs of society and government, as weak, as far as I can judge, as we ever understood him to be in America. He is also as obstinate. The unbounded popularity acquired by his temperance and facetiousness, added to the splendour of his dignity, gives him such a continual feast of flattery, that he thinks all he does is right, and he pursues his own ideas with a firmness which would become the best system of action. He has a pleasure in his own will and way, without which he would be miserable, which seems to be the true principle upon which he has always chosen and rejected ministers."*

It is a happy thing for the student of history, and indeed for the American citizen, that the letters of Washington have been preserved in remarkable completeness—a result in no small degree owing to those exact habits of business which a controlling sense of duty carried through his whole career. The manifold lessons which those letters inculcate are as legible as that admirable handwriting, which, without pretensions to elegance, or that delicacy which often belongs to the pen of men of letters, (such as Gray's, and Cowper's, and Southey's,) is eminently characteristic in its uniformity, regularity, and firmness. The historical value of the letters may readily be conceived, when it is remembered that they extend over the whole era of early American nationality, connecting it by actual presence and participation. I speak of that era in an extended completeness, beginning with the old French war, which is properly to be regarded as part of the preparation for the War of Independence, continued onward through the Revolution, its immediate sequel, the feeble period of the Confederation, and the triumphant completion of the political change in the establishment

* The recently-published diary of Mr. Adams contains, under date of 30th March, 1786, the following very characteristic entry:

"Went at nine o'clock to the French ambassador's ball, where were two or three hundred people, chiefly ladies. Here I met the Marquis of Lansdowne and the Earl of Harcourt. These two noblemen ventured to enter into conversation with me; so did Sir George Young. But there is an awkward timidity in general. This people cannot look me in the face; there is conscious guilt and shame in their countenances when they look at me. They feel they have behaved ill, and that I am sensible of it." Works of John Adams, vol. iii. p. 393.

of the Constitution, and Washington's administration; nay, beyond that, to the tranquil evening of that life so matchless in its harmony, in its freedom from contradictions, the quiet glory of its close in the rural seclusion of Mount Vernon. Now the history of that whole era may be read as it is reflected in the clear mirror of that mind, undimmed by any unworthy passion, and capacious enough to hold within it the image of his country's annals for near half a century. Nowhere can so well be seen first the dutiful and not degrading loyalty of a colonial subject, giving to his king and country a soldier's service; the no less dutiful, but far more difficult, transition from loyal obedience to resistance; the progress from peaceful to armed resistance; the magnanimous self-control and heroism alike in the prosperity and adversity of military command; the perpetual sense of subordination to law; and the willing, happy laying down of power when the purposes of that power were achieved in the public good. It needs no comment to show how the Washington letters illustrate all the eventful years of his life, but there are other portions of it less attractive and less known, on which the letters alone throw light. In a course of historical lectures I had occasion lately to treat of that uneventful, that uninviting but instructive period between the peace of 1783 and the adoption of the present Constitution—those latter years of the Confederation, when the nation seemed to be sinking from the height of its new independence down into anarchy and the world's contempt; and nothing seemed to my mind to express with so deep and sad an eloquence the gloom which was gathering over the land, as the simple words of disappointment and depression which Washington was sending from Mount Vernon to his friends and correspondents. The feeling approaching to despair, which he uttered in confidence in the darkest days of the war, before the battle of Trenton, had something far more placid and less painful than the bitterness of disappointment and distrust occasioned by what seemed so like popular degeneracy in a season of safety.

The letters of Washington serve another purpose, in completing a biographical impression which often is incomplete—made so by the very awe which his character inspires. The most usual idea of that character is perhaps that which presents it in a kind of marmoreal purity and majestic repose; a truthful idealizing of those high and heroic attributes of his nature which lift him, if not above, into a lofty region of humanity; such a conception as a great American sculptor has embodied in marble, and which Southey had in his thoughts, when, in one of his lyrics, he spake of America as the land

> "Where Washington hath left
> His awful memory,
> A light for after times."*

It is in no contradiction to, but in perfect harmony with, this aspect of his character, that other phases of it are visible in his letters. The same sense of duty and lofty self-respect, which at times produced a passionless and imperturbable dignity, admit at other times the utterance of a vehement and righteous indignation, or a placid and half-humorous tenderness for some amiable frailty of a fellow-being. This, too, is made manifest, that in all his large and varied intercourse with men, there was no repul-

* Southey's Works, vol. iii. p. 221.

sive or oppressive dignity, but a genial and modest communion with them, and even an affectionate fellowship with those who were closely associated with him in the public service or in private life. In short, the letters show, what history cannot do, the gentle side of the great man's nature, which endeared him to all who came within the influence of it; there is proof of this in a little incident which might easily have perished out of the memories of men, if it had not been witnessed by one upon whose genuine delicacy of feeling it was not lost, and who wisely judged it worthy of record. The incident is so simple, and Bishop White's little narrative of it is given with such graceful simplicity, that I almost fear the feeling cannot be communicated by repetition. It was in a letter to the biographer of Washington that Bishop White communicated what may be entitled an

ANECDOTE CONCERNING PRESIDENT WASHINGTON.

"On the day before his leaving the presidential chair, a large company dined with him. Among them were the foreign ministers and their ladies, Mr. and Mrs. Adams, Mr. Jefferson, with other conspicuous persons of both sexes. During the dinner much hilarity prevailed; but on the removal of the cloth, it was put an end to by the President—certainly without design. Having filled his glass, he addressed the company, with a smile on his countenance, as nearly as can be recollected, in the following terms: 'Ladies and gentleman, this is the last time I shall drink your health as a public man. I do it with sincerity, and wishing you all possible happiness.' There was an end to all pleasantry. He who gives this relation accidentally directed his eye to the lady of the British minister, (Mrs. Liston,) and tears were running down her cheeks."*

I have referred to this as proof of that blending of the gentle with more impressive traits of character, which may be seen in Letters and not on the pages of history.

The letters of Dr. Franklin were in like manner remarkable for their extended historical interest—more extended indeed than Washington's, both in time and place, for the correspondence, continuing nearly as late, began much earlier, and carries the reader, therefore, further back into colonial society; it was enlarged, too, by a long and renewed European residence, first in England, with intercourse with Lord Chatham and other British statesmen friendly to the colonial cause, and to Franklin personally; and afterwards in France, where the sagacious and simply-attired republican was a fashionable novelty, caressed by the nobles and ladies of the court of Louis the Sixteenth. The letters of Franklin have also an additional interest by his connection with that large community, the society of men of science, not limited to the soil of any country. It is a correspondence which has further attraction, as showing that fine mastery which Franklin—by the help of a plain but substantial education, by

* Dr. Wilson's Memoir of Bishop White. p. 191. Let me here record the expression of my regret that the editor of a work published lately in this country called "The Republican Court," (p. 305,) should have preserved, on very uncertain, and, to my mind doubtful, tradition, an anecdote of Washington's violence of language and temper in most painful contrast with this anecdote W. B. R.

native sagacity, and continued culture—acquired in the use of good English speech.*

The American diplomatic correspondence of that period is interesting, too, as containing the impressions of sagacious men trained in the simplicity of republican life, (for the British colonies in America were virtually republics before independence;) such men brought into contact with artificial European society, and with political systems fast tending towards the great revolutionary convulsions at the close of the last century. It is not the least instructive portion of American state-papers, which somewhat later describes the progress of the French Revolution, as it appeared to one with high-toned, aristocratic political views, like Mr. Gouverneur Morris, or to one with democratic inclinations, like Mr. Monroe, and whose letters have respectively recorded what they witnessed in revolutionary Paris.

It is an easy and natural transition from the statesmen of the American Revolution to one who, in Parliament, was the friend and advocate of America in the hour of need—the Earl of Chatham; he who, as William Pitt, holds a title of the world's bestowing, "the great Commoner;" who gave to England, in that corrupt and degenerate eighteenth century, the example of a pure and lofty patriotism, and whose statesmanship may be paralleled with

---

* I know of few more graceful specimens of style than one from Franklin's letter to Lord Kames on 17th August, 1762. "I am now waiting here only for a wind to waft me to America, but cannot leave this happy island and my friends in it without extreme regret, though I am going to a country and a people that I love. I am going from the Old World to the New; and I fancy I feel like those who are leaving this world for the next; grief at the parting—fear of the passage—hope of the future." Sparks's Franklin, vol. i. p. 269. W. B. R.

Washington's in magnanimity. Unlike Washington, however, in simplicity of character, he seemed impelled, by the fame he had gained as an orator, to carry a sort of oratorical ambition into all his ways of life: in a letter of advice to his nephew, he says, "Behaviour, though an external thing, which seems rather to belong to the body than to the mind, is certainly founded in considerable virtues."* It has been said of him that his very infirmities were managed to the best advantage, and that in his hands even his crutch could become a weapon of oratory; but that this striving for effect has helped to give to his private letters a forced and unnatural appearance—the style of homely texture, but here and there pieced with pompous epithets and swelling phrases.† The praise of a Roman

---

* Chatham Correspondence, p. 77.

† Lord Mahon's History, vol. iii. p. 20. As this volume is going through the press, I have received from London a little tract privately printed by Lord Mahon, called "Lord Chatham at Chevening, 1769." Chevening is the seat of Earl Stanhope; and thither in 1769, in the absence of the owners on the Continent, came the valetudinarian statesman. This tract contains the letters of Mr. Brampton, the steward, describing to his mistress the demeanour of the guests: "The two young ladies in the yellow mohair room—*Master William* in the nursery." "Lord Chatham playing at billiards with the young gentlemen and ladies, so long as to bring on the gout in his ankle," &c. &c. It would seem from the tract that the poor steward had some trouble from the Earl's changeableness, and that though but a guest, he acted (as on other occasions he was apt to do) very much like an imperious master.

I confess a strong admiration for Lord Chatham, with all his infirmities; themselves palliated by what is now conceded, his occasional intellectual prostration. Horace Walpole, whose letters are read by everybody, and who had good hereditary cause to hate him, has damaged his fame with studious posterity; and yet where is there a nobler tribute to an English statesman than in one sentence of Walpole, in a letter to Mason, written when Chatham was in his grave?—" The Admi-

spirit, in the best sense of that term, has often been justly claimed for Pitt; and when writing to his wife, he says to Lady Chatham, "*Be of cheer, noble love!*" it sounds like Coriolanus speaking to the sister of Poplicola, or Brutus to his wife, the daughter of Cato. If the Chatham correspondence—both in the public and private letters—is distinguished by this stateliness of style, it is no less so by a loftiness of feeling and by the large thoughts of genuine statesmanship.

If Lord Chatham's oratory transgressed into his letters, the reverse may be observed in a living British statesman, more illustrious as a soldier. That simple and somewhat peremptory sententiousness which marks the Duke of Wellington's writings, whether an important public despatch or a private note, is also the tone of his parliamentary speeches. Whether writing or speaking, he uses words with a stern frugality, and sends them straight to their mark. Trained by the discipline of camp to know and feel the mischief of a waste of words, he has gained, through long service as a soldier and a statesman, a soldierly command of the language, producing a practical species of eloquence, wherein the most serviceable words are marshalled in compact and effective order. It is now near fifty years since, in his camp in India, he said that, when business could be done verbally, correspondence should be forbidden, to save the time of officers in perusing, considering, and copying voluminous documents about nothing; and, as commander-in-chief, he

---

ral has relieved Gibraltar. The Spanish fleet ran into their burrows, *as if Lord Chatham was alive.*" Letters to Mason, vol. ii. p. 179.
W. B. R.

said, "If officers abroad will have no mercy upon each other in correspondence, . . . I entreat them to have some upon me; to confine themselves to the strict facts of the case, and to write no more than is necessary for the elucidation of their meaning and intentions." On another occasion, he quietly suggests how writing may be a dangerous qualification: "A very trifling degree of education and practice," he remarks, "will enable an officer to string together a few words in a letter; . . . but this ability is a most dangerous qualification to the possessor, unless he has sense to guide his pen, and discretion to restrain him from the use of intemperate and improper language."*

The voluminous publication of Wellington's letters includes only, it must be remembered, his military correspondence; and whatever subjects it treats of are either subjects of warfare, or are looked at from a military point of view. Indeed, that soldierly vision had become, in a great measure, habitual, and may be discerned in his civic career. You have probably heard the story that is told of him, that, when it was represented to him, as constable of the Tower of London, some valuable national archives were deposited very near the magazine, he replied that they could not be of any damage to the saltpetre. Thus there is a ready explanation of a letter to his adjutant-general during the Peninsular War, the subject of which has rather a quaint sound, when briefly analyzed in an index, with the title, "*Singing of psalms in the abstract innocent.*" Military discipline is, of course, a general's first thought and duty, and accordingly he

* Selections from Gurwood, p. 429.

says, "The meeting of soldiers in their cantonments to sing psalms or hear a sermon read by one of their comrades, is, in the abstract, perfectly innocent; and it is a better way of spending their time than many others to which they are addicted; but it may become otherwise: and yet, till the abuse has made some progress, the commanding officer would have no knowledge of it, nor could he interfere. Even, at last, his interference must be guided by discretion, otherwise he will do more harm than good; and it can in no case be so effectual as that of a respectable clergyman. I wish, therefore, you would turn your mind a little more to this subject, and arrange some plan by which the number of respectable and efficient clergymen with the army may be increased."*

Like Washington's, the letters of Wellington display the same solicitude for not only the discipline, but the well-being of his soldiers—the same thoughtfulness of details, coupled with the genius for planning and executing large operations. There is a pervading good sense, (to call it by the humblest name,) whether the subject of the letter be the use of currycombs or hair-brushes for the horses, the stern repression of plunder, the respectful control of impracticable allies, or the report of a great battle. In the despatches to his government, after his victories, there is always a genuine soldierly modesty. After the victory at Salamanca, he begins a letter to Earl Bathurst: "I hope that you will be pleased with our battle, of which the despatch contains as accurate an ac-

* Gurwood, vol. vii. p. 231. The odd entry in the Index is to be found in the volume of Selections, published in 1851. W. B. R.

count as I can give you. There was no mistake; every thing went on as it ought."*

One other characteristic of these letters has been thus commented on by one of the authors of the "Guesses at Truth:" "Among the heroic features in the character of our great commander, none, except that sense of duty which in him is ever foremost, and throws all things else into the shade, is grander than the sorrow for his companions who have fallen, which seems almost to overpower every other feeling, even in the flush of victory. The conqueror of Bonaparte at Waterloo wrote on the day after, the 19th of June, to the Duke of Beaufort: 'The losses we have sustained have quite broken me down; and I have no feeling for the advantages we have acquired.' On the same day, too, he wrote to Lord Aberdeen: 'I cannot express to you the regret and sorrow with which I look round me and contemplate the loss I have sustained, particularly in your brother. The glory

* Letter of July 24, 1812. Selections, p. 614. There is a passage in one of Lord Wellington's letters from India which I am tempted to quote as (so it seems to me) the concentration of practical wisdom. It embodies good counsel for others besides soldiers: "I wish to draw your attention to the secresy of your proceedings. There is nothing more certain than that, out of one hundred affairs, ninety-nine might be posted up at the market-cross without injury to the public service; but the misfortune is that, when public business is the subject of general conversation, and is not kept secret as a matter of course upon every occasion, it is very difficult to keep it a secret upon that occasion when it is necessary. There is an awkwardness in a secret which enables discerning men (of which description there are always plenty in an army) invariably to find it out; and it may be depended upon, that, whenever the public service ought to be kept secret, it always suffers when it is exposed to public view." Letter of June 28, 1804. Selections, p. 177. W. B. R.

resulting from such actions, so dearly bought, is no consolation to me, and I cannot suggest it as any to you and his friends; but I hope that it may be expected that this last one has been so decisive as that no doubt remains that our exertions and our individual losses will be rewarded by the early attainment of our just object. It is then that the glory of the actions in which our friends have fallen will be some consolation for their loss.' He who could write thus had already gained a greater victory than that of Waterloo, and the less naturally follows the greater."*

An example of the same fine spirit of humanity, of true soldierly gentleness of feeling, will no doubt readily recur to many minds in the letter of condolence on the death of a gallant son addressed to an eminent American statesman by the victor of Buena Vista. As a part of military literature, the despatches of General Taylor may be spoken of as having received the stamp of history, especially since death has set its seal upon the hero's character. They stand, unquestionably, among the most remarkable productions of the kind in the language, whether considered simply as specimens of genuine and masterly use of English words, as military narratives, or as illustrations of character. They made the soldier, President of the United States. The battles might have been won, the campaigns completed; but it was the way in which the story was told, and the character uncon-

* Hare's Guesses at Truth, Second series, p. 191. There is to this letter a very characteristic and business-like postscript about Colonel Gordon's horse. W. B. R.

sciously disclosed through that story, that gained the confidence and the heart of the nation.*

I proceed to the second division of my lecture, to be more briefly disposed of, the subject of *familiar* letters—that correspondence which, like conversation, is held with the unreserved confidence of private life, and without a purpose of publication. It is worthy of notice that this did slowly and late take a place in English literature—a fact which, if reflected upon, is, in some measure, illustrative of the character of the race, and of some worthy traits in that character. There is a passage in the brief memoir of the poet Cowley, written by his friend Dr. Sprat, and addressed to another friend, which has a bearing on this subject, and which has often been referred to with complaint. "There was," he says, "one kind of prose wherein Mr. Cowley was excellent; and that is his letters to his private friends. In those he always expressed the native tenderness and innocent gayety of his mind. I

* At this time (February, 1855) the world is studying with intense interest the despatches and other letters, public and private, from the new scene of blood in the Crimea. The Anglo-French alliance, one might imagine, has had its influence on national style. For though the despatches of Lord Raglan and his generals have all the precision and business-like simplicity of his countrymen on such occasions, florid French despatch-writing, with phrases about "the sun of Austerlitz" and "conquering a peace," has nearly disappeared. It died with Marshal St. Arnaud at Alma; for General Canrobert writes with the precision and directness of an Englishman. It is very curious, too, to observe the indifference with which, in his letters to his government, he refers to topics which, twenty years ago, a Bonapartist could not think of without fury. In his despatch of 28th November to the Minister of War, speaking of the first onset of the Russians at Inkermann, he says, "Lord Raglan tells me the firing was as severe as at any time at Waterloo!" W. B. R.

think, sir, you and I have the greatest collection of this sort. But I know you agree with me that nothing of this sort should be published; and herein you have always consented to approve of the modest judgment of our countrymen above the practice of some of our neighbours, and chiefly of the French. I make no manner of question but the English, at this time, are infinitely improved in this way above the skill of former ages; yet they have been always judiciously sparing in printing such composures, while some other witty nations have tired all their presses and readers with them. The truth is, the letters that pass between particular friends, if they are written as they ought to be, can scarce ever be fit to see the light. They should not consist of fulsome compliments, or tedious politics, or elaborate elegancies, or general fancies; but they should have a native clearness and shortness, a domestical plainness, and a peculiar kind of familiarity, which can only affect the humour of those for whom they were intended. The very same passages which make writings of this nature delightful among friends, will lose all manner of taste when they come to be read by those that are indifferent. In such letters, the souls of men should appear undressed; and in that negligent habit they may be fit to be seen by one or two in a chamber, but not to go abroad in the street."

This is, indeed, very tantalizing, especially so, for Cowley's delightful prose-essays have a savour of what must have made his familiar letters most excellent of their kind; the passage described, indeed, the very perfection of such letters in the very reason given for withholding them. However one may dissent from the reasoning, and still more regret the application of it, it is entitled to some respect as having a basis of sound sense, and expressive of a just feeling—that honourable spirit which is, I believe, an element in the character of our race. It was so formerly, more so than now; for that "modest judgment," which the biographer of Cowley spoke of as restraining the publication of private correspondence, has grown to be old-fashioned; and the barriers of reserve have been broken down by the cupidity of booksellers, the vanity of authors, and the vicious curiosity of readers. If this department of English literature has, in late years, received many and valuable additions, it has not been all clear gain: the sanctities of domestic life and the proprieties of official life have been violated; the world has intruded where it had no title to enter, and often learned what it had far better remained ignorant of; the happy confidence of social communion has been startled in its security; and the author can scarce write a familiar note without misgiving of future publication.

When Pope's correspondence was surreptitiously published by an unscrupulous bookseller, Dr. Arbuthnot wittily spoke of Curll, the publisher, as a new terror of death.* When the letters of Robert Burns were first

* Dr. Johnson once remarked that the practice of publishing the letters of literary men had grown so common, that he made it a point to put as little as possible in his own. There will be found in the London Quarterly Review, a few years back, an excellent essay on this subject in its relation to official life, on the subject of the posthumous publication of Lord Malmesbury's journals and letters. Our American diplomatic subordinates have, of late years, committed the grosser scandal of scribbling for home newspapers. A greater indecorum, and one more detrimental to public interests, can hardly be conceived. W. B. R.

given to the world, disclosing the deplorable frailties of his life—not as a wise and feeling biographer might have done, but in the dark colours of the frenzy of genius, conscious of guilt and never wholly divorced from a soul of goodness—a fellow-poet, strong in the might of a life of irreproachable purity, and yet compassionate of his frail brother, protested in earnest prose against the world's right to penetrate into the privacy of an author's life. I refer to a pamphlet of Wordsworth's, in which, among other remarks, he observed that "The Life of Johnson by Boswell had broken through many pre-existing delicacies, and afforded the British public an opportunity of acquiring experience, which before it had happily wanted." A younger poet, Mr. Tennyson, has also made his protest against the growing evil, in some vigorous stanzas addressed to a friend, and entitled "*The Age of Irreverence:*"

"You might have won the poet's name,
If such be worth the winning now,
And gained a laurel for your brow,
Of sounder leaf than I can claim.

But you have made the wiser choice;
A life that moves to gracious ends,
Through troops of unrecording friends,
A deedful life, a silent voice.

And you have missed the irreverent doom
Of those that wear the poet's crown;
Hereafter neither knave nor clown
Shall hold their orgies at your tomb.

For now the poet cannot die,
Nor leave his music as of old,
But round him, ere he scarce be cold,
Begins the scandal and the cry:—

'Give out the faults he would not show!
Break lock and seal! betray the trust!
Keep nothing sacred: 'tis but just
The many-headed beast should know.'

Ah, shameless! for he did but sing
A song that pleased us from its worth:
No *public* life was his on earth,
No blazoned statesman he, nor king.

He gave the people of his best:
His worst he kept, his best he gave.
My curse upon the clown and knave
Who will not let his ashes rest!

Who makes it sweeter seem to be,
The little life of bank and brier,
The bird that pipes his lone desire,
And dies unheard within his tree,

Than he that warbles long and loud,
And drops at glory's temple-gates,
For whom the carrion vulture waits,
To tear his heart before the crowd."*

The volume which is, I believe, the earliest collection of letters, is a singular exception to that old-fashioned English reserve which I have spoken of—the volume

* On a kindred subject, that of the rash, posthumous publication of private diaries, or rather of the faithful performance of duty to the dead in their suppression, the reader is referred to the conduct of Lady Bute, the daughter of Lady Mary Wortley Montague, in the introductory anecdotes prefixed to Lord Wharncliffe's edition, p. 21. I may here observe that nothing more clearly shows the popular and cursory character of these lectures, (and this was my brother's view of them,) than that among the poets he does not mention Thomson or Collins, or, among the letter-writers, Lady Mary Wortley Montague. W. B. R.

entitled "Familiar Letters, domestic and foreign, partly historical, political, and philosophical, by James Howell," in the times of Charles the First, and published during the Protectorate. It is the case of a writer setting such esteem upon his own letters as to collect and give them to the world; and although the volume is now a neglected and rather rare one, the welcome it had is proved by the fact that it went through eleven editions in a century. Howell was a traveller, on the continent and in England was in intercourse with men of various celebrity: while his letters show much curious matter, one cannot help thinking how high a value such a correspondence might have had, if it had given the thoughts of a stronger mind in that momentous period. The Paston Letters, though of much earlier date, were not published until the latter part of the eighteenth century, about three hundred years after they were written. It is the correspondence of the Paston family during the era of the wars of York and Lancaster, comprehending a curious variety of epistles, from the note of an Eton scholar, with thanks for a box of raisins and figs, to letters following the sad fortunes of that simple and saintly sovereign, Henry the Sixth, and his heroic queen. When these letters were brought to light, after their long sleep, they had a congenial welcome from Horace Walpole, who said, "The letters of Henry the Sixth's reign are come out, and to *me* make all other letters not worth reading. I have gone through above one volume, and cannot bear to be writing when I am so eager to be reading."*

A very pathetic interest attaches to the collection of

* Letters to Lady Ossory, vol, ii. p. 297.

the Letters of Lady Russel, the memory of her husband's tragic death on the scaffold casting a solemn light over the whole correspondence during a widowhood protracted to extreme old age, and distinguished no less by profound affection to her departed husband than by a widowed mother's untiring duty to her children. Her's was a life of genuine womanly heroism, a life with one awful sorrow in its centre, sustained, if not cheered, by thoughtful Christian piety. The correspondence is the unconscious portraiture of such a character, in which were combined the spirit of submission to affliction and an energetic fortitude that shrank from no duty. There is, perhaps, no more touching incident in British annals than that one so well-known on the trial of her husband for treason, when Lord Russel asked, "May I have somebody to write to help my memory?" The attorney-general answered, "Yes, a servant." The noble prisoner said, "My wife is here." The harshness of the chief justice (Pemberton) was softened, when, recognising Lady Russel's presence, he added, "If my lady please to give herself the trouble."

It is a transition from letters of the most intense and serious reality to a correspondence the most superficial in feeling and the most artificial in expression, to pass to the letters of Pope; another instance, like Howell's, of the letter-writer making of his letters to his intimates a book for everybody. They were modelled after the French epistolary school of Balzac and Voiture, (before the talent of Madame de Sevigné had given an attractive gracefulness to French letters,) and vitiated by the ambition, bad enough in any use of speech or writing, but odious, in a familiar letter—the ambition of fine thoughts in fine words.

Even Mr. Hallam's calm judgment stops not at calling Pope "the ape of Voiture" in his letters to ladies.* And one who so admirably conceived and executed the true idea of a familiar letter, as Cowper did, in shrinking from that applause of his correspondence which Pope was ever coveting, said a "foolish vanity would have spoiled me quite, and made me as disgusting a letter-writer as Pope, who seems to have thought that unless a sentence was well turned, and every period pointed with some conceit, it was not worth the carriage. Accordingly, he is to me, except in very few instances, the most disagreeable maker of epistles that ever I met with. I was willing, therefore, to wait till the impression your commendation had made upon the foolish part of me was worn off, that I might scribble away as usual, and write my uppermost thoughts and those only."†

Of that society identified with Pope's letters, it was well said by the late Hartley Coleridge, "Never was literary band so closely united by harmonious dissimilitude as that which comprised Swift, Pope, Gay, Arbuthnot, and Parnell: they were a perfect co-operative society, and might be said, almost without a metaphor, to feel for each other. But Swift *thought* for them all: his was the informing mind, and exercised over his associates that supremacy which philosophic power, however perverted, will always maintain over mere genius, though elegant as Pope's—over simple erudition, though extensive as Arbuthnot's. Moreover, whenever a limited number of men form a league or union, it is ten to one that the

* Literature of Europe, vol. iii. p. 641.

† Southey's Cowper, vol. iv. p. 15.

least amiable will be the most influential."* Swift's masculine power is manifest in his letters, for affectation, unless the affectation of rudeness, came not nigh him. there is, too, in his letters, a sad reality, from the connection with that strange control which his stern nature gained over the affections of two women at the same time; his mysterious marriage with one, and the final heartbreaking of them both. Whenever a letter of Bishop Berkeley's appears, it shows him always the pure, the gentle, and the virtuous, the gentleman and the divine, the most beautiful character of that generation, the moral footprints of whose life are to this day visible on American soil.†

The letters of Lord Chesterfield are a remarkable instance of celebrity gained unintentionally, and superseding, in a great measure, other grounds of reputation. For one person acquainted with his character as a statesman, at home and in diplomacy, the rare ability displayed as Lord Lieutenant of Ireland in the administration of that most unmanageable section of the British empire, and the tradition of his oratory, twenty know of his letters to his son, written in perfect parental confidence, and published years afterwards surreptitiously. I cannot better or more briefly characterize the letters, than by saying that they make a book of the minor moralities and the major immoralities of life. They profess to deal with nothing higher than those secondary motives which,

---

* Hartley Coleridge's Biographia Borealis, p. 115. Note to Life of Bentley.

† No one that heard them will ever forget Mr. Thackeray's brilliant criticism on Pope's letters, and his sketches of the society, heartless it may be, but very fascinating, which they illustrate. W. B. R.

though poor and even dangerous substitutes for moral principle, are yet not to be despised in the formation of character—considerations of expediency, reputation, personal advantage; and being addressed to a youth of uncouth manners, they laid that stress upon grace of deportment which has given to the name of Chesterfield a proverbial use. The letters embody a great deal of sound advice, the result of the large worldly experience of an acute and cultivated nobleman, too acute not to know at least the impolicy of much of the world's wickedness. When they were published, Dr. Johnson pronounced a pithy and coarse sentence of condemnation, which may recur to the minds of some of my hearers, who will recognise my restraint in not repeating it. He afterwards modified his censure, and said, "Take out the immorality, and the book ought to be in the hands of every young gentleman."*

It is to another man of the world of Chesterfield's times, and the times of a great many other people, that English literature owes its most voluminous, and, in some respects, most remarkable collection of letters—I need hardly say, I refer to Horace Walpole. His letters count by thousands: about three thousand are in print, and the publication of more is looked for. In one of Scribe's vaudevilles, Madame de Sevigné is described as the lady

* The notes to this lecture have been too far multiplied to allow me room for admiration, as a matter of rhetoric, of Lord Chesterfield. I have often thought that a biography of British statesmen by an American, and from an American point of view, would be a most useful and delightful book, and on its pages no one would appear more brightly than Lord Chesterfield. The English of his letters, not written for publication, but in the strictest confidence, is matchless. W. B. R.

who used to write letters all the while. Horace Walpole takes the palm; and has been styled the prince of letter-writers, a title well-earned by the continuity of his labours, or rather his pleasures, in this department of composition during a long life. His letters cover a period of more than threescore years, beginning in 1735, and ending in 1797, a few weeks before his death; thus touching at one end the times of George the Second, and the Pretenders, and Maria Theresa, and at the other the French Revolution and Republic. With Walpole's large political and social opportunities, his letters are full of the history, and fuller of the gossip, of sixty years—pleasant reading, but uncertain authority. A shrewd, but sometimes malevolent commentator on his fellow-men, a witty observer of manners, he sought amusement in the fopperies of a fantastic country mansion and the luxury of a private printing-press, but his happiness, rather, I think, in the luxurious indulgence of perpetual letter-writing to correspondents of both sexes and various ages; and twelve octavo volumes, with an indefinite series in prospect, are the record of this indulgence. An elegant sefishness, tempered with much kindly feeling for his friends, is undisguised in his letters; and a self-indulgent frivolity deepens into earnestness only in a fervid indignation, which he was one of the first to utter against the African slave-trade, and when, near the close of life, his imperturbable voluptuousness was startled by the atrocities of the French Revolution. The letters, faithful to the last, bring their story very near to the old man's death—the melancholy conclusion of eighty years of worldliness. It is in his last letter but one to Lady Ossory, that he describes himself as a sort of Methuselah, whom fourscore nephews and nieces were annually brought to stare at. The title of Earl of Orford came too late to be welcome; he never took his place in the House of Lords, and even evaded the dignity by either signing himself "uncle of the late Earl of Orford," or simply with a capital O, almost as if, with something of bitter self-satire, he meant by the cipher to symbolize the nothingness of his state of being.*

To turn from Walpole's letters to those of his once friend and travelling companion, the poet Gray, is like passing from the throng of the world of politics or fashion into the calm and cloistered seclusion of a college. That seclusion was connected with both the virtues and the weaknesses of Gray's character, his purity, his gentleness, his studious love of books, and with his dainty and almost effeminate shrinking, not only from active life, but even from the publicity of authorship, and social intercourse with mankind or womankind. Cowper said, "I once thought Swift's letters the best that could be written, but I like Gray's better. His humour, or his wit, or whatever it is to be called, is never ill-natured or offensive, and yet, I think, equally poignant with the Dean's."†

* The letters to Lady Ossory are certainly marked by a superior tone of seriousness and dignity, and no solemn moralist can write more genuine words of honest self-reproach, than Walpole did when he said, "When young, I wished for fame, not examining whether I was capable of attaining it, nor considering in what light fame was desirable. There are two parts of honest fame; that attendant on the truly great, and that better sort which is due to the good. I fear I did not aim at the latter, nor discover, till too late, that I could not compass the former. Having neglected the best road, and having, instead of the other, strolled into a narrow path that led to no goal worth seeking, I see the idleness of my journey." W. B. R.

† Southey's Cowper, vol. iv. p. 15.

The letters on which I should have been glad to have dwelt the most I must dispose of briefly—Cowper's own; and I can do so the more safely, in speaking of them as the purest and most perfect specimens of familiar letters in the language. Considering the secluded, uneventful course of Cowper's life, the charm in his letters is wonderful; and is to be explained, I believe, chiefly by the exquisite light of poetic truth which his imagination shed upon daily life, whether his theme was man, himself or a fellow-being, or books, or the mute creation which he loved to handle with such thoughtful tenderness. His seclusion did not separate him from sympathy with the stirring events of his time; and, alike in seasons of sunshine or of gloom, there is in his letters an ever-present beauty of quiet wisdom, and a gentle but fervid spirit. There is, I believe, no long collection of letters which can be continuously read with the same sustained interest, following the writer through cheerfulness and despondency into the cloud, from which he sent forth some words of sadness as it mysteriously closed over him.

The letters of Sir Walter Scott, in Mr. Lockhart's inimitable biography, claim the same high praise. There is the same excellent adaptation of the letter to the occasion and to the party addressed, which is essential in a true letter. There is also the same power of so expressing the writer's feelings as to move in sympathy with the correspondent, and for the correspondent's pleasure, without ever sinking into egotism or vanity. It is this—the mastery of the *subjective* character of the composition, which is at once the difficulty and virtue of the real familiar letter. A child, in its innocence and unreflectiveness, toils at so putting its heart into words; and there are those who carry into mature life so much of child-like simplicity of character as to be unfit for letter-writing. The more common fault is, however, in the other direction—a gross or insidious egotism. Scott's style of correspondence has a very high merit in combining a frank expression of his own feelings along with a perpetual mindfulness of the feelings of those to whom he writes.

The letters of Lord Byron displaying, even more than his poems, his command of vigorous English speech—make a perilous display of a morbid egotism, redeemed, indeed, at times, by flashes of kindly feeling, of generous impulse, and healthy opinion, so as to perplex the reader's judgment, or, at least, to plead for his pity to the misery of a soul distempered by nature, and far worse by a life of moral lawlessness; and by that pride which, tempting him often to brave the world's opinion by even affecting worse thoughts and worse deeds than were imputed to him, was fatal to the truthfulness of his character and of his writings.

Of Southey's letters, interwoven with his biography, just completed, it is too soon to speak otherwise than with a general allusion to the interest of them, without attempting to measure their merits and their faults.

Charles Lamb's letters resemble his inimitable essays—a quaint wisdom, a fine literary taste, and a loving and a brave heart dwelling together in that humour which was his peculiar gift.

Letters of *dedication* may be merely mentioned in connection with this general subject. The early dedications abound in noble feeling, fitly expressed, with an eloquence that is midway between oratory and the familiarity of a letter. There followed a long period during which they were vitiated by fulsome and servile flattery. Of late years, truth has been restored on the dedication page; and many a one, in verse as well as prose, is a record of a genuine feeling of reverence, of admiration, and of love. Let me refer to one for the sake of a thought I wish (in conclusion) to leave in your minds. Charles Lamb dedicated his earliest volume to his sister—that afflicted sister to whom he devoted all his days. He consulted Coleridge in a letter in which he said, "I have another sort of dedication in my head for my few things, which I want to know if you approve of. I mean to inscribe them to my sister. It will be unexpected, and it will give her pleasure; or do you think it will look whimsical at all? . . . There is a monotony in the affections, which people living together (or, as we do now, very frequently seeing each other) are apt to give into; a sort of indifference in the expression of kindness for each other, which demands that we should sometimes call to our aid the trickery of surprise."*

* These last words have suggested to me a dedication of this volume which I had not before designed. In parting with it, it seemed natural and congenial with my feelings to the dead to add a tribute, most deserved and unexpected, to the living. W. B. R.

THE END.

STEREOTYPED BY L. JOHNSON & CO.
PHILADELPHIA.

www.ingramcontent.com/pod-product-compliance
Lightning Source LLC
LaVergne TN
LVHW020105110826
845151LV00001B/62

* 9 7 8 1 4 2 5 5 4 4 7 4 4 *